enVision® Mathematics
Common Core

Volume 1 Topics 1–7

Authors

Randall I. Charles
Professor Emeritus
Department of Mathematics
San Jose State University
San Jose, California

Jennifer Bay-Williams
Professor of Mathematics
Education
College of Education and Human
Development
University of Louisville
Louisville, Kentucky

Robert Q. Berry, III
Professor of Mathematics
Education
Department of Curriculum,
Instruction and Special Education
University of Virginia
Charlottesville, Virginia

Janet H. Caldwell
Professor Emerita
Department of Mathematics
Rowan University
Glassboro, New Jersey

Zachary Champagne
Assistant in Research
Florida Center for Research in
Science, Technology, Engineering,
and Mathematics (FCR-STEM)
Jacksonville, Florida

Juanita Copley
Professor Emerita
College of Education
University of Houston
Houston, Texas

Warren Crown
Professor Emeritus of Mathematics
Education
Graduate School of Education
Rutgers University
New Brunswick, New Jersey

Francis (Skip) Fennell
Professor Emeritus of
Education and Graduate and
Professional Studies
McDaniel College
Westminster, Maryland

Karen Karp
Professor of
Mathematics Education
School of Education
Johns Hopkins University
Baltimore, Maryland

Stuart J. Murphy
Visual Learning Specialist
Boston, Massachusetts

Jane F. Schielack
Professor Emerita
Department of Mathematics
Texas A&M University
College Station, Texas

Jennifer M. Suh
Associate Professor for
Mathematics Education
George Mason University
Fairfax, Virginia

Jonathan A. Wray
Mathematics Supervisor
Howard County Public Schools
Ellicott City, Maryland

SAVVAS
LEARNING COMPANY

ISBN-13: 978-0-13-495471-4
ISBN-10: 0-13-495471-8

9 2022

Digital Resources

You'll be using these digital resources throughout the year!

Go to SavvasRealize.com

 Interactive Student Edition
Access online or offline.

 Interactive Additional Practice Workbook
Access online or offline.

 Videos
Watch Math Practices Animations, Another Look Videos, and clips to support 3-Act Math.

 Math Tools
Explore math with digital tools.

A-Z Glossary
Read and listen in English and Spanish.

 Visual Learning
Interact with visual learning animations.

 Activity
Solve a problem and share your thinking.

 Practice Buddy
Do interactive practice online.

 Games
Play math games to help you learn.

 Assessment
Show what you've learned.

SAVVAS realize™ Everything you need for math anytime, anywhere

Contents

Digital Resources at SavvasRealize.com

And remember your Interactive Student Edition is available at SavvasRealize.com!

This shows how to find the value of the digits in a number.

millions period | thousands period | ones period

hundred millions | ten millions | one millions | hundred thousands | ten thousands | one thousands | hundreds | tens | ones

3 5 6, 0 3 9

TOPIC 1 Generalize Place Value Understanding

This shows one way to add whole numbers.

$$\begin{array}{r} \overset{1\ \ 1}{9{,}263} \\ +\ \ 7{,}951 \\ \hline 17{,}214 \end{array}$$

TOPIC 2 Fluently Add and Subtract Multi-Digit Whole Numbers

This shows how to use partial products to multiply.

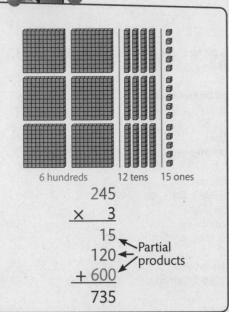

6 hundreds   12 tens   15 ones

$$245$$
$$\times \quad 3$$
$$15$$
$$120 \quad \text{Partial products}$$
$$\underline{+\ 600}$$
$$735$$

TOPIC 3 Use Strategies and Properties to Multiply by 1-Digit Numbers

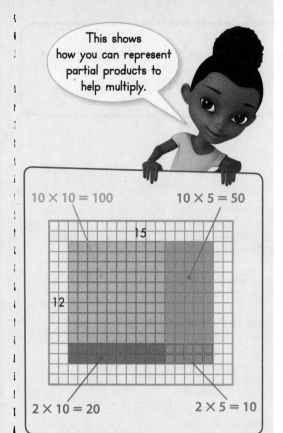

This shows how you can represent partial products to help multiply.

$10 \times 10 = 100$ $10 \times 5 = 50$

15

12

$2 \times 10 = 20$ $2 \times 5 = 10$

TOPIC 4 Use Strategies and Properties to Multiply by 2-Digit Numbers

This shows how place value can help you divide.

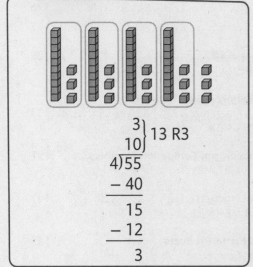

TOPIC 5 Use Strategies and Properties to Divide by 1-Digit Numbers

This shows how you can represent a comparison situation.

42

3 · *n* times as many

TOPIC 6 Use Operations with Whole Numbers to Solve Problems

This shows how you can use arrays to model factor pairs for a number.

TOPIC 7 Factors and Multiples

Grade 4 Common Core Standards

Dear Families,

The standards on the following pages describe the math that students will learn this year. The greatest amount of time will be spent on standards in the major clusters.

DOMAIN 4.OA
OPERATIONS AND ALGEBRAIC THINKING

MAJOR CLUSTER 4.OA.A
Use the four operations with whole numbers to solve problems.

4.OA.A.1 Interpret a multiplication equation as a comparison, e.g., interpret $35 = 5 \times 7$ as a statement that 35 is 5 times as many as 7 and 7 times as many as 5. Represent verbal statements of multiplicative comparisons as multiplication equations.

4.OA.A.2 Multiply or divide to solve word problems involving multiplicative comparison, e.g., by using drawings and equations with a symbol for the unknown number to represent the problem, distinguishing multiplicative comparison from additive comparison.

4.OA.A.3 Solve multistep word problems posed with whole numbers and having whole-number answers using the four operations, including problems in which remainders must be interpreted. Represent these problems using equations with a letter standing for the unknown quantity. Assess the reasonableness of answers using mental computation and estimation strategies including rounding.

SUPPORTING CLUSTER 4.OA.B
Gain familiarity with factors and multiples.

4.OA.B.4 Find all factor pairs for a whole number in the range 1–100. Recognize that a whole number is a multiple of each of its factors. Determine whether a given whole number in the range 1–100 is a multiple of a given one-digit number. Determine whether a given whole number in the range 1–100 is prime or composite.

ADDITIONAL CLUSTER 4.OA.C
Generate and analyze patterns.

4.OA.C.5 Generate a number or shape pattern that follows a given rule. Identify apparent features of the pattern that were not explicit in the rule itself.

Common Core Standards

DOMAIN 4.NBT
NUMBER AND OPERATIONS IN BASE TEN

MAJOR CLUSTER 4.NBT.A
Generalize place value understanding for multi-digit whole numbers.

4.NBT.A.1 Recognize that in a multi-digit whole number, a digit in one place represents ten times what it represents in the place to its right. *For example, recognize that 700 ÷ 70 = 10 by applying concepts of place value and division.*

4.NBT.A.2 Read and write multi-digit whole numbers using base-ten numerals, number names, and expanded form. Compare two multi-digit numbers based on meanings of the digits in each place, using >, =, and < symbols to record the results of comparisons.

4.NBT.A.3 Use place value understanding to round multi-digit whole numbers to any place.

MAJOR CLUSTER 4.NBT.B
Use place value understanding and properties of operations to perform multi-digit arithmetic.

4.NBT.B.4 Fluently add and subtract multi-digit whole numbers using the standard algorithm.

4.NBT.B.5 Multiply a whole number of up to four digits by a one-digit whole number, and multiply two two-digit numbers, using strategies based on place value and the properties of operations. Illustrate and explain the calculation by using equations, rectangular arrays, and/or area models.

4.NBT.B.6 Find whole-number quotients and remainders with up to four-digit dividends and one-digit divisors, using strategies based on place value, the properties of operations, and/or the relationship between multiplication and division. Illustrate and explain the calculation by using equations, rectangular arrays, and/or area models.

DOMAIN 4.NF
NUMBER AND OPERATIONS-FRACTIONS

MAJOR CLUSTER 4.NF.A
Extend understanding of fraction equivalence and ordering.

4.NF.A.1 Explain why a fraction $\frac{a}{b}$ is equivalent to a fraction $\frac{(n \times a)}{(n \times b)}$ by using visual fraction models, with attention to how the number and size of the parts differ even though the two fractions themselves are the same size. Use this principle to recognize and generate equivalent fractions.

4.NF.A.2 Compare two fractions with different numerators and different denominators, e.g., by creating common denominators or numerators, or by comparing to a benchmark fraction such as $\frac{1}{2}$. Recognize that comparisons are valid only when the two fractions refer to the same whole. Record the results of comparisons with symbols >, =, or <, and justify the conclusions, e.g., by using a visual fraction model.

MAJOR CLUSTER 4.NF.B
Build fractions from unit fractions.

4.NF.B.3 Understand a fraction $\frac{a}{b}$ with $a > 1$ as a sum of fractions $\frac{1}{b}$.

4.NF.B.3a Understand addition and subtraction of fractions as joining and separating parts referring to the same whole.

4.NF.B.3b Decompose a fraction into a sum of fractions with the same denominator in more than one way, recording each decomposition by an equation. Justify decompositions, e.g., by using a visual fraction model. *Examples: $\frac{3}{8} = \frac{1}{8} + \frac{1}{8} + \frac{1}{8}; \frac{3}{8} = \frac{1}{8} + \frac{2}{8}; 2\frac{1}{8} = 1 + 1 + \frac{1}{8} = \frac{8}{8} + \frac{8}{8} + \frac{1}{8}.*

4.NF.B.3c Add and subtract mixed numbers with like denominators, e.g., by replacing each mixed number with an equivalent fraction, and/or by using properties of operations and the relationship between addition and subtraction.

4.NF.B.3d Solve word problems involving addition and subtraction of fractions referring to the same whole and having like denominators, e.g., by using visual fraction models and equations to represent the problem.

4.NF.B.4 Apply and extend previous understandings of multiplication to multiply a fraction by a whole number.

4.NF.B.4a Understand a fraction $\frac{a}{b}$ as a multiple of $\frac{1}{b}$. *For example, use a visual fraction model to represent $\frac{5}{4}$ as the product $5 \times (\frac{1}{4})$, recording the conclusion by the equation $\frac{5}{4} = 5 \times (\frac{1}{4})$.*

4.NF.B.4b Understand a multiple of $\frac{a}{b}$ as a multiple of $\frac{1}{b}$, and use this understanding to multiply a fraction by a whole number. *For example, use a visual fraction model to express $3 \times (\frac{2}{5})$ as $6 \times (\frac{1}{5})$, recognizing this product as $\frac{6}{5}$. (In general, $n \times (\frac{a}{b}) = \frac{(n \times a)}{b}$.)*

Common Core Standards

4.NF.B.4c Solve word problems involving multiplication of a fraction by a whole number, e.g., by using visual fraction models and equations to represent the problem. *For example, if each person at a party will eat $\frac{3}{8}$ of a pound of roast beef, and there will be 5 people at the party, how many pounds of roast beef will be needed? Between what two whole numbers does your answer lie?*

MAJOR CLUSTER 4.NF.C
Understand decimal notation for fractions, and compare decimal fractions.

4.NF.C.5 Express a fraction with denominator 10 as an equivalent fraction with denominator 100, and use this technique to add two fractions with respective denominators 10 and 100. *For example, express $\frac{3}{10}$ as $\frac{30}{100}$, and add $\frac{3}{10} + \frac{4}{100} = \frac{34}{100}$.*

4.NF.C.6 Use decimal notation for fractions with denominators 10 or 100. *For example, rewrite 0.62 as $\frac{62}{100}$; describe a length as 0.62 meters; locate 0.62 on a number line diagram.*

4.NF.C.7 Compare two decimals to hundredths by reasoning about their size. Recognize that comparisons are valid only when the two decimals refer to the same whole. Record the results of comparisons with the symbols >, =, or <, and justify the conclusions, e.g., by using a visual model.

DOMAIN 4.MD
MEASUREMENT AND DATA

SUPPORTING CLUSTER 4.MD.A
Solve problems involving measurement and conversion of measurements.

4.MD.A.1 Know relative sizes of measurement units within one system of units including km, m, cm; kg, g; lb, oz.; l, ml; hr, min, sec. Within a single system of measurement, express measurements in a larger unit in terms of a smaller unit. Record measurement equivalents in a two-column table. *For example, know that 1 ft is 12 times as long as 1 in. Express the length of a 4 ft snake as 48 in. Generate a conversion table for feet and inches listing the number pairs (1, 12), (2, 24), (3, 36), ...*

4.MD.A.2 Use the four operations to solve word problems involving distances, intervals of time, liquid volumes, masses of objects, and money, including problems involving simple fractions or decimals, and problems that require expressing measurements given

in a larger unit in terms of a smaller unit. Represent measurement quantities using diagrams such as number line diagrams that feature a measurement scale.

4.MD.A.3 Apply the area and perimeter formulas for rectangles in real world and mathematical problems. *For example, find the width of a rectangular room given the area of the flooring and the length, by viewing the area formula as a multiplication equation with an unknown factor.*

SUPPORTING CLUSTER 4.MD.B
Represent and interpret data.

4.MD.B.4 Make a line plot to display a data set of measurements in fractions of a unit ($\frac{1}{2}, \frac{1}{4}, \frac{1}{8}$). Solve problems involving addition and subtraction of fractions by using information presented in line plots. *For example, from a line plot find and interpret the difference in length between the longest and shortest specimens in an insect collection.*

ADDITIONAL CLUSTER 4.MD.C
Geometric measurement: understand concepts of angle and measure angles.

4.MD.C.5 Recognize angles as geometric shapes that are formed wherever two rays share a common endpoint, and understand concepts of angle measurement:

4.MD.C.5a An angle is measured with reference to a circle with its center at the common endpoint of the rays, by considering the fraction of the circular arc between the points where the two rays intersect the circle. An angle that turns through $\frac{1}{360}$ of a circle is called a "one-degree angle," and can be used to measure angles.

4.MD.C.5b An angle that turns through n one-degree angles is said to have an angle measure of n degrees.

4.MD.C.6 Measure angles in whole-number degrees using a protractor. Sketch angles of specified measure.

4.MD.C.7 Recognize angle measure as additive. When an angle is decomposed into non-overlapping parts, the angle measure of the whole is the sum of the angle measures of the parts. Solve addition and subtraction problems to find unknown angles on a diagram in real world and mathematical problems, e.g., by using an equation with a symbol for the unknown angle measure.

Common Core Standards

DOMAIN 4.G.A
GEOMETRY

ADDITIONAL CLUSTER 4.G.A
Draw and identify lines and angles, and classify shapes by properties of their lines and angles.

4.G.A.1 Draw points, lines, line segments, rays, angles (right, acute, obtuse), and perpendicular and parallel lines. Identify these in two-dimensional figures.

4.G.A.2 Classify two-dimensional figures based on the presence or absence of parallel or perpendicular lines, or the presence or absence of angles of a specified size. Recognize right triangles as a category, and identify right triangles.

4.G.A.3 Recognize a line of symmetry for a two-dimensional figure as a line across the figure such that the figure can be folded along the line into matching parts. Identify line-symmetric figures and draw lines of symmetry.

MATHEMATICAL PRACTICES

MP.1 Make sense of problems and persevere in solving them.

MP.2 Reason abstractly and quantitatively.

MP.3 Construct viable arguments and critique the reasoning of others.

MP.4 Model with mathematics.

MP.5 Use appropriate tools strategically.

MP.6 Attend to precision.

MP.7 Look for and make use of structure.

MP.8 Look for and express regularity in repeated reasoning.

Math Practices and Problem Solving Handbook

The **Math Practices and Problem Solving Handbook** is available at SavvasRealize.com.

Math Practices

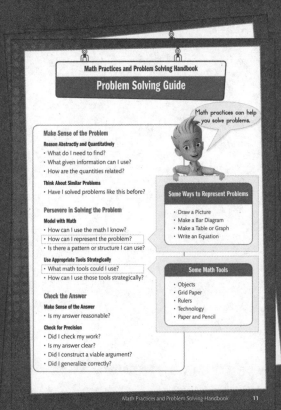

Problem Solving Guide
Problem Solving Recording Sheet
Bar Diagrams

Generalize Place Value Understanding

Essential Questions: How are greater numbers written? How can whole numbers be compared? How are place values related?

Digital Resources

Interactive Student Edition · Activity · Visual Learning · Video · Practice

Assessment · Games · Tools · Glossary

Water, wind, and ice can change the shapes of rocks over thousands of years. This is called erosion.

Kannesteinen Rock in Norway got its shape from the sea that surrounds it.

Mountains, caves, and some islands are kinds of rock formations. Here is a project about caves and greater numbers.

ēnVision STEM Project: Caves

Do Research Use the Internet or other sources to find the depths in feet of the 5 deepest caves in the world.

Journal: Write a Report Include what you found. Also in your report:

- Make a place-value chart that includes the five depths.

- Write each depth in expanded form.

- Use "greater than" or "less than" to compare the depths of two of the caves.

Name_____

Review What You Know

A-Z Vocabulary

Choose the best term from the box. Write it on the blank.

- expanded form
- place value
- number line
- rounding
- number name
- whole numbers

1. The numbers 0, 1, 2, 3, 4, and so on are called _____.

2. A number written using only words is written using a _____.

3. Replacing a number with a number that tells about how many or how much is called _____.

4. _____ is the value given to the place of a digit in a number.

Comparing Numbers

Compare each set of numbers using >, <, or =.

5. 201 ◯ 21

6. 313 ◯ 313

7. 289 ◯ 290

8. 7 ◯ 70

9. 725 ◯ 726

10. 82 ◯ 82

11. 614 ◯ 641

12. 618 ◯ 618

13. 978 ◯ 987

Place Value

Tell if the underlined digit is in the ones, tens, hundreds, or thousands place.

14. 9,482

15. 8,000

16. 1,506

17. 8,005

18. 5,100

19. 2,731

In this topic, you will learn more about place value.

Rounding

20. **Construct Arguments** Use the number line to describe how to round 450 to the nearest hundred.

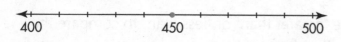

400   450   500

Pick a Project

PROJECT
1A

How many bones are in your body?

Project: Make a Bones Poster

PROJECT
1B

Would you like to be a construction manager?

Project: Design a Building

PROJECT
1C

Which stadium is your favorite?

Project: Create a Stadium Model

Before watching the video, think:

Last week, I read an entire book in one sitting. I could not put it down. How long is your reading list? Do you think this pile will take me a year to read? Time to get started.

I can ...

model with math to solve a problem that involves rounding, estimating, and computing with whole numbers.

© **Mathematical Practices** MP.3, MP.4, MP.7
Content Standards 4.NBT.A.2, 4.NBT.A.1, 4.NBT.A.3

Name _____

Solve & Share

Mrs. Darcy saved ten $100 bills. How much money did Mrs. Darcy save?

I can ...
read and write numbers through one million in expanded form, with numerals, and using number names.

Content Standard 4.NBT.A.2
Mathematical Practices MP.2, MP.7

You can use reasoning in solving a problem. Think about what you know about ten $10 bills to help you find how much money you would have if you had ten $100 bills.

$$10 \times 100 = 1000$$

Look Back! How did you decide how many zeros you needed to write in your answer?

3 zeros

Essential Question **What Are Some Ways to Write Numbers to One Million?**

A

The graph shows the attendance at a ballpark over one year. Write the total attendance in expanded form and using number names.

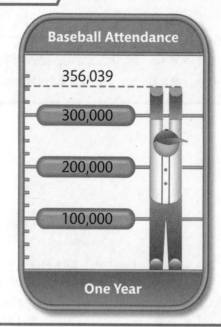

Baseball Attendance

356,039

300,000

200,000

100,000

One Year

Place value is the position of a digit in a number that tells the value of the digit.

B

The place-value chart shows periods of three places, starting at the ones period from the right and including the thousands and millions period. Each period is separated by a comma and has three place values: ones, tens, and hundreds.

Each digit in 356,039 is written in its place on the chart. Expanded form shows the sum of the values of each digit.

Expanded form: 300,000 + 50,000 + 6,000 + 30 + 9

Number name: three hundred fifty-six thousand, thirty-nine

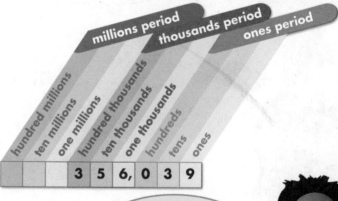

millions period   thousands period   ones period

hundred millions | ten millions | one millions | hundred thousands | ten thousands | one thousands | hundreds | tens | ones

3 5 6, 0 3 9

Notice the comma separates the periods when the number name is written.

Convince Me! **Look for Relationships** What pattern exists in the three places in each period?

Each period has ones place Tens place and hundreds place

Another Example!

21,125 can be expanded and written in different ways.

20,000 + 1,000 + 100 + 20 + 5
21,000 + 100 + 25
20,000 + 1,100 + 20 + 5

Every form is equal to 21,125.

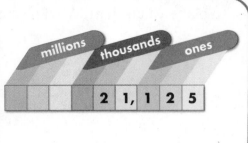

millions thousands ones

| 2 | 1, | 1 | 2 | 5 |

☆ Guided Practice

Do You Understand?

1. What do you notice about the comma in the number on the previous page?

The comma seperates the ones proid and the thousands proid

2. Write an example of a number that would include 2 commas.

606,665,466

Do You Know How?

3. Write 7,320 in expanded form.

7000 + 300 + 20-

4. Write 55,426 using number names.

fifty five thousand four hundred twenty six

5. In a recent year, 284,604 fans attended the hockey playoffs in Chicago. What digit is in the thousands place in 284,604?

4 thousand

☆ Independent Practice ☆

For **6-8**, write each number in expanded form.

6. 7,622   **7.** 294,160   **8.** 43,702

7000+ 600+20+2   *294000+100+60*   *43000 + 700 + 2*

For **9-11**, write each number name.

9. 1,688   **10.** 331,872   **11.** 44,444

1000+600+80+8   *331000+800+70+ 4*

Problem Solving

12. Letitia wrote one thousand, two hundred four in a place-value chart. What mistake did she make?

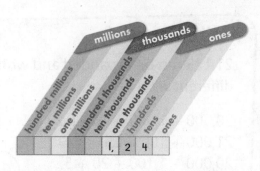

13. Reasoning In 2016, the world's oldest tree was 5,066 years old. Write the number that is one hundred more using number names.

14. Jessica wants to buy a new team jacket that costs $35. If Jessica saves $5 a week for 4 weeks and $4 a week for 3 weeks, will she have enough money to buy the team jacket? Explain.

15. **Vocabulary** Drew wrote the following sentence: "A period is a group of any 3 three digits in a number." Do you agree with Drew? If not, how would you correct him?

16. Higher Order Thinking Two numbers have the same digit in the millions period, the same digits in the thousands period, and the same digits in the ones period. Do these two numbers have the same value? Explain.

Assessment Practice

17. Wallace writes the number 72,204 in a place-value chart. Select the places that will be filled on the chart.

- ☐ Ones
- ☐ Tens
- ☐ Thousands
- ☐ Ten thousands
- ☐ Hundred thousands

18. Select all that are equal to 96,014.

- ☐ $96,000 + 10 + 4$
- ☐ $90,000 + 60,000 + 10 + 4$
- ☐ $90,000 + 6,000 + 4$
- ☐ $90,000 + 6,000 + 10 + 4$
- ☐ $96,000 + 14$

Activity

Solve & Share

Place-value blocks are shown below for 1, 10, and 100. What patterns in the shapes and sizes of the blocks do you see?

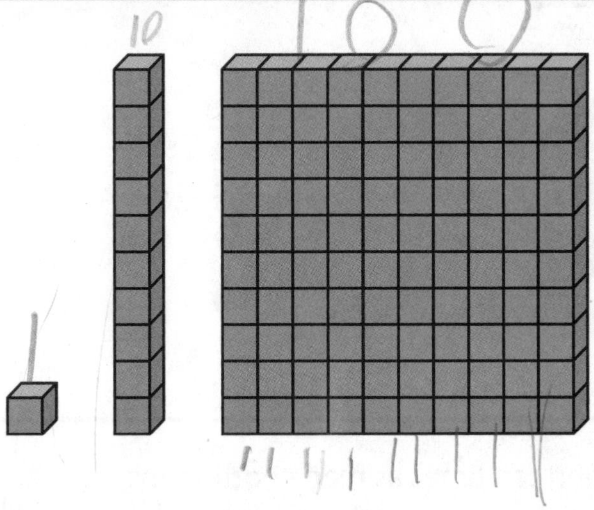

10

100

I can ...
recognize that a digit in one place has ten times the value of the same digit in the place to its right.

© **Content Standard** 4.NBT.A.2
Mathematical Practices MP.2, MP.3, MP.8

Add 1 to 100

Use reasoning. You can use place value to analyze the relationship between the digits of a number.

Look Back! Describe two ways 100 and 10 are related.

10 tens Is the sem size
One hundred,
100 is greater then ten because
100 has 3 digits and ten has 2 digit

How Are Place Values Related to Each Other?

A

Kiana had bottle caps. She wants to collect ten times as many bottle caps. How many bottle caps will Kiana have in her collection then?

Think place value.

100 bottle caps

B A hundreds flat represents 100 bottle caps.

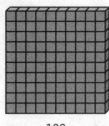

100

C To find ten times as many bottle caps, group 10 hundreds flats together.

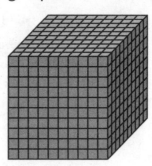

1,000

One thousand is ten times 100.

$100 \times 10 = 1,000$

One hundred is one-tenth of 1,000.

$1,000 \div 10 = 100$

Kiana will have 1,000 bottle caps in her collection.

Convince Me! **Generalize** Use place-value blocks to model 1 and 10, 10 and 100, 100 and 1,000. What pattern do you see?

Another Example!

Joe scored 2,000 points on a progressive video game. It took him 5 weeks to get his total point value to 20,000. It took him 3 months to get his total point value to 200,000 points. How many times greater than his first score were his points after 5 weeks? After 3 months?

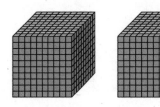

After 5 weeks, Joe's points were 10 times greater.

After 3 months, Joe's points were 100 times greater.

$2,000 \times 10 = 20,000$

$20,000 \times 10 = 200,000$

$10 \times 10 = 100$

☆ Guided Practice

Do You Understand?

1. Is the value of the 2 in 23,406 ten times as great as the value of the 3? Explain.

    2 3,406 no the valid of 2 in 23,496 is 2000 the 3 is 3000 is not 10 times greater tan 3000

Do You Know How?

For **2**, use the relationship between the values of the digits to solve.

2. Write a number in which the value of the 3 is ten times greater than the value of the 3 in 135,864.

    353,686   303,000

☆ Independent Practice ☆

For **3–5**, use the relationship between the values of the digits to solve.

3. Baseten School District bought 5,000 pencils. They are distributing the pencils evenly to 10 schools in the district. How many pencils will each school get?   *500 pencils*

4. Place Elementary School is raising money. They raise $90 a week. How long will it take them to raise $900?   *10 weeks*

5. A donation of 50 rulers was given to Value Elementary School. The school had 10 times as many erasers donated. How many erasers were donated?   *500 erasers*

Problem Solving

6. What can you say about the 3s in 43,862 and 75,398?

7. Critique Reasoning Mia says in 5,555, all the digits have the same value. Is Mia correct? Explain.

8. Number Sense In 1934, there was an extreme drought in the Great Plains. In the number 1,934, is the value of the 9 in the hundreds place ten times as great as the value of the 3 in the tens place? Explain.

9. Critique Reasoning Vin says in 4,346, one 4 is 10 times as great as the other 4. Is Vin correct? Explain.

10. Describe 2 ways to find the area of the shaded rectangle.

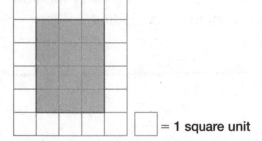

= 1 square unit

11. Higher Order Thinking In 448,244, how is the relationship between the first pair of 4s the same as the relationship between the second pair of 4s?

12. Which group of numbers shows the values of the 4s in 44,492?

ⓐ 40,000; 4,000; 400

ⓑ 40,000; 400; 40

ⓒ 4,000; 400; 4

ⓓ 400; 40; 4

13. In which number is the value of the red digit ten times as great as the value of the blue digit?

ⓐ **33**5,531

ⓑ 335,**5**31

ⓒ 335,**5**31

ⓓ 335,5**3**1

Name _____

Solve & Share

A robotic submarine can dive to a depth of 26,000 feet. Which oceans can the submarine explore all the way to the bottom? *Solve this problem any way you choose.*

I can ...
use place value to compare numbers and record my comparisons using <, =, or >.

 Content Standard 4.NBT.A.2
Mathematical Practices MP.1, MP.2, MP.4

You can model with math. Use what you know about place value to help solve the problem.

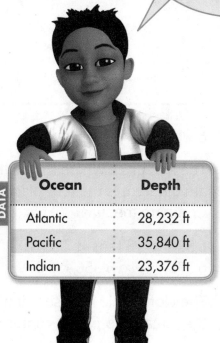

DATA

Ocean	Depth
Atlantic	28,232 ft
Pacific	35,840 ft
Indian	23,376 ft

Look Back! Which of the oceans listed is the shallowest? Explain.

Essential Question **How Do You Compare Numbers?**

A

Earth is not perfectly round. The North Pole is 6,356 kilometers from Earth's center. The equator is 6,378 kilometers from the center. Which is closer to Earth's center, the North Pole or the equator?

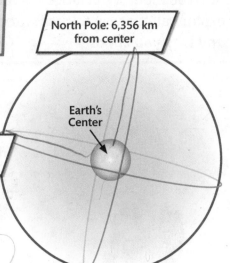

North Pole: 6,356 km from center

Earth's Center

Equator: 6,378 km from center

The symbol > means "is greater than," and the symbol < means "is less than."

B **Step 1**

Write the numbers, lining up places. Begin at the left and compare.

6,356
6,378

The thousands digit is the same in both numbers.

C **Step 2**

Look at the next digit. Compare the hundreds.

6,356
6,378

The hundreds digit is also the same in both numbers.

D **Step 3**

The first place where the digits are different is the tens place. Compare the tens.

6,356   5 tens < 7 tens,
6,378   so 6,356 < 6,378.

The North Pole is closer than the equator to Earth's center.

Convince Me! **Reasoning** Is a whole number with 4 digits always greater than or less than a whole number with 3 digits? Explain.

greater than because the greatst 3 digit number is 444

Name _____

☆ Guided Practice

Do You Understand?

1. Which place do you use to compare the numbers 60,618 and 60,647?

tens

2. Morocco has a total area of 442,300 square kilometers. Uzbekistan has a total area of 447,400 square kilometers. Use >, <, or = to compare the two areas.

442,300   442,300

Do You Know How?

For **3–7**, complete by writing >, =, or < in each ◯.

3. 2,643 ⊜ 2,643

4. 62,519 ⬳ 64,582

5. 218,701 ⊘ 118,692

6. 32,467 ⊜ 32,467

7. 19,219 ⊘ 19,209

☆ Independent Practice ☆

For **8–12**, complete by writing >, =, or < in each ◯.

8. 22,873 ⊘ 22,774

9. 912,706 ⊜ 912,706

10. 22,240 ⬳ 2,224

11. 30,000 + 5,000 + 3 ⊘ 300,000 + 5,000

12. 40,000 + 2,000 + 600 + 6 ⬳ 40,000 + 3,000 + 10

For **13–17**, write which place to use when comparing the numbers.

13. 394,284
328,234   *hundred*
tenthousand

14. 6,716
6,714
ones

15. 32,916
32,819   *one*
Hundred

16. 12,217
11,246   *tens*
ones
10 thousand

17. 812,497
736,881
10 thousand
thousand
hundred
tens
ones

Remember to compare each place value, starting on the left!

Problem Solving

For **18-19**, use the table at the right.

18. Which genres at Danny's Books did **NOT** sell better than Science?

14, 843 Humer

19. Which genres at Danny's Books sold better than Biography?

fantby fiction

Sales at Danny's Books	
Fiction	48,143
Fantasy	42,843
Biography	41,834
Science	41,843
Humor	14,843

20. Celia bought 3 bags of 4 hamburger buns and 3 bags of 8 hot dog buns. How many hamburger and hot dog buns did Celia buy?

12 humburges
24 hotdogs buns

21. Make Sense and Persevere Write three numbers for which you would use the hundreds place to compare to 35,712.

35812

22. enVision® STEM The Illinoian Stage began about 300,000 years ago. The Wolstonian Stage began about 352,000 years ago. Compare 300,000 to 352,000.

23. An orchard in Maine has 5,287 apple trees. An orchard in Vermont has 5,729 trees. Use <, >, or = to write a comparison between the number of trees in each orchard.

24. In 2010, the population of Alaska was 710,231. Write this number in expanded form, and write the number name.

70000 + 10,000 + 200 + 30 + 1

25. Higher Order Thinking Explain how you know 437,160 is greater than 43,716.

se more

Assessment Practice

26. Is each comparison true or false?

	True	False
209,999 > 210,000	☐	☐
59,546 < 59,564	☐	☐
178,614 > 178,641	☐	☐

27. Is each comparison true or false?

	True	False
111,009 > 111,110	☐	☐
28,736 < 27,736	☐	☐
69,454 > 69,455	☐	☐

Name _____

Solve & Share

List 7 numbers that round to 300. Use a variety of numbers. **Solve this problem any way you choose.**

I can ...
use place value to round numbers.

Content Standard 4.NBT.A.3
Mathematical Practices MP.2, MP.3, MP.5

Select and use appropriate tools. A number line can help you round numbers.

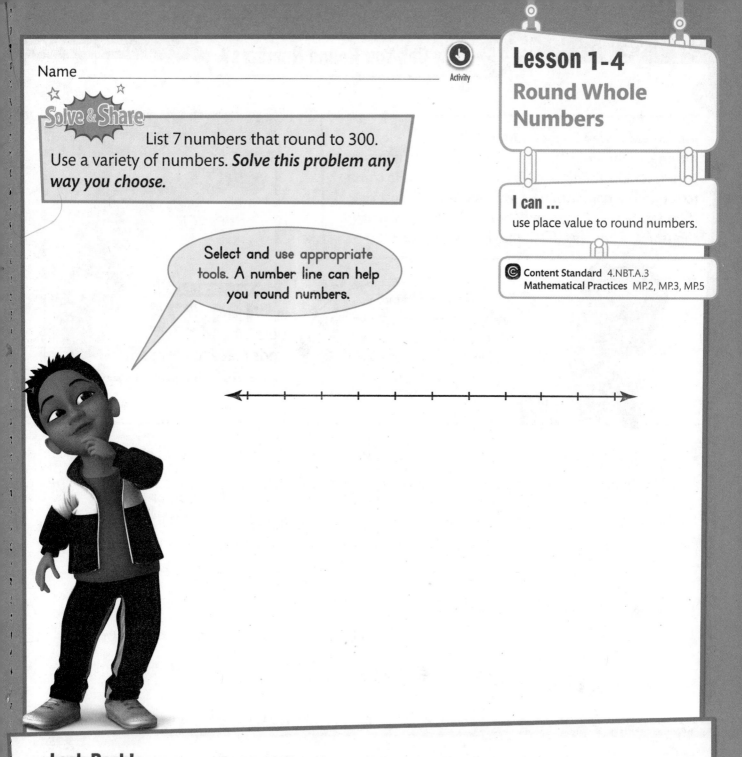

Look Back! What is the greatest number between 200 and 300 that is closer to 200 than 300? Explain.

A

James researched 10 facts about Tallahassee, Florida for an assignment. One of the facts he found was the population in Tallahassee for the year 2017. He chose to round the population on his Florida Facts poster. If James rounded the population in 2017 to the nearest thousand, what was the number James displayed?

When you round, you find which benchmark numbers, or multiples of 10, 100, 1,000, and so on, a number is closest to.

2017 Census
Tallahassee, Florida

TOTAL POPULATION
181,376

B Round 181,376 to the nearest thousand.

181,376 is between 181,000 and 182,000.

181,000 ———————————— 182,000

C Find the number 181,376 is closer to.

Mark the halfway point on the number line.

If the number is to the left of the halfway point, it rounds down. If the number is to the right of the halfway point, it rounds up.

181,376

181,000 — 181,500 — 182,000
halfway point

181,376 is to the left of the halfway point.

The poster displayed the population as 181,000.

Convince Me! **Critique Reasoning** Ellie says, "When I round these three numbers, I get the same number for two of them." Anthony says, "Hmmm, when I round these numbers, I get the same number for all three." Who is correct? Explain.

Three Numbers		
1,483	1,250	1,454

both y: because they are below 5 so the ell can Roud down

Another Example!

You can use place value to round. Round 181,376 to the nearest hundred.

- Find the digit in the rounding place.
- Look at the next digit to the right.
  If it is 5 or greater, add 1 to the rounding digit.
  If it is less than 5, leave the rounding digit alone.
- Change all digits to the right of the rounding place to 0.

181,376
↓↓↓
181,400

Since 7 > 5, the 3 becomes a 4.

☆ Guided Practice

Do You Understand?

1. Explain how to round a number when 3 is the digit to the right of the rounding place.

[handwritten: 3 ✗ 5 −3 − − Leave the rounding digit]

2. What number is halfway between 421,000 and 422,000?

[handwritten: 421,500]

[handwritten: update the digit to the right]

Do You Know How?

For **3–8**, round each number to the place of the underlined digit.

3. 128,<u>9</u>55   *[handwritten: 129,000]*

4. 8<u>5</u>,639   *[handwritten: 85,604]*

5. <u>9</u>,924   *[handwritten: 10,000]*

6. 1<u>9</u>4,524   *[handwritten: 190,000]*

7. <u>1</u>60,656   *[handwritten: 200,000]*

8. <u>1</u>49,590   *[handwritten: 100,000]*

☆ Independent Practice

For **9–24**, use a number line or place value to round each number to the place of the underlined digit.

9. 49<u>3</u>,295   *[handwritten: 500,000]*

10. <u>3</u>9,230   *[handwritten: 400,000]*

11. 2<u>7</u>7,292   *[handwritten: 30,000]*

12. 54,<u>8</u>46   *[handwritten: 54,800]*

13. 4,0<u>2</u>8   *[handwritten: 4,000]*

14. <u>6</u>38,365   *[handwritten: 700,000]*

15. 453,<u>2</u>80   *[handwritten: 453,300]*

16. 17,<u>9</u>09   *[handwritten: 18,000]*

17. 9<u>5</u>6,000   *[handwritten: 100,000]*

18. 5<u>5</u>,460   *[handwritten: 55,000]*

19. 3<u>2</u>1,679   *[handwritten: 320,000]*

20. 417,5<u>4</u>7

21. 1<u>1</u>7,821

22. <u>7</u>5,254

23. 9<u>4</u>9,999

24. 666,821

Problem Solving

25. For each zoo in the table, round the attendance to the nearest hundred thousand.

Zoo Attendance	
Zoo D	234,679
Zoo E	872,544
Zoo F	350,952

26. Number Sense Write four numbers that round to 700,000 when rounded to the nearest hundred thousand.

27. Reasoning A forest ranger correctly rounded the number of visitors to a park to be 120,000 visitors. Write a number that could be the actual number of visitors if he rounded to the nearest ten thousand.

28. Amy counted the number of boys and girls at a party. She recorded the results in the tally chart below.

Party	
Girls	///
Boys	///// //

How many more boys than girls were at the party?

29. Higher Order Thinking Liz attended class every day since she started school as a kindergartner. She said she has been in school for about 1,000 days. What numbers could be the actual number of school days if Liz rounded to the nearest ten?

Assessment Practice

30. Complete the table. Round each number to the given place.

Number	Ten	Hundred	Thousand	Ten Thousand
45,982				
128,073				
13,713				
60,827				
105,307				

Name_____

☆ ☆
Solve & Share

The land areas of three states are shown in the table. Mickey said Alaska's land area is about 10 times greater than Georgia's land area. Explain why Mickey is or is not correct. Construct a math argument to support your answer.

DATA	State	Land Area (in square miles)
	Alaska	570,641
	Georgia	57,513
	Hawaii	6,423

I can ...
construct arguments using what I know about place-value relationships.

© **Mathematical Practices** MP.3 Also MP.1, MP.2, MP.6
Content Standards 4.NBT.A.1 Also 4.NBT.A.2, 4.NBT.A.3

Thinking Habits
Be a good thinker!
These questions can help you.

• How can I use numbers, objects, drawings, or actions to justify my argument?

• Am I using numbers and symbols correctly?

• Is my explanation clear and complete?

Look Back! **Construct Arguments** Mary said Georgia's land area is about 10 times greater than Hawaii's land area. Is Mary correct? Construct a math argument to support your answer.

Essential Question

How Can You Construct Arguments?

A

The table shows the retail sales per person in three states. Bella says Arizona had more retail sales per person than Massachusetts.

DATA	State	Retail Sales per Person
	Arizona	$13,637
	Iowa	$13,172
	Massachusetts	$13,533

How can you construct a math argument that supports Bella's conjecture?

I will use what I know about place value to compare numbers.

> A conjecture is a statement that is believed to be true but has not been proven.

B

How can I construct an argument?

I can

- give an explanation that is clear and complete.

- use numbers and symbols correctly in my explanation.

- use numbers, objects, drawings, or actions to justify my argument.

- use a counterexample in my argument.

C

> Here's my thinking.

Bella's statement makes sense.

Start with the greatest place value. The digits are the same in the **ten thousands place** and in the **thousands place**. The digits are different in the **hundreds place**, so that place is compared.

$13,637

$13,533

600 > 500

So, $13,637 > $13,533.

Bella is correct. Arizona had more retail sales per person than Massachusetts.

Convince Me! **Construct Arguments** Gayle said Arizona had more retail sales than Massachusetts because 7 > 3, so $13,637 > $13,533. Construct an argument to explain whether or not Gayle is correct.

no Gayles arugumint is in corect because she needto compair other place values sht need to compair 637 and 553.

Guided Practice

Construct Arguments

Use the table on the previous page. Jorge said Massachusetts has more retail sales per person than Iowa.

When you construct arguments, you justify your conclusions.

Mes

1. What numbers would you use to construct an argument supporting Jorge's conjecture?

M. B.533 713. 172

2. How could you support Jorge's conjecture?

compair the numbers

3. Is Jorge's conjecture true? Justify your answer.

yes $135,337 172

Independent Practice

Construct Arguments

The population of Gerald's city is three hundred thousand, twenty-seven. Gerald wrote the number as 327,000. Emily lives in a city that has a population of three hundred sixteen thousand, forty-two. Gerald concluded that his city's population is greater than the population of Emily's city.

327,000 > 316,042

4. Does Gerald's explanation make sense? Identify any flaws in Gerald's thinking.

No he wrote the wrong number

5. Construct a math argument that explains why Gerald did not write the population of his city correctly.

The digit for 27 blong in the ones perod 300,027

6. Correct Gerald's argument. Explain how to compare the populations of Gerald's and Emily's cities.

300,027 316,942

Problem Solving

Planets

The planets in our solar system are different sizes, as shown below. Nora conjectured that Jupiter's equator is about 10 times as long as Earth's equator.

Length of Equators for 4 Planets

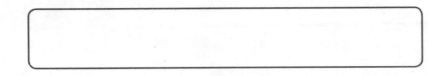

Earth 40,030 km   Jupiter 439,264 km   Venus 38,025 km   Mars 21,297 km

7. **Make Sense and Persevere** What information do you have?

8. **Be Precise** What are possible estimates for the lengths of the equators of Jupiter and Earth?

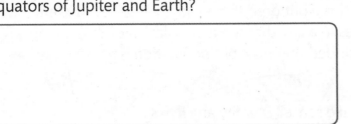

When you construct arguments, you explain clearly and completely.

9. **Reasoning** What is the relationship between the estimates you found for the lengths of the two equators?

10. **Construct Arguments** Construct an argument justifying Nora's conjecture.

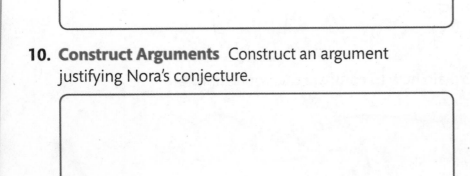

Name_____

Find a partner. Get paper and pencil. Each partner chooses a different color: Light blue or dark blue.

Partner 1 and Partner 2 each point to a black number at the same time. Both partners multiply those numbers.

If the answer is on your color, you get a tally mark. Work until one partner has twelve tally marks.

I can ...
multiply within 100.

 Content Standard 3.OA.C.7
Mathematical Practices MP.3, MP.6, MP.7, MP.8

Partner 1

| 6 |
| 9 |
| 8 |
| 5 |
| 7 |

40	28	45	56
24	24	36	20
63	48	63	64
15	42	49	32
54	27	35	21
72	72	18	81

Partner 2

| 7 |
| 4 |
| 3 |
| 9 |
| 8 |

Tally Marks for Partner 1

Tally Marks for Partner 2

Vocabulary Review

A-Z
Glossary

Understand Vocabulary

Choose the best term from the box. Write it on the blank.

1. A group of three digits, separated by commas, starting from the right is called a _period_.

2. A process that determines which multiple of 10, 100, 1,000 (and so on) a number is closest to is called _rounding_.

3. A statement that is believed to be true but has not yet been proven is called a _conjecture_.

4. The value given to a place a digit has in a number is called its _place value_.

5. In a number, a period of three places to the left of the thousands period is called the _millions_ period.

For each of these terms, give an example and a non-example.

	Example	Non-example
6. greater than symbol (>)	572	2 = 2
7. less than symbol (<)	47.5	8 = 8
8. expanded form	759	3 = 3

Use Vocabulary in Writing

9. Describe the value of the 9 in 926,415. Use at least 2 terms from the Word List in your explanation.

the 9 in the thousand period the place value of the 9 is the hundred thousand place

Name_____

Set A pages 5–8

Use a place-value chart to write 301,400.

Expanded form: 300,000 + 1,000 + 400

Number name: three hundred one thousand, four hundred

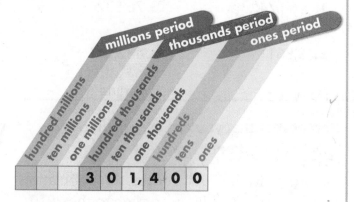

| 3 | 0 | 1, | 4 | 0 | 0 |

Remember that each period has hundreds, tens, ones, and the period name.

Write each number in expanded form and using number names.

1. 7,549   7000 + 500 + 40 +9

2. 92,065   90000 + 2 000 + 0 + 60 + 5

Set B pages 9–12

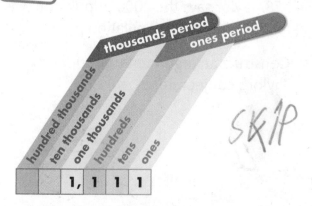

SKIP

| 1, | 1 | 1 | 1 |

1,111 = 1,000 + 100 + 10 + 1

As you move left, each numeral is 10 times greater than the digit on its right.

$1 \times 10 = 10$
$10 \times 10 = 100$
$100 \times 10 = 1,000$

Remember to use the relationship between the values of the digits.

For **1–2**, solve.

1. How many times greater is the value of the 7 in 70,048 than the value of 7 in 17,992?

    10 times greater

2. Violet has 30 glass tiles. She would like to mosaic tile a tabletop with 10 times that number of tiles. How many tiles does Violet want to use?

    300 tiles   30 × 10

Set C pages 13–16

Use place value to compare 45,423 and 44,897. Start comparing from the left. Look for the first digit that is different.

45,423   44,897

5 > 4

5,000 > 4,000

So, 45,423 > 44,897.

yes because the 5 in the thousand place

Remember that you can use place value to compare numbers.

Write < or > in the ◯.

1. 291,846 ◯ 291,864

2. 662,980 ◯ 66,298

3. 88,645 ◯ 87,645

Round 764,802 to the nearest hundred thousand.

764,802

<----+-------+-------+---->
700,000   750,000   800,000

764,802 is to the right of the halfway point. So, 764,802 rounds to 800,000.

Remember to find the halfway point to help you round.

For **1–4**, use number lines or place value to round each number to the place of the underlined digit.

1. 166,742

167000

2. 76,532

77000

3. 5,861

6000

4. 432,041

432,000

Think about these questions to help you **construct arguments**.

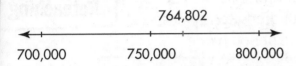

Thinking Habits

- How can I use numbers, objects, drawings, or actions to justify my argument?

- Am I using numbers and symbols correctly?

- Is my explanation clear and complete?

Remember that you can use math to show why your argument is correct.

According to the 2000 census, the population of a city was 935,426. According to the 2010 census, the population of the same city was 934,578. Taylor says the 2000 population was greater than the 2010 population.

1. Construct an argument that supports Taylor's conjecture.

Taylor is right when comparing place values that greatest place the different place

2. In 1870, the population was seventy-two thousand, five hundred six. Lupita wrote 72,560. Construct a math argument that explains whether Lupita wrote the number correctly.

In the thousand 574 Lupita wrote the number incorrect. the digit 6 belong

Name_____

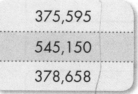
1. Choose all the numbers that round to 100,000 when rounded to the nearest hundred thousand.

☐ 9,999

☑ 89,006

☑ 109,999

☑ 119,999

☑ 999,999

2. Which symbol makes the comparison true? Write >, =, or < in the ○.

111,011 ○ 110,111

| < | ⬭ > | = |

3. Write three numbers that round to 40,000 when rounded to the nearest ten thousand.

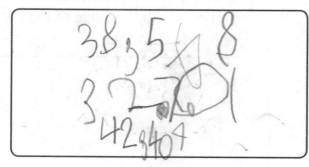

4. John wrote the numbers 678,901 and 67,890. How many times greater is the value of 7 in 678,901 than the value of 7 in 67,890?

Ⓐ 10,000

Ⓑ 1,000

Ⓒ 100

Ⓓ 10

5. Look at the numbers in the table.

375,595
545,150
378,658

Which number has one digit that represents ten times the value of the digit to its right? Explain.

375,595 the value of the 5 in the thones place is ten times greater than the 5 in the hundreds place

6. Write the number for 160,060 in expanded form and using number names.

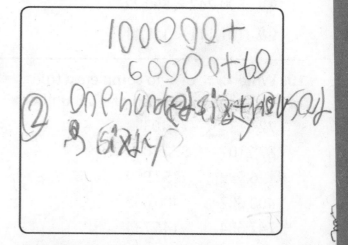

100000 + 60000 + 60

② One hundred sixty thousand & sixty

7. A. For each number, give the whole number that represents the value of the underlined digit. Write your answers in the boxes.

155,349 [5,000]

651,907 [50,000]

947,502 [500]

317,055 [50]

B. Look at your answers in **Part A**. In which number is the value of the underlined digit 10 times the value of the digit to the right of it?

(A) 155,349   (C) 947,502

(B) 651,907   (D) 317,055

---

8. Rhode Island has about three hundred fifty-six thousand acres of forested land. What is this number in standard form rounded to the nearest ten thousand?

356,000

(A) 350,000   (C) 360,000

(B) 400,000   (D) 356,000

---

9. Which one of the following comparisons is correct?

(A) 65,215 > 65,512

(B) 292,200 < 229,200

(C) 890,242 < 890,224

(D) 101,111 < 111,111

---

10. Write <, =, or > to complete a true comparison for each pair of numbers.

72,013 < 72,103

87,210 = 87,210

126,999 < 152,999

400,602 > 400,062

147,634 ___ 146,734

---

11. The table shows the areas of four states.

State	Area (square miles)
Montana	147,042
Kansas	82,278
Oregon	98,381
Wyoming	97,814

A. Which of the 4 states has the least area? the greatest area? Write the number name for the area of each of these states.

kansis eight two thousand seventy eight monto one hundred thousan 42

B. Draw a place-value chart. Record Kansas's area. Explain how the value of the 2 in the thousands place compares with the value of the 2 in the hundreds place.

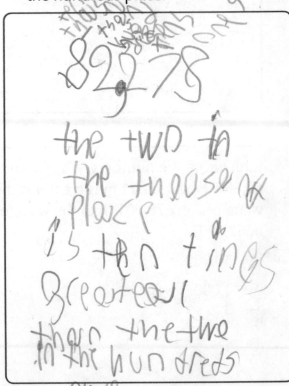

82,278

the two in the thousand place is ten times greater than the two in the hundreds place

Name_____

Video Games

Tanji, Arun, and Juanita are playing a video game with 3 levels. The opportunity to earn points increases as the levels of the game increase. To keep track of their progress, Tanji, Arun, and Juanita record and examine their scores at each level.

1. Use the **Level 1** table to answer the following questions.

Part A

Tanji noticed he was the only player with 3s in his Level 1 score. What are the values of the 3s in Tanji's score?

Part B

Arun noticed the 5s in his score were next to each other. Describe the relationship between the 5s in Arun's score.

Level 1

Player	Score
Tanji	4,337
Arun	5,519
Juanita	2,868

Part C

Juanita says the value of one 8 in her score is ten times greater than the value of the other 8. Construct an argument and draw a place-value chart to determine if Juanita is correct.

2. Use the **Level 2** table to answer the following questions.

Part A

Juanita had the greatest score at Level 2, followed by Tanji and Arun. Write each player's score in expanded form to compare each score by place value.

Level 2	
Player	**Score**
Tanji	56,899
Arun	39,207
Juanita	60,114

Part B

Write each player's score using number names.

Part C

Use >, =, or < to write comparisons between the Level 2 scores.

Part D

Arun noticed his Level 2 score has a greater value in the thousands place than Tanji's and Juanita's Level 2 scores. Round Arun's score to the nearest thousand.

Fluently Add and Subtract Multi-Digit Whole Numbers

Essential Questions: How can sums and differences of whole numbers be estimated? What are standard procedures for adding and subtracting whole numbers?

Digital Resources

Interactive Student Edition   Activity   Visual Learning   Video   Practice

Assessment   Games   Tools   Glossary

The faster an object is moving, the more energy it has.

In 1970, a rocket-powered vehicle was the first to travel over 1,000 kilometers per hour!

That takes a lot of energy! Here is a project on speed and comparing speeds.

enVision STEM Project: The World's Fastest Vehicles

Do Research Since 1970, the speed record has been broken many times. Use the Internet or other sources to find five vehicles that can go faster than 1,000 kilometers per hour.

Journal: Write a Report Include what you found. Also in your report:

- Make a table that includes the type of vehicle, whether the vehicle moves on land, water, or in space, and the speed of the vehicle.

- Use place value to find the fastest and the slowest vehicle in your table.

- Calculate the difference between the speeds of two of the vehicles in your table.

Review What You Know

A-Z Vocabulary

Choose the best term from the box.
Write it on the blank.

• equation	• period
• estimate	• rounding

1. An _____ is an approximate number or answer.

2. A process that determines which multiple of 10, 100, 1,000, and so on a number is closest to is called _____.

3. A number sentence that uses the equal sign (=) to show two expressions have the same value is an _____.

Addition Facts and Mental Math

Find each sum.

4. 4 + 6   **5.** 7 + 5   **6.** 29 + 8

7. 14 + 5   **8.** 13 + 7   **9.** 37 + 7

10. 289 + 126   **11.** 468 + 329   **12.** 157 + 211

Subtraction Facts and Mental Math

Find each difference.

13. 27 – 3   **14.** 6 – 4   **15.** 15 – 8

16. 11 – 8   **17.** 66 – 2   **18.** 17 – 8

19. 416 – 404   **20.** 220 – 205   **21.** 148 – 106

Rounding

22. Construct Arguments Why does 843,000 round to 840,000 rather than 850,000 when rounded to the nearest ten thousand?

> A good math explanation should be clear, complete, and easy to understand.

PROJECT 2A

What are the largest cities in your home state?

Project: Map the Population of Your State's Largest Cities

PROJECT 2B

How did the United States become a nation?

Project: Write a Report on U.S. Expansion

How do the sizes of the planets compare to the size of Earth?

Project: Make a Model of the Solar System

PROJECT 2D

How high is high?

Project: Compare Mountain Elevations

Name _____

Solve & Share

Luke collected 1,034 baseball cards, 1,289 football cards, and 1,566 hockey cards. Use mental math to find the number of cards in Luke's collection. *Solve this problem any way you choose.*

I can ...
use properties and strategies to change a problem to add and subtract with mental math.

© **Content Standard** 4.NBT.B.4
Mathematical Practices MP.3, MP.6, MP.7

You can break apart the addends and use mental math to find the sum. *Show your work in the space below!*

Look Back! **Construct Arguments** How could you use mental math to solve 1,289 + 1,566? 1,034 + 1,566? How is the thinking different?

Essential Question **How Can You Use Mental Math to Solve Problems?**

Visual Learning Bridge

A

Katy's dad washes windows at one of the tallest buildings in Miami, the Four Seasons Hotel. He worked Saturdays in October and earned more money than in September. How much did he earn in the two months combined?

You can use strategies based on properties to add numbers mentally.

Washing Windows
Earned $1,985 in Sept.
Earned $2,595 in Oct.

Find $1,985 + $2,595 with mental math.

B **Make Ten**

Break apart 1,985 to get a number that makes a ten, hundred, or thousand when added to 2,595. Then, use the **Associative Property of Addition** to change the grouping.

1,985 + 2,595
= (1,580 + 405) + 2,595
= 1,580 + (405 + 2,595)
= 1,580 + 3,000
= 4,580

Katy's dad earned $4,580.

C **Add On**

Break one addend apart and add on.

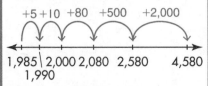
+5 +10 +80 +500 +2,000

1,985 ╲ 2,000 2,080 2,580   4,580
  1,990

You can start with either addend because of the **Commutative Property of Addition.**

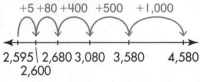
+5 +80 +400 +500 +1,000

2,595 ╲ 2,680 3,080 3,580   4,580
  2,600

Katy's dad earned $4,580.

D **Use Compensation**

Add 15 to 1,985. Then subtract 15 from 2,595 to compensate. Adding 15 and subtracting 15 is the same as adding zero. Adding zero doesn't change the sum because of the **Identity Property of Addition.**

1,985 + 2,595
= (1,985 + 15) + (2,595 − 15)
= 2,000 + 2,580
= 4,580

Katy's dad earned $4,580.

Convince Me! **Use Structure** How could you make ten by breaking apart 2,595?

Another Example!

Subtract 2,595 − 1,985 with mental math.

Count Up

Count from 1,985 up to 2,595.

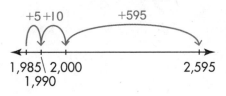

Find how much you counted up.

$5 + 10 + 595 = 610$

Count Down

Count down 1,985 from 2,595.

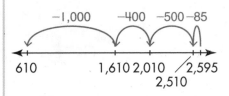

Use Compensation

Adding the same amount to both numbers in a subtraction problem doesn't change the difference.

$(2,595 + 15) − (1,985 + 15)$
$= 2,610 − 2,000$
$= 610$

☆ Guided Practice

Do You Understand?

1. Explain how to find 2,987 + 4,278 with mental math. What property does your strategy use?

Do You Know How?

For **2–4**, use mental math strategies to solve.

2. 6,794 − 999

3. 4,505 + 3,515

4. 9,100 + 2,130 + 900

Independent Practice ☆

For **5–10**, use mental math to solve.

5. 7,000 − 827

6. 1,225 + 975

7. 5,491 − 2,860

8. 6,686 − 1,443

9. 8,375 + 31,145

10. 23,100 + 74,900

Problem Solving

For **11–12**, use the table at the right.

11. **Precision** How much greater is the area of California than Montana? Explain how to use mental math to solve.

	State	Square Miles of Land
DATA	Alaska	570,641
	California	155,779
	Montana	145,546
	New Mexico	121,298
	Texas	261,232

12. Round the land area of the state with the least number of square miles to the nearest ten thousand.

---

13. The town of Worman Grove has collected 28,481 pens for a school supplies drive. Their goal is 30,000 pens. Show how to use counting on to find how many more pens they need to reach their goal.

14. Conservationists weigh two Northern elephant seals. An adult seal weighs 6,600 pounds, and its pup weighs 3,847 pounds. What is their combined weight? Explain how to use mental math to solve.

---

15. **Higher Order Thinking** Is Kelly's answer correct? What mistake did she make?

Kelly's Work

$5{,}356 + 2{,}398$

$= (5{,}356 + 2) + (2{,}398 + 2)$

$5{,}358 + 2{,}400 = 7{,}758$

Assessment Practice

16. Use mental math to find $1{,}218 + 1{,}598$.

Ⓐ 2,716

Ⓑ 2,720

Ⓒ 2,816

Ⓓ 2,820

17. Use mental math to find $5{,}280 - 1{,}997$.

Ⓐ 3,177

Ⓑ 3,180

Ⓒ 3,277

Ⓓ 3,283

Name_____

Solve & Share

A manufacturer in Detroit produces three new cars that weigh 6,127 pounds, 4,652 pounds, and 3,393 pounds. If these are are loaded on a truck, has the truck reached its 15,000-pound maximum? Use an estimate to decide. **Solve this problem any way you choose.**

I can ...
use rounding and place value to estimate sums and differences.

Content Standards 4.OA.A.3 Also 4.NBT.B.4
Mathematical Practices MP.2, MP.3

You can use reasoning and round each number to estimate the total weight.

6000
4000
3000

15,000

estumet   13000

the   His did not
much   its est limits

Look Back! Why can you solve the problem using only an estimate rather than finding the exact weight of the three cars?

Essential Question

How Can You Estimate Sums and Differences of Whole Numbers?

A

Books, magazines, and movies were checked out of the public library. About how many more books were checked out than magazines and movies combined?

Use reasoning. Use an estimate to solve. You can round to the nearest thousand or the nearest hundred to estimate.

12,642 books, 4,298 magazines, and 2,149 movies are checked out.

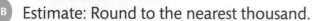

B Estimate: Round to the nearest thousand.

Find the number of magazines and movies.

$$
\begin{array}{r}
4{,}298 \longrightarrow 4{,}000 \\
+\,2{,}149 \longrightarrow +\,2{,}000 \\
\hline
6{,}000
\end{array}
$$

Subtract the number of magazines and movies from the rounded number of books.

$13{,}000 - 6{,}000 = 7{,}000$

About 7,000 more books were checked out.

C Estimate: Round to the nearest hundred.

Find the number of magazines and movies.

$$
\begin{array}{r}
4{,}298 \longrightarrow 4{,}300 \\
+\,2{,}149 \longrightarrow +\,2{,}100 \\
\hline
6{,}400
\end{array}
$$

Subtract the number of magazines and movies from the rounded number of books.

$12{,}600 - 6{,}400 = 6{,}200$

About 6,200 more books were checked out.

Convince Me! Construct Arguments The head librarian at the public library says she will establish a separate checkout desk for magazines and movies if the difference between the number of books and the number of these other materials is greater than 6,500. Which of the estimates above should you use to help her make her decision? Explain.

Name_____

Practice Tools Assessment

Another Example!

Decide if each computation is reasonable.

You can use an estimate to decide whether or not an exact answer is reasonable.

39,482 + 26,357 = 65,839

39,482 + 26,357 is about 40,000 + 26,000 = 66,000

The sum, 65,839, is reasonable because it is close to the estimate of 66,000.

8,215 − 5,852 = 3,643

8,215 − 5,852 is about 8,000 − 6,000 = 2,000

The difference, 3,643, is not reasonable because it is not close to the estimate of 2,000.

☆ Guided Practice

Do You Understand?

1. Is 2,793 a reasonable difference for 6,904 − 4,111? Explain.

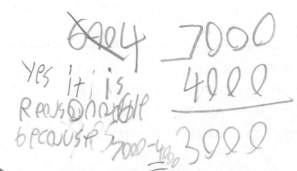

Yes it is Reasonable because 3000−4000 3000

3000 is close to 3000

Do You Know How?

For **2-4**, estimate each sum or difference.

2. 5,638 → 5,600
    + 3,753 → 3,800

3. 63,526 60000
    + 25,038 30000
    ———————
    90000

4. 262,262 260000
    − 132,147 130000
    ————————
    130000 30000

☆ Independent Practice ☆

Leveled Practice For **5-13**, estimate each sum or difference.

5. 5,323 → 6,000
    + 2,611 → + 3,000
    —————————
    8000

6. 542,817 → 543,000
    − 27,398 → − 16,200
    ——————————
    526,8

7. 49,761 → 50,000
    + 59,499 → + 60,000
    ——————————
    311,000

8. 4,225 → 4000
    +   98 → +100
    ——————
    4100

9. 738,775 700000
    + 272,044 300000
    ——————————
    1000000

10. 24,300 → 23000
     − 10,125 → 4000
     ————————
     14000 14000

11. 485,635 − 231,957

12. 9,668 − 2,489 100000

13. 368,545 + 114,254

Topic 2 | Lesson 2-2   **43**

Problem Solving

14. The table shows the number of students at each school in the district. Is 2,981 reasonable for the total number of students at Wilson Elementary and Kwame Charter School? Explain.

handwritten: 1523
handwritten: 8224~ + 1471
handwritten: Round 8000 1458
handwritten: 697
handwritten: 8224

Numbers of Students in District 37	
School	**Number of Students**
Wilson Elementary	1,523
Hearst Academy	1,471
Kwame Charter School	1,458
Evers Elementary	1,697

15. enVision® STEM A satellite moves at a speed of 27,950 kilometers per hour. A satellite at a higher orbit travels at a speed of 11,190 kilometers per hour. About how much faster is one satellite than the other? Explain how to estimate.

handwritten: 16760 27950
handwritten: more km -11190
handwritten: AR 16760

16. Critique Reasoning Elle says, "When rounding to the nearest thousand, 928,674 rounds to 930,000." Do you agree? Explain.

17. Higher Order Thinking A football team needs to sell at least 20,000 tickets to two games to cover expenses. They sell 10,184 tickets to one game and 9,723 to the other. Estimate by rounding to the nearest thousand and by rounding to the nearest hundred. Did the team sell enough tickets? Explain your answer.

handwritten: 9000 10000 19000

Assessment Practice

18. Last week, Mallory flew two round trips. They were 3,720 miles and 5,985 miles. Which is the best estimate of the total distance Mallory flew?

- Ⓐ 11,000 miles
- Ⓑ 9,700 miles
- Ⓒ 8,700 miles
- Ⓓ 8,000 miles

19. Use estimation to decide which is a reasonable difference.

38,041 − 19,558

- Ⓐ 21,374
- Ⓑ 20,973
- Ⓒ 18,473
- Ⓓ 16,483

Name _____

Solve & Share

Students collect empty plastic water bottles to recycle. How many bottles were collected in the first two months? How many bottles were collected in all three months? *Solve this problem using any strategy you choose.*

I can ...
connect place-value concepts to using addition algorithms.

Content Standards 4.NBT.B.4 Also 4.OA.A.3
Mathematical Practices MP.3, MP.5, MP.7

You can use appropriate tools, such as drawings or place-value blocks, to help you add.

Month	Water Bottles
September	357
October	243
November	468

Handwritten work:

all months

600
+468
_____
1068

2 months
11
357
+243
_____
608

the student colected 600 in 2 month

the students collected 1968 in all

1968

Look Back! When adding, how do you know when there are enough tens to make one hundred?

Essential Question

How Do You Add Whole Numbers Efficiently?

A

The Florida Legislature set a statewide recycling goal. To help meet this goal, Kennedy Elementary school students collected newspaper. How many pounds of newspaper did they collect in all?

Newspaper Collected	
Month	**Pounds**
March	358
April	277

Add 358 + 277.
Estimate.
350 + 250 = 600

Connect adding partial sums to adding using the *standard algorithm for addition.*

B **Add using partial sums.**

```
    358
  + 277
  ------
     15     8 ones + 7 ones
    120     5 tens + 7 tens
  + 500     3 hundreds + 2 hundreds
  ------
    635
```

C **Add using the standard algorithm.**

Step 1 Add ones.

```
    ¹
    358     8 ones + 7 ones = 15 ones
  + 277     Regroup. 15 ones = 1 ten + 5 ones
  ------
      5
```

Step 2 Add tens.

```
   ¹¹
   358     5 tens + 7 tens + 1 ten = 13 tens
 + 277     Regroup: 13 tens =
  -----
    35     1 hundred + 3 tens
```

Step 3 Add hundreds

```
   ¹¹
   358     3 hundreds +
 + 277     2 hundreds +
  -----    1 hundred =
   635     6 hundreds
```

The students collected 635 pounds of newspaper.

Convince Me! **Use Structure** In the problem above, when you add partial sums you can add the ones first or the hundreds. Can you do the same when you add using the standard algorithm?

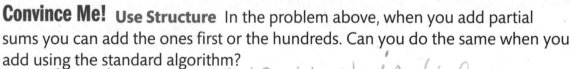
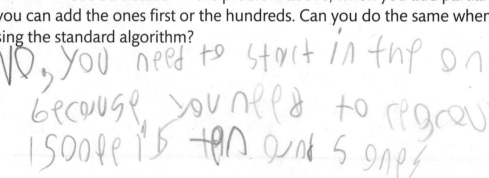

NO, you need to start in the ones because, you need to regroup
cx 15 ones it's ten and 5 ones

☆ Guided Practice

Do You Understand?

1. When you place a 1 above the tens values, what does it mean?

It means there are 10 or more only regrouped as ten

2. When you place a 1 above the hundreds values, what does it mean?

It means there are 10 more tens

Do You Know How?

Find the sum by using partial sums and by using the standard algorithm.

3.
```
   11
  378
+ 557
-----
 435
```

Find each sum using the strategy you choose.

4a. 678   **b.** 325   **c.** 185
     + 253   + 256   + 253
      843 *541*

☆ Independent Practice ☆

In **5–16**, find each sum.

7050
600+200

5.
```
  11
  148
+ 157
-----
 305
```

6.
```
  1 1
  389
+ 461
-----
 850
   1
```

7.
```
  11
  365
+ 458
-----
 423
```

8.
```
  126
+ 138
-----
 264
   1
```

9.
```
  371
+ 454
-----
 825
```

10.
```
  11
  357
+ 498
-----
 855
```

11. 142 + 178

12. 565 + 694

13. 375 + 548

14. 718 + 865

15. 909 + 624

16. 129 + 587

Topic 2 | Lesson 2-3   47

Problem Solving

17. Construct Arguments Harmony solved this problem using the standard algorithm, but she made an error. What was her error, and how can she fix it?

$$
\begin{array}{r}
\overset{1}{4}37 \\
+\ 175 \\
\hline
5{,}112
\end{array}
$$

18. Higher Order Thinking For which problems would you use a mental strategy or the standard algorithm to solve? Explain.

499 + 121

827 + 385

175 + 325

19. A Little League team played a doubleheader (two back-to-back baseball games). The first game lasted 155 minutes. The second game lasted 175 minutes. There was a 30-minute break between games. What was the total time of the doubleheader?

Assessment Practice

20. Select all the correct sums.

☐ 742 + 353 = 1,095
☐ 428 + 247 = 665
☐ 604 + 684 = 1,288
☐ 735 + 298 = 1,033
☐ 912 + 198 = 1,010

21. What is the missing digit in the addition problem?

$$
\begin{array}{r}
3\ \square\ 5 \\
+\ 6\ 5\ 9 \\
\hline
1{,}0\ 0\ 4
\end{array}
$$

Name _____

☆☆
Solve & Share

Erica's class collected 4,219 bottles for the recycling center. Ana's class collected 3,742 bottles. Leon's class collected 4,436 bottles. How many bottles did the three classes collect? **Solve this problem any way you choose.**

I can ...
use the standard algorithm and place value to add multi-digit numbers.

© **Content Standards** 4.NBT.B.4 Also 4.OA.A.3
Mathematical Practices MP.1, MP.3, MP.8

Just like you did with smaller numbers, you can break up greater numbers by place value to help you add. *Show your work in the space below!*

all three classes colected
1 hundred 23+ dousand 436

2 hundred
42

1 1
4219
3742
436
12397

Look Back! **Generalize** Which properties allow you to change the order and grouping of numbers to add? How did you use these properties?

Essential Question **How Do You Add Greater Numbers?**

A

Plans for remodeling a sports stadium include adding an additional 19,255 seats. How many seats will be in the remodeled stadium?

20,000 stadium seats
4,595 box seats

Seats in the original stadium:

$20,000 + 4,595 = 24,595$

You can use a variable to represent the unknown value. The variable, s, represents the total number of seats in the remodeled stadium.

s	
24,595	19,255

You can use an algorithm which is a set of steps used to solve a math problem.

B **Step 1**

Use the standard algorithm for addition.

To add 24,595 + 19,255, add the ones, then the tens, and then the hundreds. Regroup if necessary.

$$\begin{array}{r} 24,5\overset{1}{9}\overset{1}{5} \\ + 19,255 \\ \hline 850 \end{array}$$

C **Step 2**

Add the thousands and the ten thousands. Regroup if necessary.

$$\begin{array}{r} \overset{1}{2}4,\overset{1}{5}\overset{1}{9}5 \\ + 19,255 \\ \hline 43,850 \end{array}$$

$s = 43,850$

The remodeled stadium will have 43,850 seats.

D **Step 3**

Use an estimate to check if your answer is reasonable.

$$\begin{array}{r} 24,595 \longrightarrow \overset{1}{2}5,000 \\ + 19,255 \longrightarrow + 19,000 \\ \hline 44,000 \end{array}$$

43,850 is close to the estimate of 44,000, so the answer is reasonable.

You can add two or more numbers when you line up the numbers by place value. Add one place at a time.

Convince Me! **Construct Arguments** When using the standard algorithm to add 24,595 + 19,255, how do you regroup 1 ten + 9 tens + 5 tens?

Practice Tools Assessment

Another Example!

Find 30,283 + 63,423 + 6,538.
Explain how to check that your answer is reasonable.

Estimate:
30,000 + 63,000 + 7,000 = 100,000

$$\begin{array}{r} \overset{1\ 1\ 1\ 1}{30,283} \\ 63,423 \\ +\ \ 6,538 \\ \hline 100,244 \end{array}$$

The sum is reasonable because it is close to the estimate of 100,000.

☆ Guided Practice ☆

Do You Understand?

1. When adding 36,424 and 24,482, why is there no regrouping in the final step?

   because 3+2= 5 and it need to be above 10

2. Science-volunteer teams catalog 7,836 species of insects and 4,922 species of spiders. How many species did the volunteers catalog?

   the volentes collected 12,758 speses   7,836   4,922   2758

Do You Know How?

For **3-6**, find each sum. Check that your answer is reasonable.

3. 14,926
   + 3,382
   18308   5000 3000

4. 423,156
   + 571,607
   1111 82000

5. 3,258
   + 1,761

6. 82,385
   + 49,817
   132242 50000 132000

Independent Practice ☆

For **7-16**, find each sum. Check that your answer is reasonable.

7. 14,312
   + 9,617
   2392

8. 275,558
   + 605,131
   85069

9. 38,911
   + 45,681
   84542 40000 40000 80000

10. 5,801
   + 4,189
   9990 6000 4000 100,0

11. 8,818
   + 1,182
   10 000

12. 5,555
   + 7,412
   12967

13. 21,009
   + 5,529
   26538 21000 6000 27,000

14. 30,080
   + 19,187
   49267 30,000 20,000 50,000

15. 29,634 + 12,958 + 6,835

16. 64,673 + 48,262 + 8,918

Problem Solving

17. Aubrey writes a blog. 29,604 people read her first post. The next week, 47,684 people read her second post. Aubrey's third post had 41,582 readers. What is the total number of readers?

$$\begin{array}{r} 29604 \\ + 47684 \\ 41582 \\ \hline 118870 \end{array}$$

18. Write the number name for 21,604.

Twenty one thousand six hundred four

19. Higher Order Thinking Explain the mistake made when finding the sum at the right. What is the correct sum?

$$\begin{array}{r} 638528 \\ + 234351 \\ \hline 872874 \end{array}$$

the correct answer is 872874 they forgot to regroup

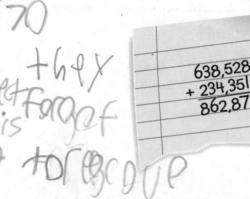

$$\begin{array}{r} 638{,}528 \\ + 234{,}351 \\ \hline 862{,}879 \end{array}$$

20. Number Sense Maria added 45,273 and 35,687 and got a sum of 70,960. Is Maria's answer reasonable? Explain.

21. Make Sense and Persevere There were 130,453 pairs of skates rented at an ice rink in one year. The next year, 108,626 pairs were rented. The following year 178,119 pairs were rented. How many pairs were rented during the busiest two years? How many pairs were rented during all three years?

✓ Assessment Practice

22. Select all the correct sums.

- ☐ $5{,}742 + 8{,}353 = 14{,}095$
- ☐ $9{,}428 + 18{,}247 = 27{,}665$
- ☐ $29{,}604 + 47{,}684 = 77{,}288$
- ☐ $66{,}288 + 145{,}280 = 211{,}568$
- ☐ $235{,}912 + 19{,}847 = 434{,}382$

23. Select all the addition expressions that have a sum of 89,405.

- ☐ $78{,}487 + 7{,}998$
- ☐ $79{,}562 + 9{,}843$
- ☐ $2{,}222 + 77{,}183$
- ☐ $52{,}514 + 36{,}891$
- ☐ $6{,}573 + 82{,}832$

Name _____

 Activity

Solve & Share

Carly's parents own a motel in Orlando with 224 rooms. Last night, 176 rooms were rented. How many rooms were not rented? **Solve this problem using any strategy you choose.**

I can ...
connect place-value concepts to using the standard algorithm for subtraction.

 Content Standards 4.NBT.B.4 Also 4.OA.A.3
Mathematical Practices MP.1, MP.5, MP.7

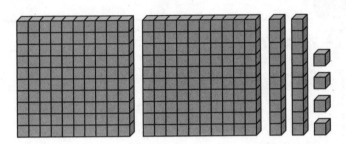

You can use appropriate tools, such as place-value blocks, to help you subtract.

Look Back! How can you use properties to find the number of rooms not rented?

Essential Question

How Can You Subtract Whole Numbers Efficiently?

A

The movie theater already sold 172 seats. How many seats are still available?

Subtract 358 − 172.

Estimate: 400 − 200 = 200

Here's a way to record subtraction, called the *standard algorithm for subtraction.*

Seats 358 people

B **What You Show**

Step 1 Subtract ones.

Step 2 Subtract tens.

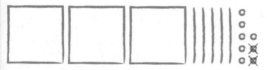

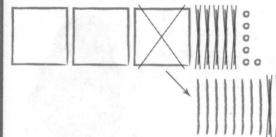

Step 3 Subtract hundreds.

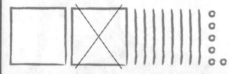

C **What You Write**

Step 1 Subtract ones.

$$\begin{array}{r} 358 \\ -172 \\ \hline 6 \end{array}$$ 8 ones − 2 ones = 6 ones

Step 2 Subtract tens.

$$\begin{array}{r} \overset{2\ 15}{3\,\cancel{5}8} \\ -172 \\ \hline 86 \end{array}$$ Regroup: 3 hundreds + 5 tens = 2 hundreds + 15 tens

15 tens − 7 tens = 8 tens

Step 3 Subtract hundreds.

$$\begin{array}{r} \overset{2\ 15}{3\,\cancel{5}8} \\ -172 \\ \hline 186 \end{array}$$ 2 hundreds − 1 hundred = 1 hundred

The theater has 186 seats available.

The difference 186 is reasonable because it is close to the estimate of 200.

Convince Me! **Use Structure** How many times do you need to regroup to subtract 483 − 295? Explain.

Name _____

☆ Guided Practice

Do You Understand?

1. To subtract 859 − 583, how do you regroup 8 hundreds 5 tens?

7 hundred 15 ten

2. What do you need to regroup to subtract 753 − 489 using the standard algorithm?

1 − Regop 5 tns
3 Oney aus lt tens
and 13 enes

Do You Know How?

In **3–6**, subtract. Use an estimate to check that your answer is reasonable.

3.
```
  154
−  89
─────
   65
```

4.
```
  592
− 357
─────
  235
```

5.
```
  915
− 288
─────
```

6.
```
  743
− 694
─────
```

Independent Practice ☆

In **7–18**, subtract. Use an estimate to check that your answer is reasonable.

7.
```
  289
− 145
─────
  144
```

8.
```
  326
− 184
─────
  142
```

9.
```
  736
− 218
─────
  518
```

10.
```
  525
− 267
─────
  258
```

11.
```
  683
− 295
─────
  388
```

12.
```
  847
− 387
─────
  460
```

13.
```
  475
−  98
─────
  377
```

14.
```
  826
− 184
─────
  642
```

15.
```
  936
− 218
─────
  718
```

16. 167 − 79

17. 284 − 167

18. 817 − 548

Topic 2 | Lesson 2-5   55

Problem Solving

19. How much greater is the area of Hernando County than Union County?

20. Make Sense and Persevere How much greater is the area of Monroe County than the area of Union County and Hernando County combined? Explain.

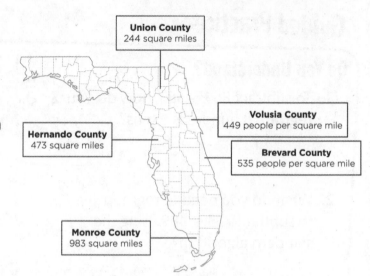

Union County
244 square miles

Volusia County
449 people per square mile

Hernando County
473 square miles

Brevard County
535 people per square mile

Monroe County
983 square miles

21. Population density is measured in people per square mile. It indicates how crowded an area is. How many more people per square mile does Brevard County have than neighboring Volusia County?

22. Higher Order Thinking What mistake did Leon make? What is the correct difference?

$$\begin{array}{r} {\scriptstyle 6\ 18\ 13} \\ 7\,9\,3 \\ -5\,7\,6 \\ \hline 1\,1\,7 \end{array}$$

Leon

---

23. What is the difference?

$$\begin{array}{r} 724 \\ -459 \\ \hline \end{array}$$

ⓐ 1,183

ⓑ 335

ⓒ 266

ⓓ 265

24. What is the missing digit in the subtraction statement?

$$\begin{array}{r} 6\ 3\ 4 \\ -2\ \square\ 7 \\ \hline 3\ 3\ 7 \end{array}$$

Name_____

Solve & Share

Nevada has a land area of 109,781 square miles. Colorado has a land area of 103,642 square miles. How much larger is Nevada than Colorado? **Solve this problem any way you choose.**

I can ...
use the standard algorithm and place value to subtract whole numbers.

Content Standards 4.NBT.B.4 Also 4.OA.A.3
Mathematical Practices MP.2, MP.3, MP.7

You can use structure and break numbers apart by place value to subtract. *Show your work in the space below!*

Nevado has 6,139 sm. Larger than colorado.

$$
\begin{array}{r}
109,781 \\
- 103,642 \\
\hline
006,139
\end{array}
$$

Look Back! Estimate the difference in the areas of the two states. Is your answer close to this estimate?

110,000
- 104,000

$$
\begin{array}{r}
110,000 \\
104,000 \\
\hline
000
\end{array}
$$

Essential Question

How Do You Subtract Greater Numbers Efficiently?

A

Three of the country's most scenic national parks are in Alaska. How much larger is the area of Gates of the Arctic than the combined area of Denali and Kenai Fjords?

Gates of the Arctic: 34,287 sq km

Denali: 19,182 sq km

Kenai Fjord: 2,711 sq km

Find the total area of Denali and Kenai Fjords.

$$\begin{array}{r} 19{,}182 \\ +\ 2{,}711 \\ \hline 21{,}893 \end{array}$$ square kilometers

Then find the difference of the areas.

34,287	
21,893	*a*

Let *a* equal the difference in the areas.

B Step 1

Find 34,287 − 21,893.

Subtract the ones. Regroup if necessary.

$$\begin{array}{r} 34{,}287 \\ -\ 21{,}893 \\ \hline 4 \end{array}$$

C Step 2

Subtract the tens, hundreds, thousands, and ten thousands.

Regroup if necessary.

$$\begin{array}{r} \overset{3\ \ 1118}{3\cancel{4}{,}2\cancel{8}7} \\ -\ 21{,}893 \\ \hline 12{,}394 \end{array}$$

Gates of the Arctic is 12,396 square kilometers larger.

D Step 3

Operations that undo each other are inverse operations. Addition and subtraction have an inverse relationship. Add to check your answer.

$$\begin{array}{r} \overset{1\ \ 1}{12{,}394} \\ +\ 21{,}893 \\ \hline 34{,}287 \end{array}$$

Convince Me! **Critique Reasoning** The work shown is **NOT** correct. What errors were made? Show how to find the correct answer.

$$\begin{array}{r} \overset{1\ 14}{4{,}2\cancel{4}8} \\ -2{,}76\cancel{4} \\ \hline 11484 \end{array}$$

$$\begin{array}{r} \overset{14}{4{,}2\cancel{4}8} \\ -\ 2{,}764 \\ \hline 2{,}584 \end{array}$$

Thy hundreds were not Regrouped

Name _____

☆ ☆
Solve & Share

London, England, is 15,710 kilometers from the South Pole. Tokyo, Japan, is 13,953 kilometers from the South Pole. How much farther is London than Tokyo from the South Pole? *Solve this problem any way you choose.*

I can ...
use the standard algorithm to subtract from numbers with zeros.

© **Content Standards** 4.NBT.B.4 Also 4.OA.A.3
Mathematical Practices MP.2, MP.3, MP.7

You can use reasoning to identify the operation you use to compare two distances. *Show your work in the space below!*

Look Back! Explain how you decided what operation to use to find how much farther London is than Tokyo from the South Pole.

Essential Question **How Do You Subtract Across Zeros?**

A

A music hall is hosting a concert. The hall sells 4,678 tickets to the show. How many tickets are still available?

When subtracting from a number with zeros, you may need to regroup several places before subtracting.

Let t equal the number of available tickets.

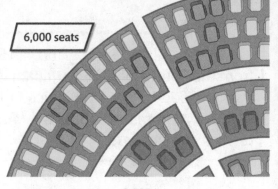

6,000 seats

6,000

| 4,678 | t |

$t = 6,000 - 4,678$

Estimate: $6,000 - 4,700 = 1,300$

B

Regroup.

$$\begin{array}{r} 6,000 \\ -\,4,678 \\ \hline \end{array}$$

Because of the zeros, you need to start regrouping from the thousands.

$$\begin{array}{r} {}^{5}\ {}^{10}\\ \cancel{6},\cancel{0}00 \\ -\,4,678 \\ \hline \end{array}$$

6 thousands = 5 thousands + 10 hundreds

$$\begin{array}{r} {}^{5}\ {}^{9}{}^{10}10\\ \cancel{6},\cancel{0}\cancel{0}0 \\ -\,4,678 \\ \hline \end{array}$$

10 hundreds = 9 hundreds + 10 tens

$$\begin{array}{r} {}^{5}\ {}^{9}10\,{}^{9}10\,10\\ \cancel{6},\cancel{0}\,\cancel{0}\,\cancel{0} \\ -\,4,678 \\ \hline \end{array}$$

10 tens = 9 tens + 10 ones

C

Subtract.

$$\begin{array}{r} {}^{5}\ {}^{9}10\,{}^{9}10\,10\\ \cancel{6},\cancel{0}\cancel{0}\cancel{0} \\ -\,4,678 \\ \hline 1,3\,2\,2 \end{array}$$

$10 - 8 = 2$ ones

$90 - 70 = 20 = 2$ tens

$900 - 600 = 300$ = 3 hundreds

$5,000 - 4,000 = 1,000$ = 1 thousand

Since the difference 1,322 is close to the estimate 1,300, the difference is reasonable.

There are still 1,322 tickets available for the concert.

Convince Me! **Use Structure** How would you regroup if the hall had 5,900 seats?

Name _____

☆ Guided Practice

Do You Understand?

1. Leesa used compensation to solve the problem on the previous page. She subtracted $(6,000 - 1) - (4,678 - 1) = 5,999 - 4,677 = 1,322$. How could you use Leesa's approach to subtract $5,000 - 1,476$?

2. One passenger flew 11,033 kilometers from Oslo to Lima. Another passenger flew 8,593 kilometers from Oslo to Los Angeles. How many more kilometers was the flight to Lima?

Do You Know How?

For **3–8**, subtract.

3. 6,000
    − 1,773

4. 231,086
    − 172,863

5. 76,810
    − 22,645

6. 90,304
    − 51,137

7. $101,001 - 8,915$

8. $9{,}\underline{}50 - 3,461$

☆ Independent Practice ☆

For **9–23**, subtract.

stimate to check if your answer is reasonable.

9. 1,902
    − 1,374

10. 6,502
     − 5,380

11. 63,000
     − 48,673

12. 84,010
     − 3,992

13. 2,025
     − 1,540

14. 31,03_
     − 27_6

15. 50,469
     − 22,917

16. 1,830
     − 644

17. 7,203
     − 847

18. 726,003
     − 282,942

19. 4,707
     − 2,016

20. 30,900
     − 22,855

21. $6,090 - 5,130$

22. $11,246 - 9,489$

23. $790,008 - 643,829$

Problem Solving

24. Construct Arguments Will the difference between 44,041 and 43,876 be greater or less than 1,000? Explain.

25. (A-Z) **Vocabulary** Define *variable* and give an example of how a variable is used in an equation.

For **26–27**, use the table at the right.

26. How many more hip-hop than country downloads were sold?

27. Higher Order Thinking How many more hip-hop and Latin downloads were sold than rock and country downloads? Explain.

Music City Sales	
Music style	**Downloads sold**
Rock	4,007
Hip-hop	7,097
Country	5,063
Latin	6,203

28. Select all the correct differences.

- ☐ $5,000 - 1,856 = 3,244$
- ☐ $10,700 - 8,243 = 2,457$
- ☐ $64,002 - 43,178 = 20,934$
- ☐ $98,000 - 59,214 = 38,786$
- ☐ $600,482 - 428,531 = 171,951$

29. Find the difference.

$$\begin{array}{r} 60,000 \\ -\ 38,243 \\ \hline \end{array}$$

- Ⓐ 17,355
- Ⓑ 20,757
- Ⓒ 21,757
- Ⓓ 98,243

Name _____

Solve & Share

A group of students collected donations for a toy drive. They collected a total of 3,288 toys one week and 1,022 toys the next week. They donated 1,560 toys to the Coal City Charity and the rest were donated to Hartville Charity. How many toys were donated to Hartville Charity? Use reasoning about numbers to show and explain how the two quantities of toys given to charity are related.

Activity

I can ...
make sense of quantities and relationships in problem situations.

 Mathematical Practices MP.2 Also MP.1, MP.4
Content Standards 4.OA.A.3 Also 4.NBT.B.4

Thinking Habits
Be a good thinker!
These questions can help you.

• What do the numbers and symbols in the problem mean?

• How are the numbers or quantities related?

• How can I represent a word problem using pictures, numbers, or equations?

Look Back! **Reasoning** Over three weeks, the students collected a total of 8,169 toys. How many toys did they collect in the third week? Complete the bar diagram to show your reasoning. Did the students collect more toys in the third week than in weeks 1 and 2 combined? Explain.

Essential Question

How Can You Use Quantitative Reasoning to Solve Problems?

A

Kara and Carl join their mother on a boat off the coast of the Florida Keys. Their mother is a scientist studying blue marlins. Each child gets to help weigh two marlins. How much more did Kara's marlins weigh than Carl's?

How can you draw a diagram to help reason how the numbers in the problem are related?

I can represent the relationship between the numbers with a bar diagram.

Here's my thinking.

DATA	Kara's Marlins	Carl's Marlins
	948 pounds	895 pounds
	1,219 pounds	973 pounds

B **How can I use reasoning to solve this problem?**

I can

- identify the quantities I know.

- draw diagrams and write equations to show relationships.

- connect the solution back to the real world problem.

C K = the total weight of Kara's marlins, and C = the total weight of Carl's marlins.

K

948 lb	1,219 lb

$K = 948 + 1,219$
$K = 2,167$

C

895 lb	973 lb

$C = 895 + 973$
$C = 1,868$

d = the difference
$d = 2,167 - 1,868$
$d = 299$

$K = 2,167$	
$C = 1,868$	d

Kara's marlins weighed 299 pounds more than Carl's.

Convince Me! **Reasoning** Write a problem that can be solved using the bar diagram below. Write an equation to solve. Use reasoning to think about the meaning of each number before starting.

16,792	
2,550	c

Guided Practice

Reasoning

A manufacturer shipped 12,875 fidget spinners one week and 9,843 of them were sold. The next week, they shipped 19,175 and 12,752 of them were sold. How many fidget spinners had not sold yet?

When you use reasoning, you use diagrams, numbers, or equations to show relationships.

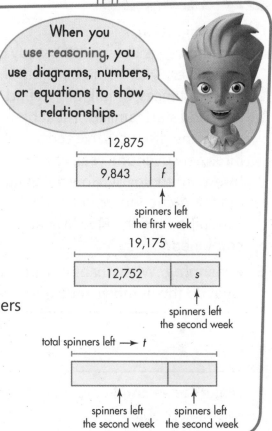

1. What quantities are given in the problem, and what do the numbers mean?

2. Use the bar diagrams that show the relationships of the numbers in the problem. Write and solve equations which could be used to find f, the spinners not sold the first week; s, the spinners not sold the second week; and t, the total spinners not sold.

Independent Practice

Reasoning

A wall is being built with 16,351 stones. The builders have placed 8,361 stones, and they have 7,944 stones left. Do they have enough stones? How many more stones do they need? Use Exercises 3–5 to answer the question.

3. What quantities are given in the problem, and what do the numbers mean?

4. Complete the bar diagram to show how to find s, the number of stones the builders have in all. Then, write and solve an equation. Do they have enough? Explain.

5. Complete the bar diagram to show how to find the difference, d, of how many more stones the builders need. Then, write and solve an equation.

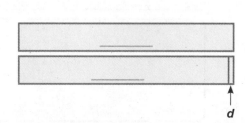

☑ **Performance Task**

Bird Migration

Ornithology is the scientific study of birds. Every year, some birds travel great distances, or migrate, to find food and start families. The table shows the distances five species of birds flew over one year, as observed by an ornithologist. How much farther did the Arctic Tern fly than the Pectoral Sandpiper and the Pied Wheatear combined?

DATA	Distances Traveled by Birds	
	Species	**Distance in Miles**
	Sooty Shearwater	39,481
	Pied Wheatear	11,184
	Arctic Tern	44,819
	Short-Tailed Shearwater	26,636
	Pectoral Sandpiper	18,247

6. **Reasoning** What quantities are given in the problem and what do the numbers mean?

7. **Make Sense and Persevere** What strategy can you use to solve the problem?

The hidden questions are the questions which must be answered before answering the main question asked in the problem.

8. **Make Sense and Persevere** What is the hidden question?

9. **Model with Math** Complete the bar diagrams to show how to find the answer to the hidden question and the main question. Write and solve equations.

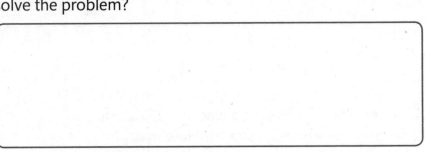

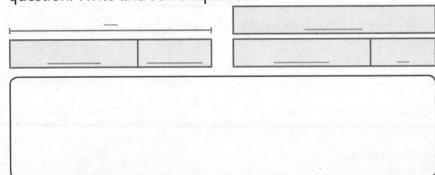

Follow the Path

Shade a path from **START** to **FINISH**.
Follow the sums that are correct. You can
only move up, down, right, or left.

TOPIC 2

Fluency Practice Activity

I can ...
add multi-digit whole numbers.

Content Standard 4.NBT.B.4
Mathematical Practices MP.2, MP.6, MP.7

Start				
213 + 675 —— 888	264 + 632 —— 896	887 + 112 —— 999	124 + 345 —— 461	414 + 111 —— 515
810 + 172 —— 762	212 + 486 —— 678	511 + 228 —— 739	245 + 322 —— 667	613 + 282 —— 891
454 + 545 —— 919	187 + 412 —— 499	676 + 322 —— 998	101 + 116 —— 218	454 + 432 —— 876
409 + 390 —— 697	340 + 340 —— 620	124 + 65 —— 189	911 + 64 —— 975	674 + 115 —— 789
374 + 613 —— 978	318 + 121 —— 429	177 + 311 —— 478	612 + 317 —— 939	678 + 321 —— 999
				Finish

Vocabulary Review

A-Z
Glossary

Word List

- add on
- algorithm
- Associative Property of Addition
- Commutative Property of Addition
- compensation
- Identity Property of Addition
- inverse operations
- variable

Understand Vocabulary

1. Circle the property of addition shown by $126 + 0 = 126$.

Associative   Commutative   Identity

2. Circle the property of addition shown by $21 + 34 = 34 + 21$.

Associative   Commutative   Identity

3. Circle the property of addition shown by $(1 + 3) + 7 = 1 + (3 + 7)$.

Associative   Commutative   Identity

4. Draw a line from each term to its example.

algorithm	$4 + 2 = 6 \longrightarrow 6 - 2 = 4$
compensation	$435 - 199 = (435 + 1) - (199 + 1)$
add on	Step 1: Add the ones. Step 2: Add the tens.
inverse operations	$x = 7$
variable	$326 + 103 : 326 + 3 = 329,$ $329 + 100 = 429$

Use Vocabulary in Writing

5. Rob found $103 + 1,875 = x$ using mental math. Use at least 3 terms from the Word List to describe how Rob could find the sum.

Name_____

Reteaching

Set A | pages 37–40 _____

Find 3,371 + 2,429. Use mental math.

Make Ten

$$3,371 + 2,429 = 3,371 + (29 + 2,400)$$
$$= (3,371 + 29) + 2,400$$
$$= 3,400 + 2,400 = 5,800$$

So, 3,371 + 2,429 = 5,800.

Remember to adjust the sum or difference when you use the compensation strategy.

1. 4,153 + 2,988   **2.** 92,425 + 31,675

3. 5,342 + 1,999   **4.** 22,283 − 14,169

5. 47,676 − 16,521   **6.** 1,089 − 961

Set B | pages 41–44 _____

Estimate the sum by rounding each number to the nearest ten thousand.

241,485
+429,693

241,485 rounds to 240,000.

429,693 rounds to 430,000.

Add.
    240,000
+ 430,000
    670,000

Remember that you can round numbers to any place when estimating sums and differences.

Estimate each sum or difference.

1. 652,198 + 49,753   **2.** 8,352 − 3,421

3. 17,586 − 9,483   **4.** 823,725 + 44,851

5. 1,440 − 933   **6.** 55,748 − 28,392

7. 4,981 + 6,193   **8.** 995,275 + 4,921

Set C | pages 45–52 _____

Find 72,438 + 6,854.

Estimate: 72,000 + 7,000 = 79,000

Add the ones. Regroup if necessary.

$$\begin{array}{r} 72,4\overset{1}{3}8 \\ +\ \ 6,854 \\ \hline 2 \end{array}$$

Add the other places, regrouping if necessary.

$$\begin{array}{r} \overset{1}{7}2,\overset{1}{4}38 \\ +\ \ 6,854 \\ \hline 79,292 \end{array}$$

The answer 79,292 is close to the estimate of 79,000, so the answer is reasonable.

Remember to regroup if necessary when adding whole numbers.

1.   32,834   **2.**   148,382
   + 17,384   +   9,243

3. 215 + 8,823   **4.** 142,968 + 44,456

5. 2,417 + 3,573   **6.** 572,941 + 181,662

Find 52,839 − 38,796.

Estimate: 53,000 − 39,000 = 14,000

Subtract the ones. Regroup if necessary.

52,839
− 38,796
_____
        3

Subtract the other places, regrouping as necessary.

$\overset{4\ 12\ \ 7\ 13}{\cancel{5}\cancel{2},\cancel{8}\cancel{3}9}$
− 3 8 , 7 9 6
_____
  1 4 , 0 4 3

The answer is reasonable.

Remember that you may need to regroup to subtract.

1. 651,784
     − 482,638
     _____

2.   18,465
      − 6,291
     _____

3. 41,542 − 32,411

4. 4,978 − 2,766

5. 735,184 − 255,863

6. 44,558 − 22,613

Find 60,904 − 54,832.

Estimate: 61,000 − 55,000 = 6,000

Subtract the ones. Regroup if necessary.

60,904
− 54,832
_____
        2

Subtract the other places, regrouping as necessary.

$\overset{5\ 10\ \ 8\ 10}{\cancel{6}\cancel{0},\cancel{9}\cancel{0}4}$
− 5 4 , 8 3 2
_____
    6 , 0 7 2

The answer is reasonable.

Remember you may need to regroup more than one place at a time to subtract across zeros.

1.   40,700
      − 23,984
     _____

2. 203,056
      − 5,213
     _____

3. 70,000 − 25,228

4. 560,043 − 312,562

5. 8,052 − 1,205

6. 20,008 − 16,074

Think about these questions to help you **reason abstractly and quantitatively.**

Thinking Habits

- What do the numbers and symbols in the problem mean?

- How are the numbers or quantities related?

- How can I represent a word problem using pictures, numbers, or equations?

Remember that you can draw a bar diagram and use it to reason about a problem.

Raahil traveled 11,469 kilometers from home to visit his mother's family in Qatar. He then traveled 12,332 kilometers from Qatar to visit his father's family in Brisbane, Australia.

1. Draw a bar diagram that shows the distance Raahil traveled to Brisbane.

2. Write and solve an equation for your bar diagram.

Name_____

1. The table shows the number of hot dogs Frank's hot dog stand sold this weekend.

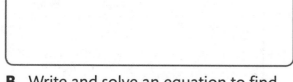

Hot Dogs Sold	
Friday	3,825
Saturday	1,297
Sunday	4,175

A. Estimate the number of hot dogs sold by rounding each number in the table to the nearest thousand and finding the sum.

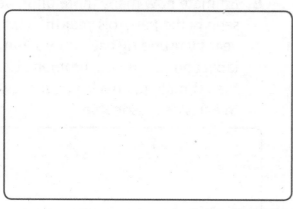

B. Write and solve an equation to find how many hot dogs were sold.

2. Find 8,000 − 6,280.

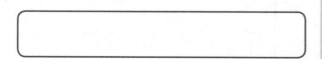

3. Enter the missing digit to complete the subtraction.

Assessment Practice

$$\begin{array}{r} 1\,0,1\,4\,6 \\ -6,4\,5\,2 \\ \hline \square\,6\,\square\,4 \end{array}$$

4. Find the difference.

$$\begin{array}{r} 6,5\,7\,2 \\ -2\,3\,9 \\ \hline \end{array}$$

Ⓐ 6,811

Ⓑ 6,351

Ⓒ 6,333

Ⓓ 6,331

5. Complete the equation to make it true. Write your answer in the box.

$12{,}769 + 16{,}065 = \boxed{} + 15{,}402$

6. Find the difference. Then use addition to check your work.

$$\begin{array}{r} 2\,4,4\,2\,1 \\ -\,1\,5,0\,2\,9 \\ \hline \end{array}$$

7. Which of the following statements is true? Select all that apply.

- ☐ $12{,}395 + 14{,}609 = 27{,}004$
- ☐ $76{,}237 - 4{,}657 = 42{,}430$
- ☐ $67{,}407 - 38{,}227 = 29{,}180$
- ☐ $69{,}844 + 1{,}014 = 70{,}452$
- ☐ $34{,}980 - 1{,}999 = 32{,}981$

8. Find the sum.

$$\begin{array}{r} 8,7\,2\,3 \\ 2,8\,4\,9 \\ +\,6,4\,1\,9 \\ \hline \end{array}$$

9. Sandra used addition properties to rewrite the equation below. Select all the equations Sandra might have written.

$$1{,}450 + 1{,}125 + 1{,}050 = n$$

- ☐ $(1{,}400 + 1{,}100 + 1{,}000) + (50 + 25 + 50) = n$
- ☐ $1{,}450 + 1{,}050 = n$
- ☐ $1{,}125 + 1{,}050 + 1{,}450 = n$
- ☐ $1{,}000 + 1{,}000 + 1{,}000 + 450 + 50 + 125 = n$
- ☐ $(1{,}450 + 1{,}050) + 1{,}125 = n$

10. Joe and Sara recorded the number of birds they saw in the park over two summers.

Birds in the Park

Year	Finches	Pigeons
Last Year	1,219	4,620
This Year	1,906	4,287

A. Write and solve equations to find how many more total birds Joe and Sara saw this year than last year.

B. Estimate how many more birds were seen in the park this year than last year by rounding each number in the table and solving the problem. Use the estimate to check if your answer to Part A is reasonable.

Name_____

Taking Inventory

Jiao runs a wholesale art supply website. She fills bulk orders for craft and hobby stores.

1. Use the **Wooden Beads** table to answer the questions.

Part A

Crafts and Stuff ordered oak and ebony beads. Explain how to use mental math and properties of addition to find how many beads Jiao sent.

Wooden Beads	
Oak	4,525
Maple	6,950
Ash	3,720
Ebony	2,475
Bayong	1,250

Part B

Jiao sends an order of oak and bayong beads to Jill's Crafts and an order of ash and ebony beads to Create. How much larger is the order for Create? Write and solve equations to find j, the number of beads in the order to Jill's Crafts; c, the number of beads in the order to Create; and d, the difference.

2. Use the **Glass Beads** table to answer the questions.

Part A

Write and solve an equation to show how many glass beads, *b*, Create will have if they order the bubble and smoky beads.

Glass Beads	
Smoky	25,236
Bubble	41,828
Stained	32,991
Molded	47,312

Part B

Jiao sends the molded and stained beads to Hometown Craft Supply. Explain how to use compensation to find how many more molded beads than stained beads were sent.

3. Use the **Metal Beads** table to answer the questions.

Part A

Write and solve an equation to show how many more beads, *b*, are in an order of gold beads than in an order of platinum beads.

Metal Beads	
Gold	14,960
Silver	8,147
Platinum	6,488
Brass	30,019
Copper	20,605

Part B

Craftology orders the brass and copper beads. After they arrive, the store sells 29,735 of them. How many beads does Craftology have left from their order? Show your computations.

Use Strategies and Properties to Multiply by 1-Digit Numbers

Essential Questions: How can you multiply by multiples of 10, 100, and 1,000? How can you multiply whole numbers?

Digital Resources

 Interactive Student Edition
 Activity
 Visual Learning
 Video
 Practice

 Assessment
 Games
 Tools
 Glossary

Maps that show the natural features of Earth's landscape are called topographic maps. Mountains, plains, and oceans are some of the features the maps show.

Did you know that Pikes Peak is the most visited mountain in North America?

We should visit! In the meantime, here is a project on maps and multiplication.

enVision STEM Project: Maps and Math

Do Research Use the Internet or other sources to find information about three of Earth's features on a topographic map, such as mountains or oceans. Write two facts about each of the features you researched.

Journal: Write a Report Include what you found. Also in your report:

• Write the height or depth of each feature you researched.

• Estimate to find 10 times the heights or depths of the features you researched.

Name_____

Review What You Know

1. Multiplication and division are
   _____.

2. A mental math method used to rewrite a number as the sum of numbers to
   form an easier problem is called _____.

3. Choosing numbers close to the numbers in a problem to make the
   computation easier, and then adjusting the answer is called _____.

Multiplication

Find each product.

4. 6×2 **5.** 8×9 **6.** 6×5

7. 7×8 **8.** 4×8 **9.** 3×7

Rounding

Round each number to the nearest ten.

10. 16   **11.** 82   **12.** 35
13. 53   **14.** 24   **15.** 49

Round each number to the nearest hundred.

16. 868   **17.** 499   **18.** 625
19. 167   **20.** 341   **21.** 772
22. 919   **23.** 552   **24.** 321

Problem Solving

25. Critique Reasoning Tyler says, "9×7 is greater than 7×9
because the greater number is first." Explain Tyler's error.

Name _____

PROJECT 3A

How zesty is Key lime pie?

Project: Create Data for Key Lime Pie Ingredients

PROJECT 3B

What do a dozen Florida panthers weigh?

Project: Draw a Captioned Picture

PROJECT 3C

What's the mass of a giraffe?

Project: Create a Song

Before watching the video, think:

Every box has three dimensions: length, width, and height. How much paper you need to wrap the box depends on all three of the dimensions. There are also other shapes you can wrap. I just wish someone had told me this wasn't a birthday party!

I can ...
model with math to solve a problem that involves estimating and computing with area models.

ⓒ **Mathematical Practices** MP.4 Also MP.2, MP.8
Content Standards 4.NBT.B.5 Also 4.OA.A.3, 4.NBT.B.4

Name _____

Lesson 3-1
**Multiply by Multiples
of 10, 100, and 1,000**

⭐ **Solve & Share**

Find the products for 3 × 4, 3 × 40,
3 × 400, and 3 × 4,000. *Solve these problems using
any strategy you choose.*

I can ...
find the products of multiples of
10, 100, and 1,000 using mental
math and place-value strategies.

ⓒ **Content Standard** 4.NBT.B.5
Mathematical Practices MP.1, MP.2, MP.7

$$3 \times 4000$$

$$
\begin{array}{r}
4000 \\
4000 \\
4000 \\
\hline
12000
\end{array}
$$

$$3 \times 4 = 12$$

$$
\begin{array}{r}
40 \\
\times \ 3 \\
\hline
120
\end{array}
$$

You can look for
relationships in the products.
How can finding the first product
help you find the remaining
products?

$$3 \times 4000$$

$$
\begin{array}{r}
4000 \\
4000 \\
4000 \\
\hline
12000
\end{array}
$$

Look Back! What pattern do you notice in the products?

Each problem started with
a 12 and has the same
number of zeros as the factors.

Essential Question: How Can You Multiply by Multiples of 10, 100, and 1,000?

A

Calculate 3 × 50, 3 × 500, and 3 × 5,000 using basic multiplication facts and properties of operations.

The Associative Property of Multiplication states that you can change the grouping of the factors and the product stays the same.

n

B One Way

Find 3 × 50, 3 × 500, and 3 × 5,000.

Use basic facts and place value.

$3 \times 50 = 3 \times 5$ tens
$ = 15$ tens
$ = 150$

$3 \times 500 = 3 \times 5$ hundreds
$ = 15$ hundreds
$ = 1,500$

$3 \times 5,000 = 3 \times 5$ thousands
$ = 15$ thousands
$ = 15,000$

C Another Way

Find 3 × 50, 3 × 500, and 3 × 5,000.

Break apart numbers. Use the Associative Property of Multiplication.

$3 \times 50 = 3 \times (5 \times 10)$
$ = (3 \times 5) \times 10$
$ = 15 \times 10$
$ = 150$

$3 \times 500 = 3 \times (5 \times 100)$
$ = (3 \times 5) \times 100$
$ = 15 \times 100$
$ = 1,500$

$3 \times 5,000 = 3 \times (5 \times 1,000)$
$ = (3 \times 5) \times 1,000$
$ = 15 \times 1,000$
$ = 15,000$

Convince Me! **Reasoning** What patterns do you see in the number of zeros in the products above?

Another Example!

Use place value to calculate 5 × 400 and 6 × 5,000.

5 × 400 = 5 × 4 hundreds
         = 20 hundreds
         = 2,000

6 × 5,000 = 6 × 5 thousands
           = 30 thousands
           = 30,000

> If the product of the basic fact ends in zero, the product has one more zero than you see in the factors.

☆ Guided Practice

Do You Understand?

1. Show how you can use the basic fact 5 × 8 = 40 to determine the product of 5 × 800.

    5 X 800 = 4000
    200 is less than

2. Bob said 4 × 500 = 200. Explain his error using place value.

    4 X 500 ≠ 2000
    200 is less than 500 Bob needed to add one more zero

Do You Know How?

For **3–5**, use strategies you learned to help multiply.

3. 8 × 7 = __*56*__
   8 × 70 = __*560*__
   8 × 700 = __*5600*__
   8 × 7,000 = __*56000*__

4. 7 × 70 __*490*__

5. 2 × 700 __*1400*__

☆ Independent Practice ☆

> You can use place-value strategies to calculate each product.

Leveled Practice For **6–11**, use basic facts, place value, and properties to help multiply.

6. 3 × 70 = __*210*__
   3 × 700 = __*2100*__
   3 × 7,000 = __*21000*__

7. __*240*__ = 6 × 40
   __*2400*__ = 6 × 400
   __*24000*__ = 6 × 4,000

8. 8 × 50 = __*400*__
   8 × 500 = __*4000*__
   8 × 5,000 = __*40000*__

9. 4 × 2,000 = *8000*

10. 700 × 4 = *2800*

11. 6 × 60 = *120*

Problem Solving

12. enVision® STEM The Mississippi River is about 8 times the length of the Hudson River. If the Hudson River is about 300 miles long, about how many miles long is the Mississippi River? Write and solve an equation.

$8 \times 300 = 2400$

the mississippi river is 2400 miles long

13. Ted, Jason, and Angelina are trying to raise $200 for a local shelter. Ted raised $30. Jason raised $90. How much money, *m*, does Angelina need to raise to reach their goal?

$+80$
$+30$
720
80

$200		
$30	$90	*m* 80

$120 + 80 = 200$ ↑

For **14–15**, use the table at the right.

14. Make Sense and Persevere There are 9 girls and 4 adults in Aimee's scout troup. How much did the troop pay for tickets to the amusement park?

$30 \times 4 =$

15. Higher Order Thinking Tina visited Funland with her mom and a friend. They bought tickets for Plan C. How much money did they save on the two children's tickets for Plan C instead of buying separate tickets for Plan A and Plan B?

Funland Ticket Prices

Plans	Adult	Child
Plan A Waterpark	$30	$20
Plan B Amusement Park	$40	$30
Plan C Combined A + B	$60	$40

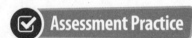
Assessment Practice

16. Brandon says 4 × 800 is greater than 8 × 4,000. Renee says 4 × 800 is less than 8 × 4,000.

A.

Without calculating the answer, explain how to use place-value strategies or the Associative Property to find which is greater.

B.

Without calculating the answer, explain how to use relationships or basic facts to find which is less.

Name _____

Solve & Share

Sarah earns $48 a week babysitting. She saves all of her earnings for 6 weeks. Estimate to determine about how much money Sarah saves. **Solve this problem using any strategy you choose.**

I can ...
use rounding to estimate products and check if my answer is reasonable.

Content Standards 4.OA.A.3 Also 4.OA.A.2
Mathematical Practices MP.2, MP.3

How can reasoning about place value make it easier to estimate products? *Show your work in the space above!*

Look Back! Is your estimate more or less than the amount Sarah actually earned? Explain.

Essential Question

How Can You Estimate When You Multiply?

A

Mr. Hector's class sold calendars and note pads for 3 weeks as a class fundraiser. About how much did Mr. Hector's class make selling calendars? selling note pads?

Note Pads $3

Calendars $4

DATA

Item	Number Sold Week 1	Number Sold Week 2	Number Sold Week 3
Calendar	28	73	63
Note Pads	272	475	232

B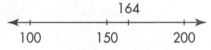

Use compatible numbers to estimate how many calendars c, were sold.

$28 + 73 + 63 = c$
$164 = c$

Estimate $\$4 \times 164$.

```
        164
◄──┼────────┼────────┼──►
  100      150      200
```

Estimate by using compatible numbers. 164 is close to 150.

$4 \times 150 = 600$

Mr. Hector's class made about $600 selling calendars.

C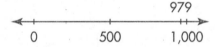

Use rounding to estimate how many note pads n, were sold.

$272 + 475 + 232 = n$
$979 = n$

Estimate $\$3 \times 979$.

```
                    979
◄──┼────────┼────────┼┼─►
   0       500     1,000
```

To the nearest thousand, 979 rounds to 1,000.

$3 \times 1,000 = 3,000$

Mr. Hector's class made about $3,000 selling note pads.

Convince Me! **Construct Arguments** Could you solve the problem above by rounding to estimate the total number of calendars and the total number of note pads? Explain.

Another Example!

Mrs. Li's class made $2,089 selling neon pencil packs. A student calculated that Mr. Hector's class and Mrs. Li's class together made $8,865 selling the school supplies. Is the student's calculation reasonable?

You can estimate to check if an answer is reasonable.

Round Mrs. Li's total to the nearest thousand: $2,000. Then, add the rounded amounts. $2,000 + $600 + $3,000 = $5,600

The student's calculation is not reasonable because $8,865 is not close to $5,600.

Guided Practice

Do You Understand?

1. Mr. Harm's class sold 1,275 items at $5 per item. One of his students calculates the class raised $2,375. Is the student's calculation reasonable? Explain.

   $1000 \times 5 = 5000$

   no not reasonable $100 \times 5 = 5000$

   5000 is not reasonable to

Do You Know How?

For **2-5**, estimate the product.

2. 6 × 125

   $6 \times 100 = 600$

3. 4 × 2,610

   $4 \times 3000 = 12000$

4. 538 × 3

   $500 \times 3 = 1500$

5. 314 × 7

   $300 \times 7 = 2100$

Independent Practice

Leveled Practice For **6-8**, estimate the product.

6. 3 × 287

   Round 287 to __290__.

   $3 \times 300 = 900$

7. 6 × 1,310

   Round 1,310 to _____.

   6 × ___ = ___

8. 9 × 62

   Round 62 to _____.

   9 × ___ = ___

For **9-11**, estimate to check if the answer is reasonable.

9. 7 × 486 = 3,402

   Round 486 to __500__.

   $7 \times 500 = 3,500$

   (Reasonable) Not Reasonable

10. 5 × 1,240 = 9,200

    Round 1,240 to _____.

    5 × ___ = ___

    Reasonable   Not Reasonable

11. 9 × 287 = 2,583

    Round 287 to _____.

    9 × ___ = ___

    Reasonable   Not Reasonable

Problem Solving

For **12-13**, use the graph at the right.

12. The students voted on a school mascot. Which mascot had 4 times as many of votes as the flamingo?

13. Construct Arguments Explain how you could estimate the number of students who voted on a school mascot. Then give your estimate.

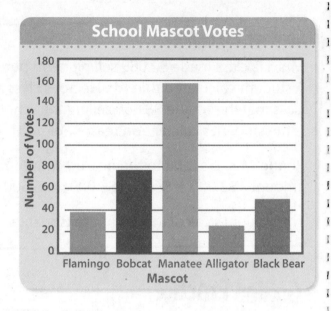

School Mascot Votes

14. Number Sense Ellie says the product of 211 and 6 is 1,866. Is this calculation reasonable? Explain.

15. Higher Order Thinking An adult sleeps about 480 minutes per day. An infant sleeps about 820 minutes per day. About how many more minutes does an infant sleep than an adult in one week? Solve the problem two different ways.

16. Gul can run 800 meters in 139 seconds. About how long would it take her to run 6 times as far if she runs at the same speed? Choose the best estimate.

Ⓐ About 140 seconds

Ⓑ About 600 seconds

Ⓒ About 1,200 seconds

Ⓓ About 6,000 seconds

17. A new two-seater car weighs 1,785 pounds. About how much would 8 of the two-seater cars weigh? Choose the best estimate.

Ⓐ About 160 pounds

Ⓑ About 1,600 pounds

Ⓒ About 16,000 pounds

Ⓓ About 60,000 pounds

Name_____

Solve & Share

A music room has chairs arranged in rows. There are 6 rows. Each row has 18 chairs. How many chairs are in the music room? *Solve this problem any way you choose.* Explain your answer.

I can ...
use arrays and partial products to multiply.

Ⓒ **Content Standard** 4.NBT.B.5
Mathematical Practices MP.4, MP.7

$6 \times 18 = 18$

$10 \quad \times 8$
$\times 6 \quad 6$

$60 + 48 = 108$

You can model with math. You can represent how the chairs are arranged to help solve the problem. *Show your work in the space above!*

Look Back! Would the answer be different if there were 18 rows with 6 chairs in each row? Explain.

Essential Question

How Can You Use an Array and Partial Products to Multiply?

A The windows of a building on International Drive are in an array. There are 5 rows with 13 windows in each row. How many windows are in this array?

B **What You Show**

13 windows per row

5 rows

> An array is an arrangement of objects in equal rows.

C **What You Think**

Find 5×13.

Estimate: 5×13 is about $5 \times 10 = 50$.

5 rows, 1 ten in each
$5 \times 10 = 50$

5 rows, 3 ones in each
$5 \times 3 = 15$

$50 + 15 = 65$

The numbers 15 and 50 are called **partial products**. 65 is the product.

D **What You Record**

$$
\begin{array}{r}
13 \\
\times\ 5 \\
\hline
15 \\
+\ 50 \\
\hline
65
\end{array}
$$

5×3 ones
5×1 ten

There are 65 windows in the array.

The product, 65, is close to the estimate of 50. The answer is reasonable.

> You can use place value to break factors apart and the Distributive Property to find partial products.

Convince Me! **Use Structure** How are the partial products represented with the place-value blocks?

Another Example!

Find 2 × 126.

Estimate:

2 × 126 is about 2 × 100 = 200.

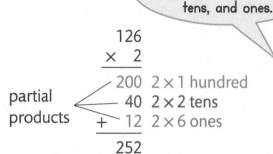

You can find partial products for hundreds, tens, and ones.

$$
\begin{array}{r}
126 \\
\times\ \ 2 \\
\hline
\end{array}
$$

partial products

200 2 × 1 hundred
 40 2 × 2 tens
+ 12 2 × 6 ones
_____
252

2 rows, 1 hundred in each   2 rows, 2 tens in each   2 rows, 6 ones in each
2 × 100 = 200   2 × 20 = 40   2 × 6 = 12

☆ Guided Practice

Do You Understand?

1. Explain how an array shows multiplication.

   An array shows the number

Do You Know How?

For **2-3**, complete each calculation.

2. 2 × 24 = 48   3. 3 × 218

Independent Practice ☆

Leveled Practice For **4-5**, multiply. Complete each equation.

4. Find 3 × 13.

3 rows, 1 ten in each   3 rows, 3 ones in each

3 × 10 = 30   3 × 3 = 9

30 + 9 = 39

5. Find 2 × 105

$$
\begin{array}{r}
105 \\
\times\ 2 \\
\hline
40 \\
\end{array}
$$
← 2 rows, 5 ones in each

+ 200 ← 2 rows, 1 hundred in each
_____
210

Problem Solving

6. Model with Math What multiplication equation do the place-value blocks show? Find the product. Then write a problem that could be solved using this model.

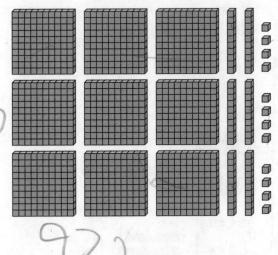

$309 \times 390 = 800$

$30 \times 2 = \overset{7}{\cancel{10}}$

$3 \times 4 = \overset{\uparrow}{12}$ 972

---

7. How many marbles are in 3 large bags and 4 small bags?

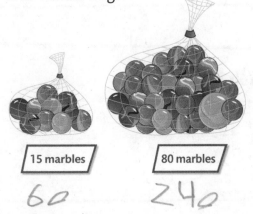

| 15 marbles |
| 80 marbles |

60   240

8. Higher Order Thinking How can the Distributive Property be used to find 4×875? Draw an array.

---

9. Select all the expressions that have a value of 312.

- ☐ $(3 \times 100) + (3 \times 4)$
- ☐ 3×12
- ☐ 3×112
- ☐ $(30 \times 10) + (3 \times 12)$
- ☐ 3×104

10. Which are correct partial products for 54×9?

- Ⓐ 36, 45
- Ⓑ 36, 450
- Ⓒ 540, 36
- Ⓓ 32, 450

Name _____

Solve & Share

Use only the numbers shown on the diagram and the operation symbols (+, −, ×, ÷) to determine the area of the unshaded rectangle below. **Solve this problem using any strategy you choose.**

I can ...
use area models and partial products to multiply.

© **Content Standard** 4.NBT.B.5
Mathematical Practices MP.4, MP.7

Use structure and what you know about calculating area to solve this problem. *Show your work in the space below!*

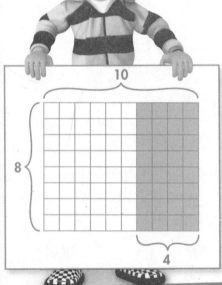

Look Back! **Use Structure** Are these equations equal? Explain.

$8 \times (10 - 4) = n$

$(8 \times 10) - (8 \times 4) = n$

Essential Question

How Can You Use an Area Model and Partial Products to Multiply?

A A garden is in the shape of a rectangle. It is 8 feet wide and 25 feet long. What is the area of the garden?

A numerical expression contains numbers and at least one operation. 8 × 25 is a numerical expression.

B **What You Show**

25 ft

8 ft | 20 | 5

You can use a rectangular area model to show multiplication. The product of 8 × 25 is the area of the rectangle.

C **What You Think**

Estimate: 8 × 25 is about 8 × 30 = 240.

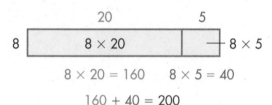

20   5

8 | 8 × 20 | ┤ 8 × 5

8 × 20 = 160   8 × 5 = 40

160 + 40 = 200

The Distributive Property says that multiplying a sum by a number is the same as multiplying each part of the sum by that number and adding the partial products.
8 × 25 = (8 × 20) + (8 × 5)

D **What You Record**

$$\begin{array}{r} 25 \\ \times\ 8 \\ \hline 40 \\ +\ 160 \\ \hline 200 \end{array}$$

8 × 5 ones
8 × 2 tens

The area of the garden is 200 square feet.

The product, 200, is close to the estimate of 240. The answer is reasonable.

Convince Me! **Use Structure** Does 12 − (4 × 2) = (12 − 4) × (12 − 2)? Explain.

---

94   **Topic 3** | Lesson 3-4

Another Example!

Find 5 × 123.

	100		20	3
5	5 × 100			— 5 × 3
			5 × 20	

$$5 \times 100 = 500$$
$$5 \times 20 = 100$$
$$5 \times 3 = 15$$

```
  123
×   5
─────
   15   5 × 3
  100   5 × 20
+ 500   5 × 100
─────
  615
```

You can use what you know about multiplying 2-digit numbers to multiply 3-digit numbers.

☆ Guided Practice

Do You Understand?

1. What numerical expression is shown by the area model below?

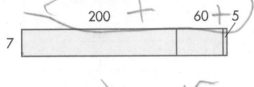

	200 +		60 + 5
7			

7 × 265

Do You Know How?

2. Multiply. Use the area model and partial products.

	500	60	560
7	3500	420	× 7
			3720

☆ Independent Practice ☆

Leveled Practice For **3–6**, multiply. Use the area model and partial products.

3.

	30	4	34
6	180	24	× 6

```
  180
+  24
─────
  204
```

4.

	90	9	99
2	180	18	× 2

148

5. 3 × 185

	100	80	5
3	300	240	15

300
240
15
555

6. 8 × 440

	400	40
8	3200	320

3200
320
3520

Problem Solving

7. Model with Math Last year, Anthony's grandmother gave him 33 silver coins and 16 gold coins to start a coin collection. Now Anthony has six times as many coins in his collection. How many coins does Anthony have in his collection? Complete the bar diagram to show your work.

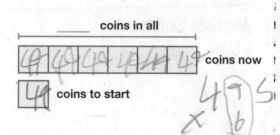

coins in all

49 49 49 49 49 49 coins now

49 coins to start

495
× 6
294

---

8. Wyatt said he used partial products to write $7 \times 870 = 5{,}600 + 49$. Explain Wyatt's error and use math to justify your explanation.

9. Higher Order Thinking Tod Mountain is a mountain peak near Tyler, Texas. A ranger hiked 607 feet to and from the peak, each way. The ranger hiked 3 times in the past four weeks. How far did the ranger hike on Tod Mountain over the past four weeks?

1821 Feet

---

10. Wendy plans to bring beverages for the school picnic. She has 5 gallons of iced tea. Also, she will bring 2 gallons of lemonade for every 10 people. How many total gallons of lemonade and iced tea does Wendy need to bring for 40 people? Complete the table.

Number of People	Gallons of Lemonade	Gallons of Iced Tea	Total Gallons
10	2	5	7
20	4	10	14
30	6	15	21
40	8	29	28

✓ **Assessment Practice**

11. What is the missing factor?

$6 \times ? = 264$

44

6 [44 | 4]

- Ⓐ 50
- Ⓑ 44
- Ⓒ 40
- Ⓓ 30

12. Which are the partial products for this area model?

7×228

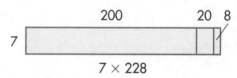

200   20 8

7 [| |]

7×228

- Ⓐ 1,400, 144, 56
- Ⓑ 14,000, 140, 56
- Ⓒ 56, 14, 1,400
- Ⓓ 56, 140, 1,400

Name_____

☆ ☆
Solve & Share

The horseshoe-pit model below has an area of 228 square feet. The length of one part of the pit was erased by mistake. What is the length of the missing section, *x*? **Solve any way you choose.** Explain how you found the answer.

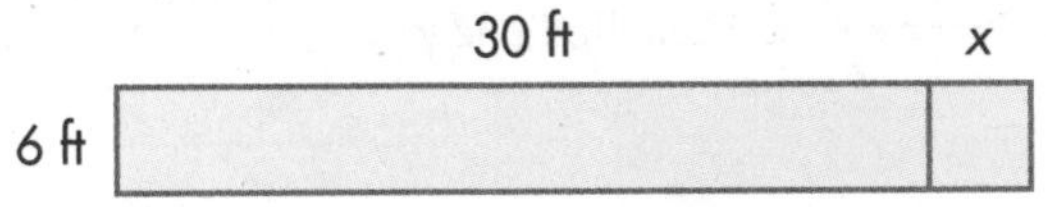

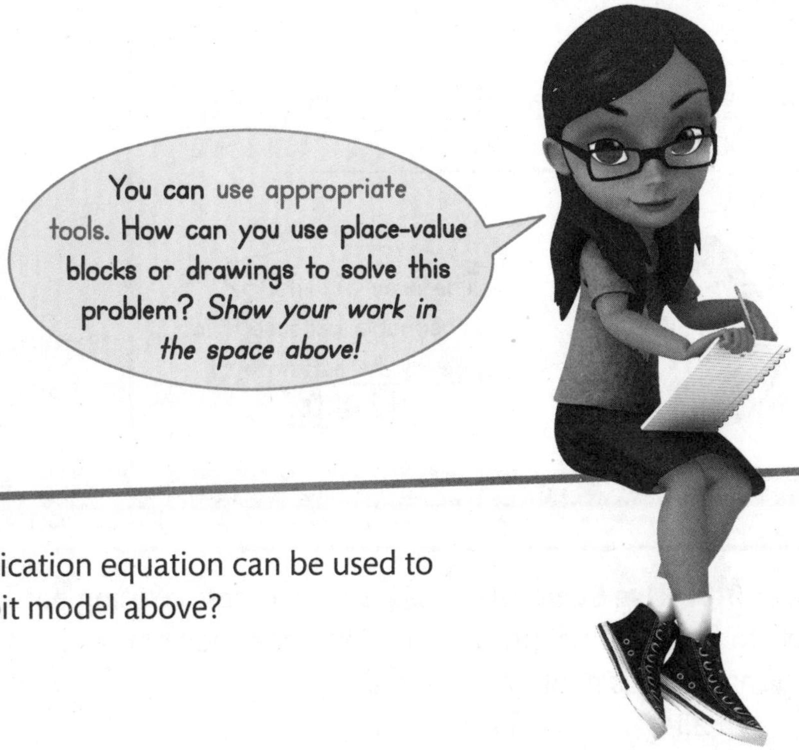

I can ...
use area models and partial products to multiply.

© **Content Standards** 4.NBT.B.5 Also 4.OA.A.3
Mathematical Practices MP.5, MP.6, MP.7

	30 ft		x
6 ft			

You can use appropriate tools. How can you use place-value blocks or drawings to solve this problem? *Show your work in the space above!*

Look Back! What multiplication equation can be used to represent the horseshoe-pit model above?

Essential Question | # How Do You Multiply with Greater Numbers?

A

The Rails-to-Trails Preservation opened a new section of a biking trail. The section is 6 yards wide. What is its area? Calculate 6 × 1,842.

The process for multiplying is the same regardless of the number of digits.

Trail Length: 1,842 yards

B Find 6 × 1,842 using an area model and partial products.

Estimate: 6 × 1,842 is about 6 × 2,000 = 12,000.

	1,000	800	40	2
6	6 × 1,000	6 × 800	6 × 40	6 × 2

The area of 11,052 is reasonable because it is close to the estimate of 12,000.

C Remember you can find partial products in any order.

$$
\begin{array}{r}
1,842 \\
\times \quad 6 \\
\hline
12 \\
240 \\
4,800 \\
+ \ 6,000 \\
\hline
11,052 \\
\end{array}
$$

6×2
6×40
6×800
$6 \times 1,000$

The new section is 11,052 square yards.

Convince Me! **Use Structure** How is the process of using partial products to find the final product the same for each of these calculations? How is it different? Explain.

$$
\begin{array}{r}
34 \\
\times 5 \\
\end{array}
\qquad
\begin{array}{r}
234 \\
\times 5 \\
\end{array}
\qquad
\begin{array}{r}
1,234 \\
\times 5 \\
\end{array}
$$

Name _____

☆ Guided Practice

Do You Understand?

1. What multiplication expression is shown by the area model below?

1,000	400	5
4 | 4000 | 1600 | 20 |

$1,405 \times 4 = 4000$
1600
20
5620

Do You Know How?

For **2**, multiply. Use the area model and partial products.

2. $5 \times 1,117$

1,000	100	7
5 | 5000 | 50 | 10 |

$$\begin{array}{r} 1,117 \\ \times \quad 5 \\ \hline 5000 \\ 500 \\ 50 \\ 35 \\ \hline 5,585 \end{array}$$

Use an estimate to check if your answer is reasonable.

☆ Independent Practice ☆

For **3–8**, multiply. Use the area model and partial products.

3.
1,000	90	2
8 | 8000 | | |

$$\begin{array}{r} 1,092 \\ \times \quad 8 \\ \hline 16 \\ 720 \\ 8000 \end{array}$$
$1\ 16\ 16$
726
$\boxed{8,736}$

4.
4,000	200	1
3 | 12000 | 600 | 60 |

180
3
42
$$\begin{array}{r} 4,261 \\ \times \quad 3 \\ \hline 12000 \\ 600 \\ 180 \\ 3 \end{array}$$
$\boxed{12783}$

5.
1,000	900	90
2 | 2000 | 1800 | 180 |

$$\begin{array}{r} 1,990 \\ \times \quad 2 \\ \end{array}$$
2000
$+1800$
$+180$
$\boxed{3980}$

6.
2,000	300	7
6 | 12000 | 1800 | 40 |

240
$$\begin{array}{r} 2,347 \\ \times \quad 6 \\ \hline 12000 \\ 1800 \\ 240 \\ 42 \end{array}$$
$\boxed{13082}$

7.
3,000		2
5 | 15000 | | |

10
20
100
$$\begin{array}{r} 3,022 \\ \times \quad 5 \\ \hline 15000 \\ 100 \\ 10 \end{array}$$
$\boxed{15110}$

8.
1,000	900	9
7 | 7000 | 6300 | 90 |

63
630
$$\begin{array}{r} 1,999 \\ \times \quad 7 \\ \hline 7000 \\ 6300 \\ 630 \\ 63 \\ \hline 13993 \end{array}$$

Problem Solving

9. **Be Precise** There are usually 365 days in each year. Every fourth year is called a leap year and has one extra day in February. How many days are there in 8 years if 2 of the years are leap years?

$$
\begin{array}{r}
365 \\
\times \ 8 \\
\hline
2720
\end{array}
$$

10. There are 1,250 seeds in each package. There are 5 packages. How many seeds are there in all?

11. A cat breeder has 6 Sphynx kittens and 7 Persian kittens for sale. If all 13 kittens sell, how much money will the breeder earn? Write and solve equations. Tell what your variables represent.

KITTENS
Sphynx $775
Persian $698
FOR SALE

12. **Higher Order Thinking** Patricia creates a design using 1,025 tiles. She doubles the number of tiles to make a second design. Her third design uses 3 times as many tiles as the second design. How many tiles does Patricia use in her third design? Explain.

Assessment Practice

13. Which are the correct partial products of $3 \times 3{,}672$?

Ⓐ 6; 21; 1,800; 9,000

Ⓑ 9,000; 1,800; 210; 6

Ⓒ 210; 1,800; 9,000

Ⓓ 6; 210; 180; 9,000

14. Select all the expressions that have 1,600 as a partial product.

☐ $4 \times 4{,}381$

☐ $8 \times 3{,}240$

☐ $4 \times 1{,}408$

☐ $2 \times 7{,}881$

☐ $8 \times 2{,}021$

Name _____

Lesson 3-6
Mental Math Strategies for Multiplication

Solve & Share

Determine the products for the expressions given below. Use mental math to solve. Explain your thinking. **Solve these problems using any strategy you choose.**

You can use structure to multiply the numbers in any order and make the computations easier. *Show your work in the space below!*

25 × 9 × 4

50 × 5 × 2

2 × 8 × 25

I can ...
use mental math strategies based on place value and properties of operations to multiply.

© **Content Standard** 4.NBT.B.5
Mathematical Practices MP.3, MP.7

Look Back! Describe two different ways to find 4 × 97.

A

Essential Question **How Can You Multiply Mentally?**

Three cyclists rode their bikes the distances shown in the table. Use mental math to calculate the total distance Pam and Anna each rode.

You can use properties of operations to help multiply mentally. According to the Commutative Property of Multiplication, you can multiply in any order.

DATA

Cyclist	Distance
Pam	325 miles a month for 4 months
Anna	25 miles a week for 8 weeks
George	398 miles a month for 3 months

B

Multiply 4 × 325 to find the distance Pam rode.

To multiply mentally, you can break apart numbers using place value and the Distributive Property.

Think:
$$4 \times 325 = 4 \times 300 + 4 \times 25$$
$$= 1{,}200 + 100$$
$$= 1{,}300$$

Pam rode 1,300 miles.

C

Multiply 8 × 25 to find the distance Anna rode.

To multiply mentally, you can break apart and rearrange numbers using the Commutative and Associative Properties.

Think:
$$8 \times 25 = (4 \times 2) \times 25$$
$$= 2 \times (4 \times 25)$$
$$= 2 \times 100$$
$$= 200$$

Anna rode 200 miles.

Convince Me! **Use Structure** In the work for 4 × 325 above, why was 25 not broken into 20 and 5? Explain.

Another Example!

Determine the distance George rode.

Find 3×398. 400 is close to 398.
Find 3×400 and adjust the answer.

$3 \times 400 = 1,200$
$398 + 2 = 400 \qquad 3 \times 2 = 6$

Adjust the answer by subtracting 6.
$1,200 - 6 = 1,194$

George rode 1,194 miles in 3 months.

Handwritten: $398 + 2 = 400$ / $398 + 2 = 400$ / $398 + 2 = 400$ / 398

You can use compensation to multiply mentally. Choose numbers close to the numbers in the problem and then adjust the answer.

☆ Guided Practice

Do You Understand?

1. Why was 6 subtracted from 1,200 in the problem above?

Handwritten: because you aded 2 three times and to get the corect answer we dep to subtract6 to get the corect anser

Do You Know How?

For **2**, multiply mentally to find the product. Explain which strategy you used.

2. $8 \times 903? = (900 + 3) \times 8 =$
   Handwritten: $900 \times 8 + 3 \times 8 = 9200 - 24 =$ (7224)

☆ Independent Practice

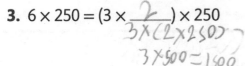

Leveled Practice For **3–10**, multiply mentally to find each product. Explain which strategy you used.

3. $6 \times 250 = (3 \times \underline{2}) \times 250$
   Handwritten: $3 \times (2 \times 250)$ / $3 \times 500 = 1500$

4. $4 \times 506 = 4 \times (\underline{500} + \underline{6})$
   Handwritten: C4

5. $4 \times 1,995$

6. 22×5
   Handwritten: 110

7. 404×6

8. 7×250
   Handwritten: 1700

9. 2×395

10. 9×56

Problem Solving

11. Each elephant at a zoo eats 100 pounds of hay and 5 pounds of fruits and vegetables every day. How many pounds of food does the zoo need to feed one elephant for one week? Use mental math to solve.

There are 7 days in 1 week.

---

12. Ashley and 3 friends are planning a trip. The cost of the trip is $599 per person. How much will the trip cost Ashley and her friends? Explain the mental math strategy you used to find the answer.

13. Kyle has a rock collection. On Monday, he found 16 new rocks. On Tuesday, he gave 9 rocks to his friends. After giving away the rocks, Kyle had 122 rocks left in his collection. How many rocks did Kyle have to start with?

---

14. Critique Reasoning Quinn used compensation to find the product of 4 × 307. First, she found 4 × 300 = 1,200. Then she adjusted the product by subtracting 4 groups of 7 to get her final answer of 1,172. Explain Quinn's mistake and find the correct answer.

15. Higher Order Thinking Do you think it would be better to use breaking apart and the Distributive Property or compensation to find the product of 5 × 328? Explain why and show how to find the product.

✓ Assessment Practice

16. Select all of the expressions that show how to use mental math to find the product of 4 × 27.

- ☐ (4 × 20) + (4 × 7)
- ☐ 4 × (20 × 7)
- ☐ (4 × 30) − (4 × 3)
- ☐ (4 × 25) + (4 × 2)
- ☐ 4 × 2 × 7

Some mental math strategies include both compensation and properties of operations.

Name _____

☆ ☆
Solve & Share

A cineplex has 4 movie theaters. Each theater has 342 floor seats and 85 mezzanine seats. How many people can the cineplex seat? *Solve this problem using any strategy you choose*. Explain your solution.

I can ...
choose an appropriate strategy to multiply.

© **Content Standards** 4.NBT.B.5 Also 4.OA.A.3
Mathematical Practices MP.1, MP.2, MP.6

You can be precise and use the information given to calculate accurately. *Show your work in the space above!*

Look Back! What strategy or strategies did you use to solve this problem? Explain why.

Essential Question **What Strategy Will You Use to Multiply?**

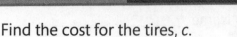
A

Paying for pothole damage to cars can be costly. The table shows the cost of some car repairs. What is the total cost of the repairs?

Think about the numbers you need to multiply to help you choose a strategy.

Repairs Due to Pothole Damage

Item	Cost	Amount Purchased
Tires	$125 each	4
Paint	$1,450 per coat	2

B Find the cost for the tires, c.

$4 \times \$125 = c$

Estimate: 4×125 is about $4 \times 120 = 480$.

Break apart 125 using place value and the Distributive Property.

$$4 \times 125 = 4 \times (100 + 25)$$
$$= 4 \times 100 + 4 \times 25$$
$$= 400 + 100$$
$$= 500$$

$c = 500$

The tire repairs cost $500.

C Find the cost of the paint, y. $2 \times \$1,450 = y$

Estimate: $2 \times 1,450$ is about $2 \times 1,500 = 3,000$.

Use an area model and partial products.

```
        1,000    400  50
   2 |                    |
```

$$\begin{array}{r} 1,450 \\ \times \quad 2 \\ \hline 100 \\ 800 \\ + \ 2,000 \\ \hline 2,900 \end{array}$$
2×50
2×400
$2 \times 1,000$

$y = 2,900$

To paint the car costs $2,900.

D Find the total cost of the repairs, z.

$\$500 + \$2,900 = z$

Estimate: $500 + 2,900$ is about $500 + 3,000 = 3,500$.

Use compensation to add.

$500 + 3,000 = 3,500$
3,000 is 100 more than 2,900.
Subtract 100.
$3,500 - 100 = 3,400$

$z = 3,400$

The total cost of the repairs was $3,400.

Convince Me! **Reasoning** Explain why the answers to each part of the problem above are reasonable.

Name _____

Solve & Share

Kevin took 120 color photos and 128 black and white photos on a field trip. Marco took 2 times as many photos as Kevin. How many photos did Marco take? *Solve this problem using any strategy you choose. Use the bar diagram to help.*

Problem Solving

Lesson 3-8
Model with Math

I can ...
apply the math I know to solve problems.

© **Mathematical Practices** MP.4 Also MP.1
Content Standards 4.OA.A.3 Also 4.NBT.B.5

348

Kevin | 120 | 120 | 128 | and

$2 \times 100 = 200$
$2 \times 40 = 40$

120
100
20

+228
240   348

Marco

$300 \times 2 = 600$
$40 \times 2 = 80$ st
$2 \times 2 = 4$

348
$\times 2$

684
marco   took 336

684 14
− 348
336

more Photos keven. 336

Thinking Habits

Be a good thinker! These questions can help you.

- How can I use math I know to solve this problem?

- How can I use pictures, objects, or an equation to represent the problem?

- How can I use numbers, words, and symbols to solve the problem?

Look Back! **Model with Math** What representation did you use to solve the problem and show relationships?

Essential Question: How Can You Represent a Situation with a Math Model?

A

An art show uses 9 teams of art judges. If each team judges the work of 13 painters and 14 sculptors, how many artists attend the show?

What do you need to find?

I need to find how many artists each team judges.

I need to find the total number of artists.

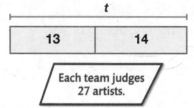

t

| 13 | 14 |

Each team judges 27 artists.

B How can I model with math?

I can

- use bar diagrams and equations to represent and solve this problem.

- decide if my results make sense.

C Find 9 × 27.

Here's my thinking.

Use a bar diagram. Write and solve an equation.

a artists

| 27 | 27 | 27 | 27 | 27 | 27 | 27 | 27 | 27 |

↑
number of artists
for each team
of judges

$a = 9 \times 27$

$a = 243$

There are 243 artists at the show.

Convince Me! **Model with Math** How could you decide if your answer makes sense?

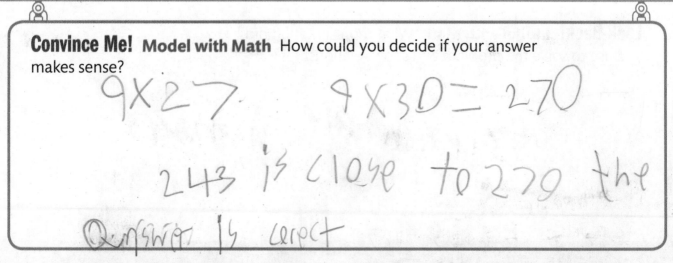

9 X 27.   9 X 3D = 270

243 is close to 270 the

answer is correct

☆ Guided Practice

Model with Math

Sharon's Stationery Store contains 1,219 boxes of cards. May's Market contains 3 times as many boxes of cards. How many boxes, *b*, does May's Market contain?

When you model with math, you can draw a bar diagram and write an equation to represent the relationships in the problem.

1. Explain how to use a picture to represent the problem and show relationships.

| 1219 | 1219 | 1219 |

1219   mX9

2. What equation can you write to represent the problem?

$1,219 \times 3 = b$

×3
1000

3. What is the solution to the problem?

3,657

200
10 3

☆ Independent Practice ☆

Model with Math

Annie has 6 albums of stamps in her stamp collection. Each album contains 440 stamps. How many stamps, *s*, does Annie have in her collection? Use Exercises 4–6 to answer the question.

4. Draw a picture and write an equation to represent the problem.

| 440 | 440 | 440 | 440 | 440 | 440 |

$6 \times 440 = s$

5. What previously learned math can you use to solve the problem?

multiply whole numbers

6. What is the solution to the problem? Explain why your solution makes sense.

It makes sense because 6 rows. time x 6

440   440   400
× 6   × 6   ×6
2400   2400

440 stamps = 6x6= 2400 2400
2,640

Problem Solving

Hauling Fuel

A truck like the one shown delivers a load of gasoline to a gas station 3 times a week. The storage tank at the gas station holds 9 loads of fuel. How much more gas does the storage tank hold than the truck?

Hauls 2,700 gallons

7. **Make Sense and Persevere** What do you know and what do you need to determine?

When you model with math, you use math to represent real-world situations.

8. **Make Sense and Persevere** What do you need to know to determine how much more the tank holds than the truck?

9. **Model with Math** Explain how to use bar diagrams and equations to represent the problem and solve.

Name _____

Shade a path from **START** to **FINISH**. Follow the differences that are correct. You can only move up, down, right, or left.

I can ...
subtract multi-digit whole numbers.

 Content Standard 4.NBT.B.4
Mathematical Practices MP.2, MP.6, MP.7

Start				
812 − 44 768	929 − 879 150	511 − 423 112	767 − 31 636	698 − 12 586
621 − 85 536	341 − 299 142	486 − 230 256	825 −789 36	333 − 111 222
543 − 97 446	836 − 788 48	178 − 98 80	123 − 53 30	342 − 88 254
111 − 87 76	876 − 55 72	912 − 842 170	282 − 32 150	293 − 95 198
684 − 485 299	922 − 87 865	312 − 219 193	986 − 887 199	876 − 543 333

Finish

TOPIC 3 — Vocabulary Review

Glossary

Word List

- array
- Associative Property of Multiplication
- Commutative Property of Multiplication
- compensation
- Distributive Property
- estimate
- numerical expression
- partial product

Understand Vocabulary

1. Circle the property shown by $4 \times (6 + 2) = (4 \times 6) + (4 \times 2)$.

Associative   Commutative   ⟨Distributive⟩

2. Circle the property shown by $2 \times 134 = 134 \times 2$.

Associative   ⟨Commutative⟩   ~~Distributive~~

3. Circle the property shown by $(1 \times 3) \times 7 = 1 \times (3 \times 7)$.

⟨Associative⟩   Commutative   ~~Distributive~~

4. Draw a line from each vocabulary word to its example.

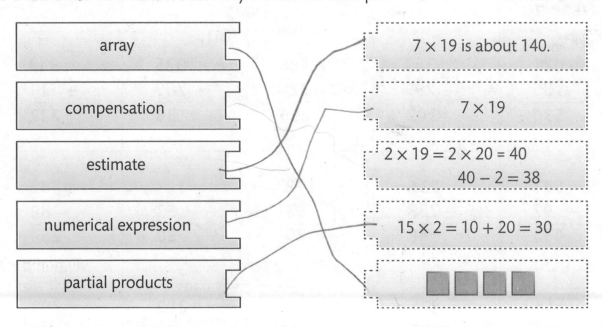

array		7 × 19 is about 140.
compensation		7 × 19
estimate		$2 \times 19 = 2 \times 20 = 40$; $40 - 2 = 38$
numerical expression		$15 \times 2 = 10 + 20 = 30$
partial products		▮ ▮ ▮ ▮

Use Vocabulary in Writing

5. Find 4×114. Use at least three terms from the Word List to describe how to find the product.

To solve the numeral exprettion 4X114 you can use the assiative property

114
×4
400

1. Use numbers from the box to show how to multiply 126 by 3.

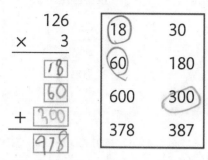

```
    126
  ×   3
   [18]
   [60]
 + [300]
   [978]
```

(18)	30
(60)	180
600	(300)
378	387

2. Alberto rode the train 198 miles round trip 4 times last month. Explain how to use mental math to find the total distance Alberto traveled.

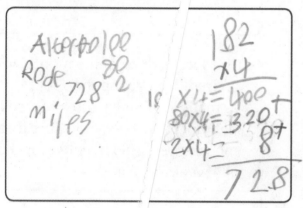

Alberto
Rode 728 80 2
miles   is ×4=400 +
         80×4=320 +
         2×4= 8 +
              728

182
×4
728

3. Mr. Ortiz sells tortillas in bags of 25 and in bags of 50. If he sells 4 bags of 50 and 6 bags of 25, how many tortillas did Mr. Ortiz sell?

Ⓐ 10 tortillas   Ⓒ 350 tortillas

Ⓑ 170 tortillas   Ⓓ 3,500 tortillas

4. A. What are the partial products when finding 1,874 × 3? Select all that apply.

☐ 5,400   ☐ 2,000

☑ 3,000   ☑ 210

☑ 2,400   ☑ 12

B. Find the product of 1,874 and 3.

5. A science class is growing some fruit and vegetable plants on a plot of land behind their school. Each section is laid out in rows.

DATA	Produce	Number of Rows
	Strawberries	65
	Peppers	18
	Squash	11
	Tomatoes	22

A. There are 9 strawberry plants planted in each row. Write and solve an equation to find how many strawberry plants were planted.

585
strawberry
plants

65
×9
60×9=540
5×9= 45
     585

B. There are 9 pepper plants planted in each row. Draw an area model and show the partial products to find how many pepper plants are planted behind the school.

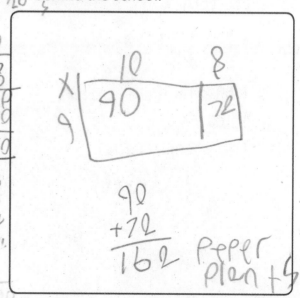

162 pepper
plants

6. Select all the expressions that could be used to find 1,235 × 9.

☐ 9 × (1,000 + 200 + 20 + 5)

☒ 9 × (1,000 + 200 + 30 + 5)

☒ (9 × 1,000) + (9 × 200) + (9 × 30) + (9 × 5)

☒ 9 × 1,235

☐ 1,235 + 9

---

7. Draw a model to find 365 × 3.

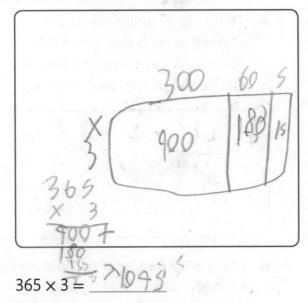

300   60   5

x 3   900   180   15

365
x 3
900
180
75

365 × 3 = _1095_

---

8. Select all of the expressions that have a product of 640.

☒ (6 × 100) + (4 × 10)

☐ 9 × 54

☐ 60 × 4 × 1

☒ 160 × 4

☒ (6 × 100) × (4 × 10)

100   60
400
240
640

---

9. The table shows the number of hot drinks sold in a busy coffee shop in 1 week.

Type	Number
Coffee	835
Latte	567
Mocha	200
Cappuccino	139

A. If the same number of cups of coffee were sold for 6 weeks in a row, how many cups would be sold in all?

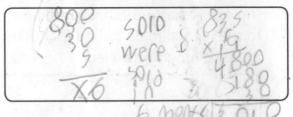

800
30
5
sold
were
sold
in

835
x 6
4800
180
30

6 months 5,010

B. The special drink of the month was an iced mocha. The shop sold 5 times as many iced mochas in one week as hot mochas. How many more iced mochas were sold than hot mochas in 4 weeks? Explain.

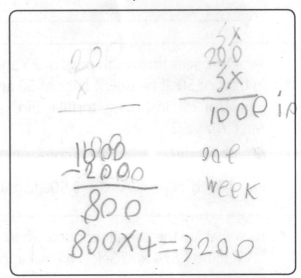

200
x

1000
-2000
800

5x
200
5x
1000 in

one
week

800 × 4 = 3200

10. Tickets for a resort cost $1,182 each for adults and $459 each for children. Find the cost for 3 adult tickets and 3 child tickets. Explain how you know your answer is reasonable.

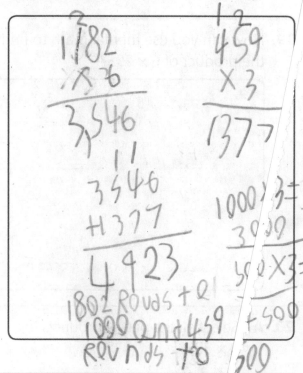

11. Which expression has the same value as 5 × 617?

Ⓐ (5 × 6) + (5 × 1) + (5 × 7)

Ⓑ (5 × 60) + (5 × 10) + (5 × 70)

Ⓒ (5 × 600) + (5 × 1) + (5 × 7)

Ⓓ (5 × 600) + (5 × 10) + (5 × 7)

12. Which of the following is equivalent to (400 × 3) + (36 × 3)?

Ⓐ 436 ÷ 3

Ⓑ 400 × 10

Ⓒ 436 × 3

Ⓓ 400 × 3 + 36

13. Find 3 × 312. Draw a bar diagram to solve.

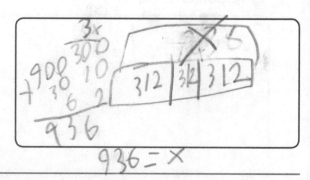

14. Bea's Bakery bakes 215 cookies and 45 muffins every hour. How many baked goods are baked in 4 hours?

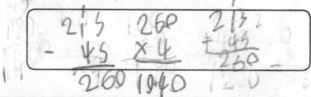

15. Write and solve an equation that represents the given bar diagram.

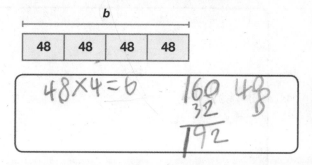

16. Which of the following is equivalent to 8 × 493? Select all that apply.

☑ (8 × 400) + (8 × 90) + (8 × 3)

☐ (8 × 400) + 93

☑ 493 × 8

☐ (8 × 500) − (8 × 93)

☐ (8 × 500) − (8 × 7)

17. Mr. Luca would like to purchase a digital keyboard for each of his 3 nieces and 1 nephew. The keyboard costs $105.

A. Mr. Luca thinks the total cost should be about $200. Is this amount reasonable? Explain.

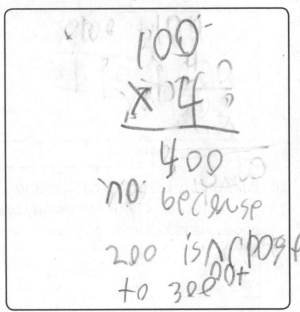

100

$\times 4$

400

no because 200 is not close to 300 + 100

B. Write and solve an equation to find the total cost of the keyboards. Explain why your answer is reasonable.

300 | 100
15 | 5
315 | $\times 3$

yes because 315 is close to 200.

18. What is the product of 5 × 1,903?

Ⓐ 9,515

Ⓑ 9,505

Ⓒ 9,155

Ⓓ 965

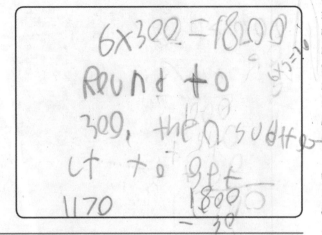

5000 | 1000
900
3
$\times 5$

19. How can you use mental math to find the product of 6 × 295?

6×300 = 1800

Round to 300, then subtract to get 1800 − 30

1170

20. A. Select all the partial products for 8 × 321.

☑ 8

☐ 80

☑ 160

☐ 1,600

☑ 2,400

300 | 321
20 | × 8
2400
160
8
2568

B. Find the product for **Part A** using the partial products.

2568

Buying Classroom Computers

Jorge's school can purchase computers and printers for the prices shown.
Information about the fourth-grade classes are given in the table.

Fourth Grade Classes		
Teacher	**Money Raised**	**Number of Students**
Mr. Jones	$6,000	25
Ms. Sanchez	$9,000	24
Ms. Katz	$7,500	26

Desktop computer: $1,050

Laptop computer: $798

Printer: $128

1. Jorge's teacher is Ms. Sanchez. His class wants to buy
8 desktop computers and 3 printers.

Part A

What is the total cost of 8 desktop computers? Use
place-value strategies and properties of operations.

$$\begin{array}{r} \overset{4}{1050} \\ \times\ 8 \\ \hline 8400 \end{array} \qquad 8400$$

Part B

What is the total cost of 3 printers? Draw an array and
show the partial products to find the cost.

Part C

Did Jorge's class raise enough money to buy 8 computers
and 3 printers? Explain.

2. Rachel's teacher is Mr. Jones. Her class wants to buy 7 computers and 2 printers.

Part A

How much more do 7 desktop computers cost than 7 laptop computers? Use bar diagrams and equations to represent and solve the problem.

Part B

What is another way to find the difference in the cost of 7 desktop computers and 7 laptop computers? Explain.

3. Miranda's teacher is Ms. Katz. Her class wants to buy 9 laptop computers and 4 printers. Miranda said the total cost should be $7,494. Is this amount reasonable? Explain. Does the class have enough money?

Use Strategies and Properties to Multiply by 2-Digit Numbers

Essential Questions: How can you use a model to multiply?
How can you use the Distributive Property to multiply?
How can you use multiplication to solve problems?

Digital Resources

Interactive Student Edition Activity Visual Learning Video Practice

Assessment Games Tools Glossary

ēnVision STEM Project: Renewable Energy and Multiplication

Do Research Use the Internet or other sources to find information about different sources of renewable energy.

Journal: Write a Report Include what you found. Also in your report:

- A wind farm is an area of land with a large number of turbines. Draw an array with 15 rows to show the turbines in a wind farm. How many turbines are in your wind farm?

- Some turbines produce 63 megawatt-hours of energy every week. Find how much energy one of these turbines would produce in one year. Remember, one year is 52 weeks.

Name _____

Review What You Know

Vocabulary

Choose the best term from the box.
Write it on the blank.

| • algorithm | • product |
| • array | • variable |

1. You multiply numbers to find a(n) _____.

2. A(n) _____ shows the number of objects in rows and columns.

3. A symbol or letter that stands for a number is called a(n) _____.

Multiplication

Find each product.

4. 4×8

5. 2×9

6. 9×5

7. 6×8

8. 16×4

9. 6×68

10. 87×5

11. 19×9

12. 128×6

Rounding

Round each number to the nearest hundred.

13. 164

14. 8,263

> You will use rounding to estimate products in this topic.

15. 527

16. 2,498

17. 7,892

18. 472

Round each number to the nearest thousand.

19. 8,685

20. 4,991

21. 62,549

22. 167,241

23. 77,268

24. 34,162

25. 1,372

26. 9,009

27. 121,619

28. Construct Arguments Explain how to round 608,149 to the nearest thousands place.

Name _____

**PROJECT
4A**

How high would a stack of sabal palms be?

Project: Explain the Processes

**PROJECT
4B**

Can you estimate the weight of dozens of birds?

Project: Write a Report About the Northern Mockingbird

How many soccer players start in the Women's World Cup ?

Project: Create an Array Poster

How much weight can shotputters throw ?

Project: Compare Shot Masses

Name_____

☆ Solve & Share ☆

The principal of a school needs to order supplies for 20 new classrooms. Each classroom needs the following items: 20 desks, 30 chairs, and 40 pencils. How many of each item does the principal need to order? *Solve these problems using any strategy you choose.*

You can use structure. What basic facts can you use to help solve these problems? How are they related? *Show your work in the space below!*

Activity

I can ...
use place-value strategies or properties of operations to multiply by multiples of 10.

© Content Standard 4.NBT.B.5
Mathematical Practices MP.2, MP.7

Look Back! Look at the factors and products. What patterns do you notice?

Essential Question

How Can You Multiply by Multiples of 10?

A

The number of visitors of each age group for the Sunny Day Amusement Park are shown below. How many children visit the park in 30 days?

You can use place-value strategies or properties of operations to multiply by multiples of 10.

Adults under 65: **60**

Adults 65 and over: **40**

Children: **80**

Number of visitors each day

B

One Way

Find 30 × 80.

Use basic facts and place value.

$30 \times 80 = 3 \text{ tens} \times 8 \text{ tens}$
$= 24 \text{ hundreds}$
$= 2,400$

2,400 children visit the park in 30 days.

$10 \times 10 = 100$

C

Another Way

Find 30 × 80.

Break apart numbers.
Use the Commutative Property and the Associative Property of Multiplication.

$30 \times 80 = (3 \times 10) \times (8 \times 10)$
$= 3 \times 8 \times 10 \times 10$
$= (3 \times 8) \times (10 \times 10)$
$= 24 \times 100$
$= 2,400$

2,400 children visit the park in 30 days.

Convince Me! **Look for Relationships** Use place value or properties of operations to determine how many adults age 65 and older visit the park in 30 days.

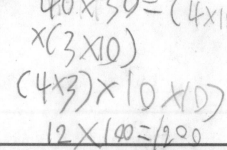

$4 \text{ tens} \times 3 \text{ tens}$

$40 \times 30 = 12 \text{ hundreds}$
$= 1200$

$40 \times 30 = (4 \times 10) \times (3 \times 10)$
$(4 \times 3) \times 10 \times 10$
$12 \times 100 = 1200$

Practice Tools Assessment

Another Example!

Use the properties of operations to find 50 × 60.

$50 \times 60 = 5 \times 10 \times 6 \times 10$
$= (5 \times 6) \times (10 \times 10)$
$= 30 \times 100$
$= 3,000$

If the product of the basic fact ends in zero, the product has one more zero than you see in the factors.

☆ Guided Practice

Do You Understand?

1. Find 50 × 20. How many zeros are in the product? Explain.

$50 \times 20 = 5 \times 10 \times 2 \times 10$
$5 \times 2 \quad 10 \times 10$
$10 \times 100 = 1000$

2. How many adults under 65 visit the park in 30 days?

$60 \times 30 = 1800$

Do You Know How?

For **3-8**, use basic facts and place-value or properties of operations to find each product.

3. $30 \times 10 = 390$ 4. $50 \times 10 = 500$

5. $20 \times 10 = 209$ 6. $60 \times 20 = 1200$

7. $90 \times 40 = 3609$ 8. $80 \times 50 = 4000$

☆ Independent Practice ☆

For **9-16**, use basic facts and place-value or properties of operations to find each product.

4 pt
4 independent

9. $20 \times 70 = 1400$ 10. $70 \times 90 = 6300$ 11. 40×20 12. 40×30

13. $70 \times 40 = 2800$ 14. $20 \times 30 = 6100$ 15. 60×40 16. 60×90

2h partple
3
80   independent x

For **17-22**, find the missing factor.

17. $10 \times \underline{10} = 100$ 18. $\underline{80} \times 20 = 1,600$ 19. $\underline{50} \times 30 = 1,500$

20. $20 \times \underline{50} = 1,000$ 21. $\underline{90} \times 90 = 8,100$ 22. $60 \times \underline{} = 4,200$

Problem Solving

23. Reasoning The product of two factors is 4,200. If one of the factors is 60, what is the other factor? Explain.

24. Algebra There are 30 players on each high school football team. Explain how you can find the total number of players if there are 40 teams. Write and solve an equation.

25. Bob uses 2 gallons of water while brushing his teeth. He uses 10 gallons of water to wash clothes. How many more cups of water did Bob use while washing his clothes than brushing his teeth?

There are 16 cups in 1 gallon.

26. James walked 30 minutes each day for 90 days. Show how you can use place value or properties to find how many minutes James walked.

27. Higher Order Thinking What is one example of a product that will have the same number of zeros in the factors and the product? What is one example of a product that will NOT have the same number of zeros in the factors as the product?

☑ Assessment Practice

28. Select all of the expressions that have a product of 1,600.

- ☐ 20 × 80
- ☐ 20 × 60
- ☐ 40 × 40
- ☐ 60 × 30
- ☐ 90 × 20

29. Which expression has 50 as the missing factor?

- Ⓐ 20 × ? = 1,000
- Ⓑ 50 × ? = 3,000
- Ⓒ 30 × ? = 1,800
- Ⓓ 10 × ? = 1,000

Name_____

☆ ☆
Solve & Share

There are 10 teams in a baseball league. Each team has 25 players. How many players are in the league? *Solve this problem using any strategy you choose.*

Lesson 4-2

Use Models to Multiply 2-Digit Numbers by Multiples of 10

I can ...
use models and properties of operations to help multiply.

© **Content Standard** 4.NBT.B.5
Mathematical Practices MP.2, MP.4, MP.5

You can use appropriate tools. Place-value blocks or grid paper can help you visualize the problem. *Show your work in the space above!*

Look Back! How many players are in the league if there are 30 teams?

Explain how you can use your answer above to help solve this problem.

Essential Question

How Can You Use an Array or an Area Model to Multiply?

A

Max's Moving Company has boxes for packing books. If each box holds 24 books, how many books would fit into 20 boxes?

Making an array with place-value blocks or using an area model helps to visualize the partial products.

24 Books

B Use place-value blocks to make an array.

Find $20 \times 24 = b$.

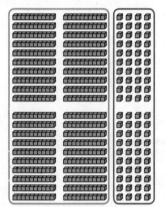

$$\begin{array}{r} 400 \\ +\ 80 \\ \hline 480 \end{array}$$ ← Partial Products

$20 \times 24 = 480$

$b = 480$

$20 \times 20 = 400 \quad 20 \times 4 = 80$
480 books will fit into 20 boxes.

C Draw an area model.

Find $20 \times 24 = b$.

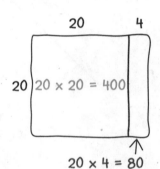

20   4

20 | $20 \times 20 = 400$

$20 \times 4 = 80$

$$\begin{array}{r} 400 \\ +\ 80 \\ \hline 480 \end{array}$$ ← Partial Products

$20 \times 24 = 480$

$b = 480$

480 books will fit into 20 boxes.

Convince Me! Reasoning In the problem above, is the product, 480, reasonable? Explain.

$20 \times 24 > 20 \times 25 = 500$

$20 \times 20 = 400$

Yes because 500 is close to 480

Name _____

☆ Guided Practice

Do You Understand?

1. Draw an area model to show 20 × 26. Then find the product.

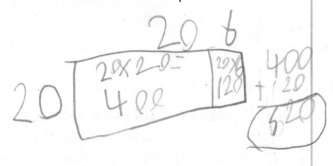

Do You Know How?

2. The place-value block array shows 10 × 16. Find the product.

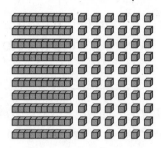

 ← 10 groups of 10

+ ← 10 groups of 6

 ← Sum of the partial products

Independent Practice ☆

Leveled Practice For **3–8**, use place-value blocks, area models, or arrays to find each product.

3. 10 × 22

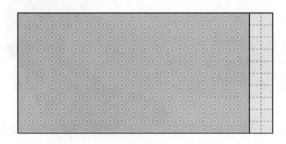

2 0 0 ← 10 groups of 20

+ 2 0 ← 10 groups of 2

2 2 0 ← Sum of the partial products

4. 10 × 13

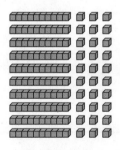

You can use a sheet of grid paper to draw arrays or area models.

1 0 0 ← 10 groups of 10

+ 3 0 ← 10 groups of 3

1 3 0 ← Sum of the partial products

5. 20 × 35

20 X 30 = 600 +
20 X 5 = 10 0 +
700

6. 20 × 41

20 X 40 = 800 +
29 X 1 = 20 +
820

7. 30 × 29

30 X 29 = 600
30 X 9 = 20
870

8. 40 × 37

1200
280
1480

40 X 3 = 12
40 X 7 = 28

Topic 4 | Lesson 4-2   **135**

Problem Solving

9. Algebra In the first 3 months of the year, an electronics store sold 1,446 cameras. How many cameras did the store sell in March? Write and solve an equation.

$$1446$$
$$-\ \ 48$$

Camera Sales	
Month	**Number Sold**
January	486
February	385

10. For every camera sold in February, the store donated $2 to a charity. How much did the store donate?

---

11. Model with Math During a basketball game, 75 cups of fruit punch were sold. Each cup holds 20 fluid ounces. How many total fluid ounces of fruit punch were sold?

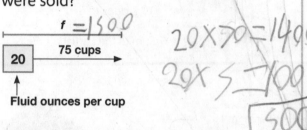

f = 1500

20 × 70 = 1400
20 × 5 = 100
1500

12. Higher Order Thinking Describe how to correct the partial product that is not correct in the worked problem below. What is the correct product?

```
    27
  × 73
  ─────
  1,400
     49
     60
  +  21
  ─────
  1,530
```

20 × 70 = 1400

✓ Assessment Practice

13. Which is greater?

15 × 30 or 22 × 20
Show your thinking.

> Representations can help you write a complete explanation.

15 × 30 = (10 × 30) + (30 × 5) = 300 + 150 = 450

450 > 440

greater

440

22 × 20 = (20 × 20) + (20 × 2) = 400 + 40

Name _____

Activity

Solve & Share

Choose two factors from the numbers below to find a product that is as close to 1,600 as possible. **Solve this problem using any strategy you choose.**

24	32	61	78

What strategies do you know that can help you estimate a product? *Show your work in the space below!*

I can ...
use rounding or compatible numbers to estimate.

© **Content Standards** 4.OA.A.3 Also 4.NBT.B.5
Mathematical Practices MP.2, MP.3

Look Back! **Construct Arguments** Why did you choose the two factors that you did? How do you know your factors will give the closest estimate of the product?

A

Essential Question: What Strategies Can I Use When Estimating?

The workers picked 14 dozen apples at Ms. Piper's apple grove and 12 dozen apples at Mr. Stuart's apple grove. There are 12 apples in one dozen. About how many apples did the workers pick?

14 + 12 = 26 dozen apples picked in total

1 dozen apples

There is more than one strategy you can use to estimate.

B

One Way

Use rounding to estimate 26 × 12.

Round 26 to the nearest ten.
Round 12 to the nearest ten.

$$26 \times 12 = n$$
$$\downarrow \qquad \downarrow$$
$$30 \times 10 = 300$$

The workers picked about 300 apples.

Some problems do not need an exact answer.

C

Another Way

Use compatible numbers to estimate 26 × 12.

Replace the factors with numbers that are close and easy to multiply.

26 is close to 25.   12 is close to 10.

$$25 \times 10 = n$$
$$250 = n$$

The workers picked about 250 apples.

Convince Me! **Reasoning** Sue said she could find an estimate for 26 × 12 by rounding only 1 factor and multiplying 26 × 10. Do you agree? Explain.

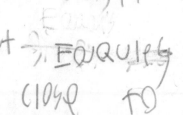

Yes, if she mutimpys 26 × 10 that EQRures 206 witch is close to 300.

Name_____

☆ Guided Practice

Do You Understand?

1. In the example on the previous page, how do you know you only need an estimate and not an exact answer?

When there is a ibouts in the sentence

2. In the example on the previous page, what is another way you can multiply using compatible numbers by changing only one of the factors? Explain how you would find the estimated product.

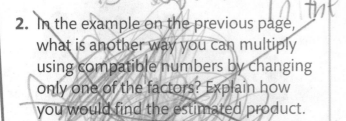

Do You Know How?

For **3-6**, estimate each product. Explain why you chose the strategy you used to estimate the product.

3. 24 × 18   **4.** 33 × 31

20×20=400   30×30=900

5. 38 × 22   **6.** 45 × 48

40×20=800   50×50= 2500

☆ Independent Practice ☆

For **7-12**, estimate each product. Explain why you chose the strategy you used to estimate the product.

7. 39 × 19
40×20=800

8. 28 × 27
30×30=900

9. 64 × 13
60×10=600

10. 42 × 17
40×20=800

11. 82 × 36
80×40=3200

12. 54 × 18
50×20=1000

For **13-14**, estimate to check if the given answer is reasonable.

13. 66 × 41 = 2,706

Rounds to ___70___ × ___40___ = (2800)

(Reasonable)   Not Reasonable

14. 34 × 52 = 2,288

Rounds to ___30___ × ___50___ = (1500)

Reasonable   (Not Reasonable)

Compare your estimate to the given answer to check if the answer is reasonable.

Problem Solving

For **15–16**, use the table at the right.

15. About how many more Valencia orange trees than Temple orange trees does Mr. Gonzalez have? Explain.

$50 \times 30 = 1500$

16. About how many orange trees does Mr. Gonzalez have? Explain.

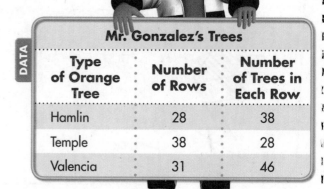

Your answer can be an estimate because an exact answer is not necessary.

Mr. Gonzalez's Trees

DATA

Type of Orange Tree	Number of Rows	Number of Trees in Each Row
Hamlin	28	38
Temple	38	28
Valencia	31	46

17. Higher Order Thinking How is using compatible numbers to estimate similar to using rounding? How is it different?

18. Construct Arguments Explain how you would use estimation to decide which has the greater product, 39×21 or 32×32.

Assessment Practice

19. Select all of the expressions that could be used to estimate 32×14.

- ☐ 30×20
- ☐ 30×10
- ☑ 14×32
- ☐ 40×10
- ☐ 32×10

20. Select all of the equations that use compatible numbers to find an estimate for 28×24.

- ☐ $30 \times 25 = 750$
- ☐ $28 \times 10 = 280$
- ☐ $28 \times 25 = 700$
- ☐ $25 \times 20 = 500$
- ☐ $30 \times 300 = 9,000$

Name _____

Solve & Share

A theater contains 14 rows of seats with 23 seats in each row. How many seats are in the theater? *Solve this problem using any strategy you choose.*

I can ...
use place-value concepts and properties to multiply.

© **Content Standards** 4.NBT.B.5 Also 4.OA.A.3
Mathematical Practices MP.4, MP.7

You can use grid paper or arrays to show the problem. *Show your work in the space below!*

$$23 \times 14 = (20 \times 10) + (3 \times 4) =$$
$$12 + 200 = 212$$

Look Back! **Use Structure** Theater seating is an example of objects that are arranged in rows and columns, or arrays. How do the number of rows and the number of seats in each row relate to the total number of seats?

Essential Question

How Can You Multiply Using an Array?

A

There are 13 toy dogs in each row of a carnival booth. Twenty rows contain toy bulldogs and 4 rows contain toy huskies. How many toy dogs are there?

To solve this problem, you need to first find how many rows of toy dogs are in the booth.

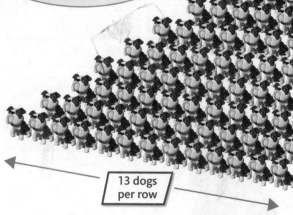

20 rows of toy bulldogs
+ 4 rows of toy huskies
───────────────────
24 rows of toy dogs

There are 24 rows of toy dogs with 13 toy dogs in each row.

13 dogs per row

B Use an array to find 24×13.

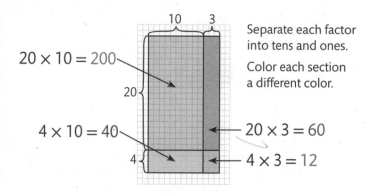

$20 \times 10 = 200$

$4 \times 10 = 40$

$20 \times 3 = 60$

$4 \times 3 = 12$

Separate each factor into tens and ones.

Color each section a different color.

12, 40, 60, and 200 are partial products.

C Add the number of squares in each part of the array.

12	4×3 ones
40	4×1 ten
60	20×3 ones
+ 200	20×1 ten
312	

There are 312 toy dogs in the booth.

$24 \times 13 = 312$ is close to $25 \times 10 = 250$. The answer is reasonable.

Convince Me! **Model with Math** What 2-digit by 2-digit multiplication is shown by the model at the right? What is the product? Explain how you used the model to find the product.

(handwritten) 100 80 50 40 270

(handwritten) 18x5=270

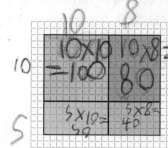

(handwritten) 10x10 =100   10x8= 80   5x10= 50   5x8= 40

(handwritten) We Used Partil produces then added

☆ Guided Practice

Do You Understand?

1. In the example on the previous page, what four simpler multiplication problems were used to find 24 × 13?

$20 \times 10 = 200$
$20 \times 3 = 60$
$4 \times 10 = 40$
$4 \times 3 = 12$

2. How can you use properties to help find the product of 24 × 13?

$24 \times 13 = (20+4) \times (10 \times 3)$
$= (20 \times 10) + (20 \times 3) + (4 \times 10) + $ 200
(4×3) 129
$+ 40$
$200 + 60 + 40 + 12 = $ $+ 24$
312 384

Do You Know How?

For **3**, use the array drawn on a grid to find the product. Check if your answer is reasonable.

3.   24
× 16

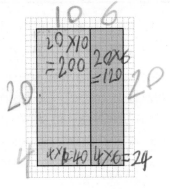

$20 \times 10 = 200$ $20 \times 6 = 120$
$4 \times 10 = 40$ $4 \times 6 = 24$

☆ Independent Practice ☆

For **4-7**, use the array drawn on a grid to find each product.

> Using the Commutative Property of Addition, you can add the partial products in any order.

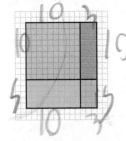

4. 14 × 21

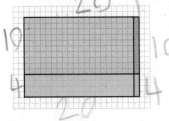

200
+ 80
10
4

5. 14 × 12

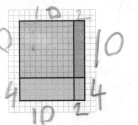

100
40
20
8
168

6. 18 × 18

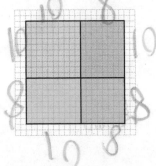

100
80
80
64
314

284

7. 15 × 13

100
50
30
15

Problem Solving

8. Find the missing factor.
$$20 \times ? = 420$$
Explain how you solved.

9. The flagpole in front of City Hall in Lou's town is 35 feet tall. How many inches tall is the flagpole? Remember, there are 12 inches in 1 foot.

$$35 \times 12 = 420$$

For **10–11**, use the array at the right.

10. Model with Math Maggie is making a balloon game for the school fair. Students throw darts to pop the balloons. Draw lines on the array to separate each factor into tens and ones. How many balloons are used to set up the game?

11. Higher Order Thinking Maggie knows she will have to completely refill the balloon board about 15 times. Write an equation to show the number of balloons Maggie will need.

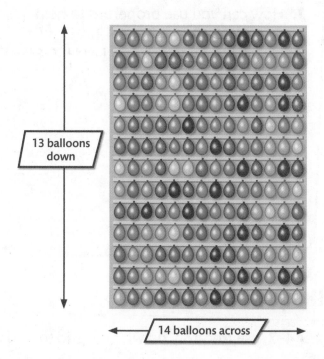

13 balloons down

14 balloons across

12. Insert the missing partial products. Then add to find the product.

| 200 60 6 1,200 120 30 12 |

$$
\begin{array}{r}
13 \\
\times\ 23 \\
\hline
9 \\
\boxed{} \\
60 \\
+\ \boxed{} \\
\end{array}
$$

$$
\begin{array}{r}
33 \\
\times\ 42 \\
\hline
6 \\
\boxed{} \\
\boxed{} \\
+\ 1{,}200 \\
\end{array}
$$

13. Insert the missing factor in each equation.

| 49 53 79 15 47 25 28 84 |

$$19 \times \boxed{} = 1{,}007$$

$$62 \times \boxed{} = 1{,}736$$

$$\boxed{} \times 37 = 1{,}813$$

$$15 \times \boxed{} = 1{,}260$$

Name _____

A playground is divided into four sections as shown in the diagram below. Find the area of the playground. Explain how you found the answer. **Solve this problem using any strategy you choose.**

You can use drawings, area models, and properties of operations to model the math.

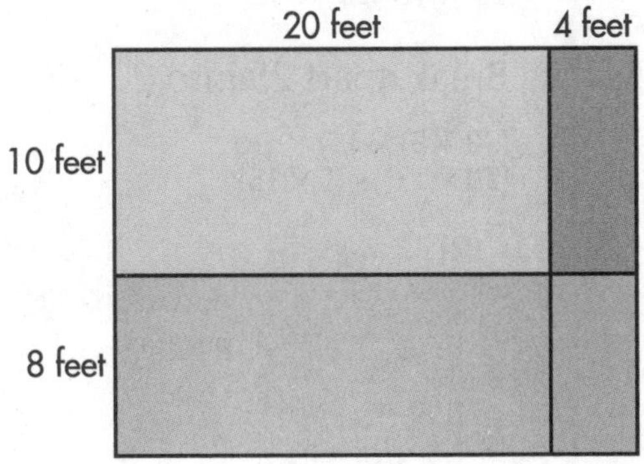

	20 feet	4 feet
10 feet		
8 feet		

Look Back! Explain how you found the area of the blue part of the playground.

Essential Question # How Can You Use the Distributive Property to Multiply?

A

There are 15 players on each baseball team of the Strike Out Club. How many players are on all of the teams in the Strike Out Club?

 You can use an area model to show the Distributive Property.

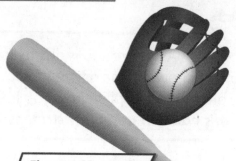

There are 25 teams in the Strike Out Club.

B ## One Way

Use an area model and the Distributive Property to find 25×15.

Break apart 15 into $10 + 5$.

$25 \times (10 + 5)$
$(25 \times 10) + (25 \times 5)$

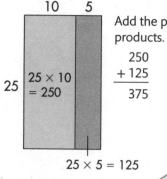

Add the partial products.
$$\begin{array}{r} 250 \\ + 125 \\ \hline 375 \end{array}$$

$25 \times 5 = 125$

C ## Another Way

Use an area model and the Distributive Property to find 25×15.

Break apart 25 into $20 + 5$.

$(20 + 5) \times 15$
$(20 \times 15) + (5 \times 15)$

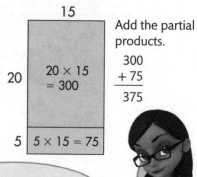

Add the partial products.
$$\begin{array}{r} 300 \\ + 75 \\ \hline 375 \end{array}$$

$5 \mid 5 \times 15 = 75$

There are 375 players on the team.

D ## Another Way

Use an area model and the Distributive Property to find 25×15.

Break apart both factors.

Break apart 25 into $20 + 5$.
Break apart 15 into $10 + 5$.

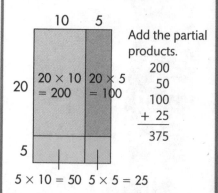

Add the partial products.
$$\begin{array}{r} 200 \\ 50 \\ 100 \\ + 25 \\ \hline 375 \end{array}$$

$5 \times 10 = 50 \quad 5 \times 5 = 25$

Convince Me! Use Structure How does an area model illustrate the Distributive Property?

☆Guided Practice

Do You Understand?

1. What four simpler multiplication problems are used to find 24 × 23?

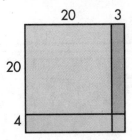

2. How can an area model and the Distributive Property help you multiply? Use 12 × 16 to explain.

Do You Know How?

3. Use the area model and the Distributive Property to find 35 × 12.

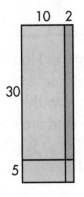

35 × 12 = _____

30 × 10 = _____

5 × 10 = _____

30 × 2 = _____

5 × 2 = _____

_____ + _____ + _____ + _____ = _____

☆Independent Practice ☆

For **4–10**, draw an area model to find each product.

4. 18 × 25

5. 14 × 25

6. 22 × 88

7.   41
     × 12

8.   30
     × 27

9.   58
     × 19

10.   29
      × 50

Problem Solving

11. Write 652,079 using number names and in expanded form.

12. Number Sense Sara estimated 23 × 43 using 20 × 40. Sam estimated 23 × 43 using 25 × 40. Will Sara's or Sam's method give an estimate closer to the exact answer? Explain.

13. Use Structure Each family of Florida Scrub Jays inhabits 25 acres of land. No other Scrub Jay families live within this area. How many acres of land are needed for 24 families of Florida Scrub Jays? Show how you can use the Distributive Property to solve this problem.

Inhabits 25 acres of land

14. Marla wants to buy a new tablet that costs $565, including tax. She saved $15 per week for 30 weeks. Does Marla have enough money saved to buy the tablet? Explain.

15. Higher Order Thinking Which costs less: 13 oranges that cost 29 cents each or 17 apples that cost 25 cents each? How much less?

☑ Assessment Practice

16. Select all of the partial products which would be used to find 19 × 26.

- ☐ 45; 60; 180; 200
- ☐ 200; 180; 60; 54
- ☐ 6; 45; 180; 200
- ☐ 200; 60; 180; 54
- ☐ 0; 54; 180; 200

17. Select all of the ways you can use breaking apart and the Distributive Property to find the product of 35 × 12.

- ☐ 35 × (10 + 2)
- ☐ (12 × 30) + (12 × 5)
- ☐ (12 × 5) + (35 × 5)
- ☐ (30 × 5) + (10 × 2)
- ☐ (30 × 10) + (5 × 10) + (30 × 2) + (5 × 2)

Name _____

☆ Solve & Share ☆

There are 11 regular players and 5 substitute players on a soccer team. How many players are on 15 soccer teams? *Solve this problem using any strategy you choose.*

I can ...
use place value and partial products to multiply.

Content Standards 4.NBT.B.5 Also 4.OA.A.3
Mathematical Practices MP.2, MP.3, MP.7

You can use structure and what you know about the Distributive Property and area models to find the product. *Show your work in the space below!*

Look Back! How could you use an array and rounding or an array and compatible numbers to estimate the product for the problem above?

Essential Question **How Can You Record Multiplication?**

A

Marcia put 7 oranges and 8 apples into each of 12 bags. How many pieces of fruit did Marcia put into all of the bags?

> Some problems have more than one step to solve.

$7 + 8 = f$
$15 = f$

Marcia put 15 pieces of fruit in each of the 12 bags.

$10 \times 10 = 100$ $10 \times 5 = 50$

15

12

$2 \times 10 = 20$ $2 \times 5 = 10$

B Find 12×15.

Estimate: 12×15 is about
$10 \times 15 = 150$.

First, multiply the ones.

```
    15
 ×  12
─────
    10   2 × 5 ones
    20   2 × 1 ten
```

> 10 and 20 are partial products.

C Then, multiply the tens.

```
     15
  ×  12
─────
     10
     20
     50   10 × 5 ones
 + 100   10 × 1 ten
─────
    180
```

Marcia put 180 pieces of fruit into the bags.

> 50 and 100 are partial products.

> The answer is reasonable because 180 is close to 150.

Convince Me! Reasoning Which partial products are incorrect? What is the correct final product?

```
       26
   ×   12
─────
       12
       40
      600
 + 2000
─────
    2,652
```

Name_____

☆Guided Practice

Do You Understand?

1. In the example on the previous page, why do you find 2 × 1 ten, rather than 2 × 1?

In the factor is, you have sames ten

2. In the example on the previous page, could you record the 4 partial products in a different order? Explain.

Yes as long as you Recored all of the partial products

Do You Know How?

For **3–4**, find all the partial products. Then add to find the final product. Draw area models as needed.

3.
```
     23
   × 14
3×4  12
     80
    130
    200
    322
```

4.
```
     41
   × 25
      5
    200
     29
    800
```

Independent Practice ☆

For **5–12**, estimate. Find all the partial products. Then add to find the final product. Draw area models as needed.

Remember to check if your final product is reasonable.

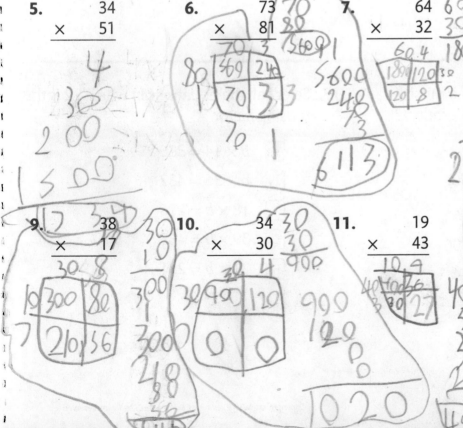

5.
```
     34
   × 51
```

6.
```
     73
   × 81
```

7.
```
     64
   × 32
```
113

8.
```
     26
   × 53
```
1000
300
60
18
1378

9.
```
     38
   × 17
```

10.
```
     34
   × 30
```
1020

11.
```
     19
   × 43
```

12.
```
     19
   × 52
```
500
450
20
18
988

Topic 4 | Lesson 4-6 **151**

Problem Solving

13. The Castillo de San Marcos is a Spanish fortress that was built between 1672 and 1695.

a. Rounded to the nearest ten thousand, how many pesos did it cost to build the fortress?

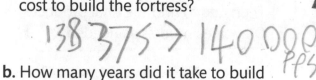

138375 → 140 000 pesos

b. How many years did it take to build the fortress?

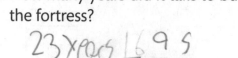

23 x pags 1695
            72
           23

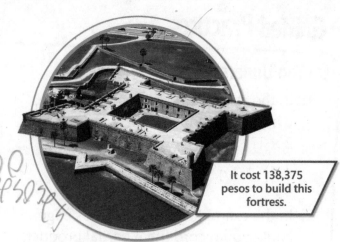

It cost 138,375 pesos to build this fortress.

---

14. Construct Arguments A school has 2 large patios. One is rectangular and is 24 feet long by 18 feet wide. The other is square and each side is 21 feet long. Which patio has a greater area? Explain.

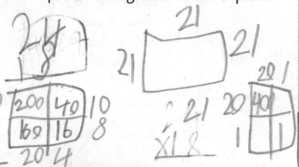

15. Higher Order Thinking Show two ways to break apart the factors, and then find the product of 14 × 22.

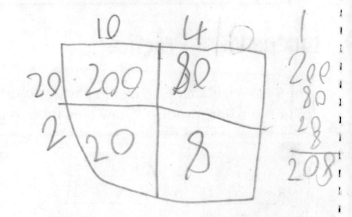

---

16. Which set of numbers has the missing partial product and the final product?

```
   13
 × 62
 ─────
    6
   20
  [180]
+ 600
 ─────
 [866]
```

Ⓐ 210; 836
Ⓑ 18; 806
Ⓒ 180; 806
Ⓓ 18; 644

17. Select all the equations in which 12 is the missing factor.

- [✓] $b \times 14 = 336$
- [✓] $b \times 36 = 432$
- [ ] $18 \times b = 216$
- [✓] $39 \times b = 468$
- [ ] $21 \times b = 231$

Name _____

Solve & Share

Five students set a goal to raise $500 from their charity walk. Sponsors donated $25 for each mile walked. By how much did these students exceed or miss their goal? *Solve this problem using any strategy you choose.*

DATA

Student	Miles Walked
Susan	5
Maxine	5
Charlie	3
Fillip	4
Rachael	4

I can ...
make sense of problems and keep working if I get stuck.

© **Mathematical Practices** MP.1 Also MP.2, MP.4 , MP.6
 Content Standards 4.NBT.B.5 Also 4.MD.A.3

Thinking Habits

Be a good thinker!
These questions can help you.

• What do I need to find?

• What do I know?

• What's my plan for solving the problem?

• What else can I try if I get stuck?

• How can I check that my solution makes sense?

Look Back! **Make Sense and Persevere** Is there more than one way to solve the problem? Explain.

Essential Question How Can You Make Sense of and Persevere in Solving Problems with More Than One Step? **Visual Learning Bridge**

A

The park has a large garden with a walkway around it. The park's ground crew are going to paint the walkway. What is the area of the walkway?

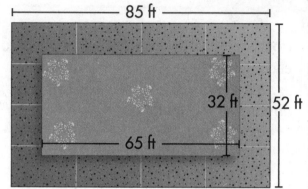

85 ft — 32 ft · 52 ft — 65 ft —

What is a good plan for solving this problem?

I need to find the area of the garden and walkway together. Then I need to subtract to find only the area of the walkway.

B **How can I make sense of and solve this problem?**

I can

- identify the quantities given.
- understand how the quantities are related.
- choose and implement an appropriate strategy.
- check to be sure my work and answer make sense.

C First find the area of the whole park.

$52 \times 85 = p$
$4,420 = p$

Next, find the area of the of the garden.

$32 \times 65 = g$
$2,080 = g$

Subtract to find the area of the walkway.
$4,420 - 2,080 = w$

The area of the walkway is 2,340 square feet.

```
    85
×   52
    10
   160
   250
+4,000
 4,420
    65
×   32
    10
   120
   150
+1,800
 2,080
  3 12
 4,4̸2̸0
-2,080
 2,340
```

Convince Me! **Make Sense and Persevere** Can you solve the problem a different way and still calculate the same answer? Explain.

Name _____

☆ Guided Practice

Make Sense and Persevere

On her vacation, Julia filled 3 memory cards like the one shown. She printed 2 copies of each picture. How many pictures did Julia print?

A memory card holds 28 pictures.

1. What do you know and what do you need to find?

[handwritten] 28 pictures on each memory card
— she printed 2 copies of each pic
— she has 3 memory cards

> When you make sense and persevere, you regularly check if your work is reasonable.

2. What steps might you take to solve the problem?

[handwritten] 3 × 28 to find the answer then multiply the product

3. How many pictures did Julia print? Explain.

[handwritten] 3 × 28 = 84   84 × 2 = 168
she printed (168 photos)

☆ Independent Practice ☆

Make Sense and Persevere

Jarrod delivers 63 newspapers each Monday through Saturday and 78 newspapers each Sunday. Last month consisted of 4 Sundays and 26 other days. How many newspapers did Jarrod deliver last month? Use Exercises 4–6 to solve this problem.

[handwritten] 63 — M–Sat   news paper   78 — Sun

4. What strategies can you use to find how many newspapers Jarrod delivered last month?

[handwritten] I can multiply to find the product delivered M–Sat   4–Sun   26 other sunday days

5. How are the quantities related?

[handwritten] 78 × 4 = 312   63 × 26 = 1638   → 1950

6. Explain how to solve the problem.

[handwritten] add the total

Uniforms

The Stillwater Storm soccer team consists of 16 players. Each player needs a uniform set. The uniform set includes two jerseys, a pair of shorts, and a pair of socks. The price for each separate item is shown. Nine of the players need a medium size and the others need a small size. If the team buys more than 10 sets, the team price for each set is $56. How much money is saved if the team buys all the uniform sets together rather than separately?

Uniform Item	Price
Jersey	$23
Pair of Shorts	$17
Pair of Socks	$8

7. **Reasoning** What are the quantities in the problem and how are they related?

8. **Model with Math** Use the bar diagram to write an addition equation and find the total cost of the uniform sets when purchased separately. Then find the total cost if 10 sets or more are purchased.

u, cost of 1 set

| $___ | $___ | $___ | $___ |

When you make sense and persevere, you think about the amounts given.

9. **Be Precise** What is the difference in cost if the team bought all the uniform sets together or if they bought them separately?

☆ ☆
Find a Match
☆

Work with a partner. Point to a clue. Read the clue.

Look below the clues to find a match. Write the clue letter in the box next to the match.

Find a match for every clue.

I can ...
add and subtract multi-digit whole numbers.

© **Content Standard** 4.NBT.B.4
Mathematical Practices MP.3, MP.6, MP.7, MP.8

Clues

A The difference is between 950 and 1,000.

E The difference is between 700 and 800.

B The difference is exactly 913.

F The sum is greater than 300 but less than 400.

C The sum is between 600 and 700.

G The sum is exactly 753.

D The sum is exactly 500.

H The difference is exactly 413.

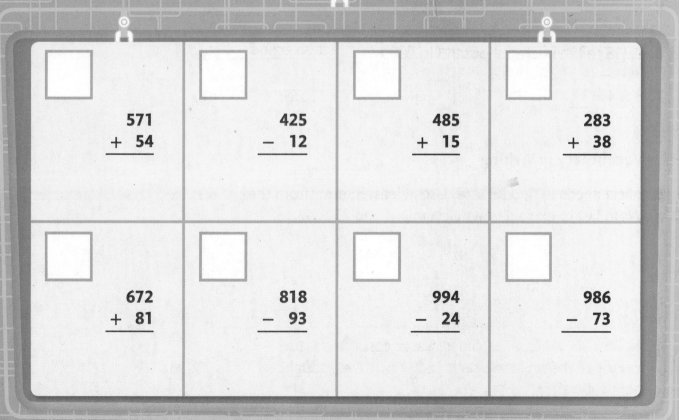

☐	☐	☐	☐
571 + 54	425 − 12	485 + 15	283 + 38

☐	☐	☐	☐
672 + 81	818 − 93	994 − 24	986 − 73

Word List

- array
- compatible numbers
- estimate
- factors
- partial product
- product
- rounding
- variable

Understand Vocabulary

1. Cross out the numbers that are **NOT** factors of 12.

1   3   ~~5~~   6   ~~8~~   O x O = 12

2. Cross out the numbers that are **NOT** good estimates for the product of 17 × 23.

~~600~~   400   300   200   ~~100~~

3. Cross out the numbers that are **NOT** partial products for 12 × 41.

~~2~~   10   18   ~~80~~   400

Label each example with a term from the Word List.

4.

array

5. *n*

variable

6. 2,318 to the nearest thousand is 2,000

rounding

7. 3 × 4 = <u>12</u>

product

Use Vocabulary in Writing

8. Alicia needs to find 23 × 47. Use at least 3 terms from the Word List to explain how Alicia might find 23 × 47.

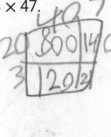

Alicia can use an model by setting the numbers

Name_____

1. Don works 18 hours a week. Which expression shows a good way to use rounding to estimate how many hours Don will work in 52 weeks?

Ⓐ 10 × 50   Ⓒ 20 × 50
Ⓑ 10 × 60   Ⓓ 18 × 60

2. Find the product 21 × 40. Show your work.

3. The product of two factors is 2,000. One of the factors is 50. What is the other factor?

Ⓐ 20   Ⓒ 200
Ⓑ 40   Ⓓ 400

4. Select all the expressions that are equal to 260.

☐ 23 × 10
☐ 20 × 10 + 3 × 10
☐ 13 × 20
☐ 1 × 20 + 3 × 20
☑ 10 × 20 + 3 × 20

5. A florist makes centerpieces. He puts 18 roses in each centerpiece. Which is the best way to use compatible numbers to estimate the number of roses the florist needs for 24 centerpieces? What is the exact number of roses?

Ⓐ 10 × 25 = 250; 360
Ⓑ 20 × 25 = 500; 432
Ⓒ 25 × 30 = 750; 672
Ⓓ 30 × 30 = 900; 784

6. Margo hiked 12 miles 13 times last month. She hiked 14 miles 12 times this month.

A. Draw arrays or area models to find the number of miles Margo hiked during the past two months.

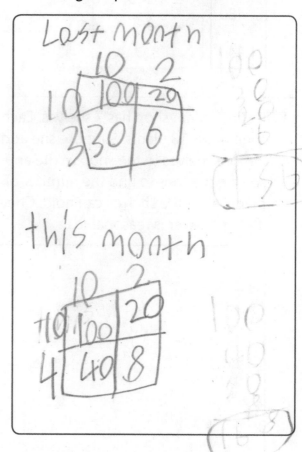

B. Write and solve equations to represent your arrays or area models.

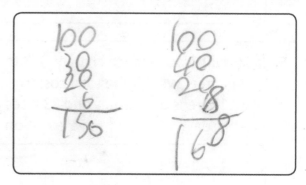

7. Liz makes necklaces. Each has 16 beads. Use the numbers in the box to complete the table.

50
90
160
480
1,440

Number of Necklaces	Number of Beads
10	160
30	480
50	800
90	1440

8. Justine's plant shop has 7 shelves. Each shelf holds 18 plants. Suppose she adds 2 more shelves to the shop. Write and solve equations to find the number of plants all of the shelves can hold. Check if your answer is reasonable.

7+2=9 shelves

$$18 \times 9$$

162 Plants

$$20 \times 10$$

200

200 is close to 162

9. Jack's landscape service charges $78 to plant a tree. What is the total cost to plant 18 trees on Tuesday and 23 trees on Wednesday? Write and solve equations.

Work on
paper: anser: 3

10. Which of the following uses properties of operations to help find 27 × 14?

(A) 20 + 7 + 10 + 4

(B) 20 × 7 × 10 × 4

(C) 27 + 14

(D) (20 + 7) × (10 + 4)

11. Lorin drew an area model to find 19 × 15. Write the partial product for each rectangle in the area model.

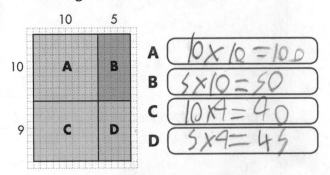

A: $10 \times 10 = 100$
B: $5 \times 10 = 50$
C: $10 \times 9 = 90$
D: $5 \times 9 = 45$

12. The biggest painting in an art show is 31 inches long and 28 inches wide. The smallest painting is 14 inches long and 11 inches wide. What is the difference between the areas of the two paintings? Use equations to show your work.

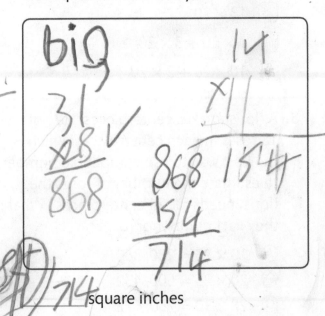

big

$$31 \times 28 = 868$$

$$14 \times 11 = 154$$

$$868 - 154 = 714$$

714 square inches

Name_____

Raising Money
The fourth-grade students at Skyline School sold candles to raise money. The money raised will be used to buy toys for children who live in a group home. The **Candle Fundraiser** table shows how many candles each class sold.

Beehive candles sell for $20 each. The class raised $12 for each candle sold.

Soybean candles sell for $22 each. The class raised $14 for each candle sold.

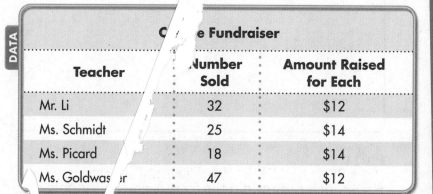

Candle Fundraiser		
Teacher	Number Sold	Amount Raised for Each
Mr. Li	32	$12
Ms. Schmidt	25	$14
Ms. Picard	18	$14
Ms. Goldwasser	47	$12

1. About how much money did the fourth-grade students raise? Explain.

2. The school secretary needs to know exactly how much money was raised.

Part A

How much money did Ms. Schmidt's class raise? Use an area model and partial products to find the product.

Part B

How much money did Ms. Picard's class raise? Use the Distributive Property to find the product.

Part C

How much money did the fourth-grade students raise? Explain.

Part D

Is the total amount of money raised from Part C reasonable based on the estimate you found in Exercise 1? Explain.

The fourth-grade students at Skyline School decide to buy the toys shown.

Buying Toys

- They buy 68 toys in all.
- They buy at least 25 of each type.
- They cannot spend more money than was raised.

Teddy bear $17

Scooter $28

3. How many of each toy can be bought following the directions from the **Buying Toys** list? Find the total cost for the numbers you choose.

Use Strategies and Properties to Divide by 1-Digit Numbers

Essential Questions: How can mental math be used to divide? How can quotients be estimated? How can the steps for dividing be explained?

Musical instruments make sounds when motion that causes vibrations creates sound waves.

This piano uses a series of keys and hammers to strike the strings, which play different notes depending on their length.

Instruments use energy to make sounds in all different ways! Here is a project about music and division.

enVision STEM Project: Music and Division

Do Research: Use the Internet or other resources to find an example of a woodwind instrument, a brass instrument, a stringed instrument, and a percussion instrument.

Journal: Write a Report Include what you found. Also in your report:

- Explain how each instrument you researched uses energy to make sounds. Include information about how the sounds are produced.

- An octave spans 8 white keys on a piano. The last key of an octave begins the next octave. Explain why you can divide by 7 to find the number of octaves on a piano with 52 white keys.

Name _____

Review What You Know

A-Z **Vocabulary**

Choose the best term from the box.
Write it on the blank.

- compatible numbers
- equation
- divisible
- round
- division
- variable

1. A(n) _____ uses the equal sign (=) to show two expressions have the same value.

2. One way to estimate a product is to _____ each factor.

3. You use _____ when you find the number of equal groups.

4. Numbers that are easy to compute mentally are called _____.

Division Facts

Find each quotient.

5. $27 \div 9$

6. $30 \div 5$

7. $32 \div 4$

8. $54 \div 9$

9. $28 \div 7$

10. $72 \div 9$

11. $56 \div 8$

12. $18 \div 3$

13. $15 \div 5$

Rounding

Round each number to the nearest hundred.

14. 864

15. 651

16. 348

17. 985

18. 451

19. 749

You will round or use compatible numbers to estimate quotients in this topic.

Division as Sharing

20. **Make Sense and Persevere** Julio has 47 marbles. He keeps his two favorite marbles, then equally shares the remaining marbles between 5 friends. How many marbles does each friend receive? Explain.

Name_____

PROJECT 5A

How many passengers did trains like those in the Gold Coast Railroad Museum carry?

Project: Make a Model of a Train

PROJECT 5B

How far do sailfish migrate?

Project: Make a Migration Map

PROJECT 5C

How much food do Portuguese Water Dogs need?

Project: Create a Brochure on Portuguese Water Dogs

Math Modeling

Snack Attack

Video

Before watching the video, think:

Healthy snacks are good for you. The best snacks include fruits and vegetables and whole grains. I wonder if I can feed this fish to my cat.

I can ...
model with math to solve a problem that involves rounding, estimating and computing with whole numbers.

Ⓒ **Mathematical Practices** MP.4, MP.6, MP.8
Content Standards 4.NBT.B.6
Also 4.OA.A.3, 4.NBT.B.5, 4.MD.A.3

Name _____

Activity

Solve & Share

José has 270 hockey cards to arrange equally in 9 boxes. Each box can hold the same number of cards. How many cards should José place in each box? **Solve this problem using any strategy you choose.**

I can ...
make sense of quantities and use mental math and place-value strategies to divide.

© **Content Standard** 4.NBT.B.6
Mathematical Practices MP.2, MP.4, MP.7

You can use structure and the relationship between multiplication and division. A multiplication fact can help you divide.

Look Back! **Reasoning** What multiplication equation could help you find the number of cards José should place in each box?

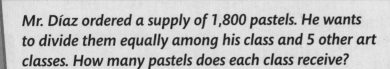

Essential Question **How Can You Divide Mentally?**

A

Mr. Díaz ordered a supply of 1,800 pastels. He wants to divide them equally among his class and 5 other art classes. How many pastels does each class receive?

If Mr. Diaz stores the pastels so each class will receive new pastels 5 times a year, how many pastels are handed out each of the 5 times?

1,800 pastels

Division is used to find equal groups. Dividend ÷ Divisor = Quotient

You can use basic division facts and place value to divide.

B Find $1,800 \div 6$.

1,800 pastels

p	p	p	p	p	p

↑ pastels for each class

The basic division fact is $18 \div 6 = 3$.

18 hundreds ÷ 6 = 3 hundreds or 300.
$1,800 \div 6 = 300$

Each class will receive 300 pastels.

C Find $300 \div 5$.

300 pastels

p	p	p	p	p

↑ pastels given out 5 times

The basic division fact is $30 \div 5 = 6$.

30 tens ÷ 5 = 6 tens or 60.
$300 \div 5 = 60$

Each class will receive 60 pastels 5 times a year.

Convince Me! Use Structure Write the missing dividends for each of the following equations. How did you determine each dividend?

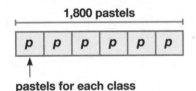

$\underline{490} \div 7 = 70$ $\underline{400} \div 8 = 50$ $\underline{3200} \div 4 = 800$

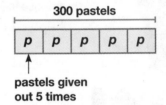

70 X 7 = 440   8 X 50 = 400   4 X 800 = 3200

Name_____

☆ Guided Practice

Do You Understand?

1. Explain how 32 ÷ 4 can help you solve 320 ÷ 4.

You can use the basic fact of 32÷4 to answer 320÷4

2. Mrs. Gall orders 240 folders and divides them equally among 3 classes. How many folders does each class receive? What basic fact did you use?

240 ÷ 3 = 80 folders

24 ÷ 3 = 8

Do You Know How?

For **3–4**, use basic facts and place value to find each quotient.

3. 28 ÷ 7 = __4__

280 ÷ 7 = __40__

2,800 ÷ 7 = __400__

7 × 4 = 28

4. __8__ = 64 ÷ 8

__80__ = 640 ÷ 8

__800__ = 6,400 ÷ 8

8 × 8 = 64

Independent Practice ☆

Leveled Practice For **5–24**, use basic facts and place value to divide.

5. 36 ÷ 9 = __4__

360 ÷ 9 = __40__

3,600 ÷ 9 = __400__

6. __5__ = 10 ÷ 2

__50__ = 100 ÷ 2

__500__ = 1,000 ÷ 2

7. 45 ÷ 5 = __9__

450 ÷ 5 = __90__

4,500 ÷ 5 = __900__

8. __3__ = 24 ÷ 8

__30__ = 240 ÷ 8

__300__ = 2,400 ÷ 8

9. 2,000 ÷ 5 = 100

10. 360 ÷ 4 = 90

11. 540 ÷ 9 = 60

12. 160 ÷ 4 = 40

13. 900 ÷ 3 = 30

14. 3,200 ÷ 8 = 400

15. 360 ÷ 6 = 60

16. 1,800 ÷ 3 = 600

17. 7,200 ÷ 8 = 900

18. 500 ÷ 5 = 25

19. 350 ÷ 7 = 50

20. 6,300 ÷ 9 = 700

21. 1,600 ÷ 2 = 800

22. 210 ÷ 7 = 30

23. 4,800 ÷ 6 = 80

24. 600 ÷ 6 = 10

Problem Solving

25. If you know 20 ÷ 5 = 4, how does that help you calculate 200 ÷ 5?

The basic fact helps to solve for larger numbers, there 20 tens in 200

26. A bakery produced two batches of bread with 80 loaves in each batch. It sold 30 loaves each hour. How many loaves of bread were sold in 4 hours? How many loaves of bread were left to sell?

_80 X 2 = 160   160 - 30 = 130_

30 X 4 = 120 loaves of bread in four hours

_160 - 120 → 40_

27. An engineer designed and built a solar race car. If there are 810 solar cells arranged in 9 rows, how many solar cells are in each row?

9 rows of solar cells

810 ÷ 9 = 90 cells

28. **Model with Math** On Saturday afternoon, 350 people attended a play. The seating was arranged in 7 equal rows. Draw a bar diagram and solve an equation to find _p_, how many people sat in each row.

_350_

_p | p | p | p | p | p | p_

_350 ÷ 7 = p_

p people in each row

29. **Higher Order Thinking** Molly and five friends picked a total of 300 oranges. If they each picked the same number of oranges, how many oranges did Molly pick? Explain.

30. Find 240 ÷ 8.

Ⓐ 3

Ⓑ 10

Ⓒ 30

Ⓓ 80

31. What basic fact helps to solve 180 ÷ 6? What is 180 ÷ 6?

Ⓐ 18 ÷ 3; 60

Ⓑ 18 ÷ 3; 30

Ⓒ 18 ÷ 6; 60

Ⓓ 18 ÷ 6; 30

Name_____

Lesson 5-2
Mental Math: Estimate Quotients

☆ Solve & Share ☆

Three friends at a video arcade win a total of 248 tickets. They decide to share the tickets equally. About how many tickets will each friend receive? **Solve this problem using any strategy you choose.**

I can ...
use compatible numbers to estimate quotients when dividing with 3-digit dividends.

© **Content Standards** 4.OA.A.3 Also 4.NBT.B.5, 4.NBT.B.6
Mathematical Practices MP.2, MP.3

You can use reasoning to estimate quotients using mental math. *Show your work in the space below!*

Look Back! Is an exact answer or an estimate needed for the problem above? Explain.

Essential Question **How Can You Estimate Quotients to Solve Problems?**

A

Max wants to make 9 rubber band balls using about the same number of rubber bands for each ball. He bought a jar of 700 rubber bands. Estimate to find about how many rubber bands Max can use for each ball.

> Max does not need to know the exact number of rubber bands to use for each ball. An estimate is all that is needed.

> There is more than one way to estimate a quotient.

700 rubber bands

B **Use Compatible Numbers**

Estimate 700 ÷ 9.

What number close to 700 is easily divided by 9?

Try multiples of ten near 700.
710 is not easily divided by 9.
720 is 72 tens and can be divided by 9.
720 ÷ 9 = 80

Max can use about 80 rubber bands for each ball.

C **Use Multiplication**

Estimate 700 ÷ 9.

9 times what number is about 700?

9 × 8 = 72, so 9 × 80 = 720.
700 ÷ 9 is about 80.

Max can use about 80 rubber bands for each ball.

Convince Me! **Construct Arguments** What compatible numbers can you use to estimate 132 ÷ 6? Why is rounding not a good way to estimate 132 ÷ 6?

Guided Practice

Do You Understand?

1. Max wants to make 9 rubber band balls using 80 bands each from his package of 700. Will Max be able to make more or fewer balls than he wanted?

   fewer because 4x80=720 bands he only has 700.

2. Max decides to use 700 rubber bands to make 8 balls. Is it reasonable to say he would use about 90 rubber bands to make each ball? Explain.

   8x90= 720
   yes it is resonable
   because 720
   is close to 700.

Do You Know How?

For **3-10**, estimate each quotient. Use multiplication or compatible numbers. Show your work.

3. $48 \div 5$
   45÷5=9
   About 4

4. $235 \div 8$
   240÷8=30
   About 30

5. $547 \div 6$
   540÷6=90
   About 90

6. $192 \div 5$
   200÷5=40
   About 40

7. $662 \div 8$

8. $362 \div 3$

9. $41 \div 2$

10. $211 \div 4$

Independent Practice

For **11-26**, estimate each quotient.

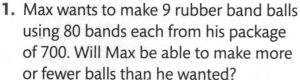

Think of basic multiplication facts to help find compatible numbers.

11. $430 \div 9$
    450÷4=
    About 50

12. $620 \div 7$
    620÷7=9
    About 90

13. $138 \div 5$

14. $232 \div 6$

15. $342 \div 8$
    320÷8=4
    About 40

16. $652 \div 6$
    660÷6
    =about 11

17. $59 \div 9$
    54÷9=6
    about 6

18. $813 \div 8$

19. $637 \div 6$
    600÷6=100
    About 100

20. $481 \div 4$
    480÷4=
    12

21. $747 \div 8$

22. $232 \div 9$

23. $552 \div 7$
    560÷7=80
    About 80

24. $52 \div 5$
    50÷5

25. $392 \div 2$

26. $625 \div 3$

Problem Solving

For **27–28**, use the table at the right.

27. Ada sold her mugs in 3 weeks. About how many mugs did Ada sell each week?

28. Ben sold his mugs in 6 weeks. About how many mugs did Ben sell each week?

Mugs Sold in Fundraiser
Each Mug = 50 mugs

Ada

Ben

29. enVision® STEM The International Space Station takes 644 minutes to orbit Earth 7 times. About how long does each orbit take?

30. There are 60 minutes in 1 hour and 24 hours in 1 day. About how many times does the International Space Station orbit Earth each day?

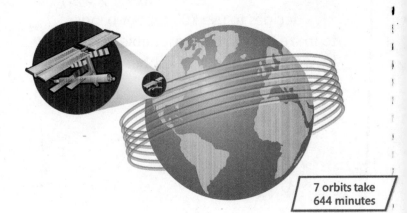

7 orbits take 644 minutes

31. Construct Arguments Complete by writing > or < in the ◯. Without dividing, explain how you know which quotient is greater.

$$930 \div 4 \bigcirc 762 \div 4$$

32. Higher Order Thinking Explain how to find a better estimate for $260 \div 5$ than the one shown below.

Round 260 to 300, and then estimate $300 \div 5$.

$300 \div 5 = 60$, so $260 \div 5$ is about 60.

☑ Assessment Practice

33. Kaylee wanted to divide 133 pieces of candy equally into 7 boxes. She decides to put 19 pieces in each box. Use estimation to determine if this answer seems reasonable.

Name _____

Solve & Share

Jimi has 3,000 tickets to sell at the school carnival. Jimi separated the tickets into groups of 8 tickets. About how many groups did Jimi make? **Solve this problem using any strategy you choose.**

You can use reasoning and compatible numbers to estimate. Dividing with compatible numbers makes estimating easier.

Lesson 5-3
Mental Math: Estimate Quotients for Greater Dividends

I can ...
estimate quotients for 4-digit dividends.

© **Content Standards** 4.OA.A.3 Also 4.NBT.B.5, 4.NBT.B.6
Mathematical Practices MP.2, MP.3, MP.4

Look Back! **Reasoning** What basic fact did you use to solve the problem above? How does this help you?

Essential Question

How Can You Estimate Quotients Using Patterns and Place Value?

A

On "Clean Up Your Town Day," 1,320 people volunteered to clean up the Springville parks. The volunteers were divided equally into teams to work in each of the town's parks. About how many people were on each team?

Multiplication and division are related. Mentally multiplying by tens or hundreds can help to estimate the quotient of a multi-digit division problem.

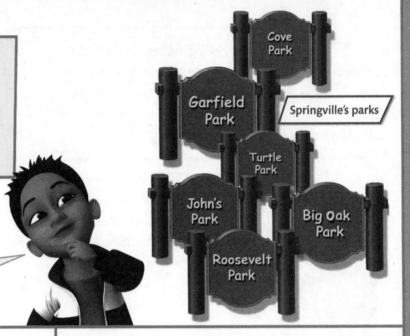

Springville's parks: Cove Park, Garfield Park, Turtle Park, John's Park, Big Oak Park, Roosevelt Park

B Use Multiplication Patterns

Estimate $1,320 \div 6$.

6 times what number is about 1,320?

You know $6 \times 2 = 12$, and
$6 \times 20 = 120$, so
$6 \times 200 = 1,200$.

1,200 is close to 1,320.

There are about 200 people on each team.

C Use Division Facts and Place-Value Patterns

Find compatible numbers to estimate $1,320 \div 6$.

You know $12 \div 6 = 2$, and
$120 \div 6 = 20$, so
$1,200 \div 6 = 200$.

$1,320 \div 6$ is about 200.

There are about 200 people on each team.

Convince Me! **Construct Arguments** Complete the calculations at the right. Explain how you can use the calculations to estimate $1,296 \div 4$.

$4 \times 100 = \underline{\hspace{2cm}}$

$4 \times 200 = \underline{\hspace{2cm}}$

$4 \times 300 = \underline{\hspace{2cm}}$

$4 \times 400 = \underline{\hspace{2cm}}$

Another Example!

You can use rounding to estimate quotients.

Estimate 357 ÷ 8 by rounding the dividend.

Round: 400 ÷ 8
400 ÷ 8 = 50
So, 357 ÷ 8 is about 50.

Estimate 5,582 ÷ 7 by rounding the dividend.

Round: 5,600 ÷ 7
5,600 ÷ 7 = 800
So, 5,582 ÷ 7 = is about 800.

☆ Guided Practice

Do You Understand?

1. When estimating 1,320 ÷ 6, why is rounding not a good strategy?

2. When dividing a 4-digit number by a 1-digit number, how many digits can the quotient have?

Do You Know How?

For **3-8**, estimate each quotient.

3. 3,340 ÷ 8

3200 ÷ 8 = 400
About 400

4. 2,943 ÷ 7

2,800 ÷ 7 = 400
About 400

5. 552 ÷ 9

540 ÷ 9 = 60
About 60

6. 776 ÷ 4

800 ÷ 4 = 200

7. 2,013 ÷ 5

8. 281 ÷ 3

☆ Independent Practice ☆

partner

For **9-20**, estimate each quotient.

9. 61 ÷ 2

about 30

10. 7,779 ÷ 7

1111 ÷ 7
about 1111

11. 3,688 ÷ 6

3,600 ÷ 6 = 600
About 600

12. 497 ÷ 8

480 ÷ 8 = 60
About 60

13. 5,684 ÷ 9

5400 ÷ 9 = 600
About 600

14. 5,346 ÷ 6

5400 ÷ 6
= 900
About 900

15. 508 ÷ 7

490 ÷ 7 = 70
About 70

16. 92 ÷ 3

90 ÷ 3 = 3
About 3

17. 647 ÷ 3

648 ÷ 3 = 216

18. 3,958 ÷ 8

4,000 ÷ 8 = 500
About 500

19. 224 ÷ 3

210 ÷ 3 =
30   About 30

20. 2,438 ÷ 5

2,500 ÷ 5 = 500
About 500

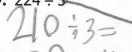

Problem Solving

21. Laura's dog eats 1 bag of dog food every 6 days. About how many bags will her dog eat in 1 year? About how many bags will Laura's dog eat in 10 years? Explain.

22. **Model with Math** During the school year, a bus driver made 7 trips to the museum. The distance from the school to the museum is 36 miles. Write and solve equations to find how many miles the bus driver drove for the 7 trips.

23. **A-Z Vocabulary** Use a vocabulary word to complete the statement.

    Multiplication and division are _____ operations because they undo each other.

24. Ramón's sister wants to buy a car that costs $7,993. She earns $9 for every hour she works. About how many hours must Ramón's sister work to earn enough money to buy the car?

25. **Number Sense** Eight students can sit at one cafeteria table. About how many tables are needed for 231 students? Explain.

26. **Higher Order Thinking** At Camp Summer Fun, 4 campers share a tent. The camp is expecting 331 campers. About how many tents will they need? Will the actual number of tents needed be more or less than your estimate? Explain.

Assessment Practice

27. Nadine has 1,424 pictures to put in 7 folders on her computer. She wants the same number in each folder. Which is the best estimate of the number of pictures she should put in each folder?

    (A) About 200

    (B) About 300

    (C) About 2,000

    (D) About 3,000

28. Sven needs to save $239 to buy a bike. Which is the best estimate of the amount he needs to save each month to have enough in 3 months?

    (A) About $60

    (B) About $70

    (C) About $80

    (D) About $90

Name_____

☆ ☆
Solve & Share

There are 47 students taking a field trip. The students are being driven in cars to a play by adult volunteers. Each driver can take at most 4 students. How many cars are needed for the field trip? Will each car have four students? Use counters or draw pictures to solve this problem. Explain how you found your answer.

I can ...
apply what I know about dividing items into equal groups to solve problems.

© **Content Standards** 4.OA.A.3, 4.NBT.B.6
Mathematical Practices MP.3, MP.4

You can draw a picture to model with math. *Show your work in the space below!*

Look Back! Suppose there were only 46 students. Would the number of cars needed for the field trip change? Explain.

Essential Question

After Dividing, What Do You Do with the Remainder?

A

When you divide with whole numbers, any whole number that remains after the division is complete is called the remainder.

Ned has 27 soccer cards in an album. He put 6 cards on each page. He knows 27 ÷ 6 = 4 with 3 left over, because 6 × 4 = 24 and 24 + 3 = 27.

Use an R to represent the remainder: 27 ÷ 6 = 4 R3

How do you use the remainder to answer questions about division?

The remainder must be less than the divisor.

B *How many pages did Ned fill?*

To answer this question, find how many groups of 6 there are. The remainder can be ignored.

27 ÷ 6 = 4 R3

Ned filled 4 pages.

C *How many pages did Ned work on?*

To answer this question, find how many groups of 6 are filled or started. Because there is a remainder, add 1 to the quotient.

27 ÷ 6 = 4 R3

Ned worked on 5 pages.

D *How many cards did Ned put on the fifth page?*

The answer to this question is the remainder.

27 ÷ 6 = 4 R3

Ned put 3 cards on the fifth page.

Convince Me! **Critique Reasoning** The calculation to the right is incorrect. What error was made? What is the correct answer?

45 ÷ 6 = 6 R9

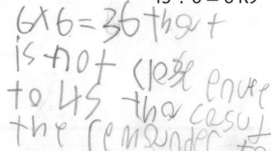

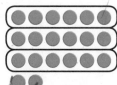
Another Example!

There are 20 apples to arrange in gift baskets, with 6 apples in each basket. How many baskets can be filled? Explain the meaning of the remainder.

3 equal groups of 6 with 2 left over

$20 \div 3 = 6$ R2, because

$3 \times 6 = 18$ and $18 + 2 = 20$.

The remainder, 2, represents the number of apples not placed into gift baskets.

☆ Guided Practice

Do You Understand?

1. When a divisor is 3, can the remainder be 5? Explain.

The remainder count be five so we can divid it by 3 to make 2 so that is t+ Rem ainder

2. Dave is packing 23 sweaters into boxes. Each box will hold 3 sweaters. How many boxes will he need? Explain how the remainder affects your answer.

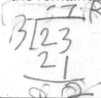

He needs 8 boxes one box

Do You Know How?

For **3–6**, find the number of groups and the number left over. Draw an array if needed.

3. $47 \div 3 =$ __15__ with __2__ left over

4. $29 \div 2 =$ __14__ with __1__ left over

5. $62 \div 5 =$ __12__ with __2__ left over

6. $86 \div 6 =$ __12__ with __2__ left over

☆ Independent Practice ☆

For **7–10**, find the number of groups and the number left over.

7. $18 \div 4 =$ __4__ with __2__ left over

8. $22 \div 6 =$ __3__ with __4__ left over

9. $31 \div 8 =$ ____ with ____ left over

10. $32 \div 9 =$ ____ with ____ left over

For **11–13**, interpret each remainder.

11. 59 football cards
    3 cards on each page

    How many pages can Alex complete?

12. 55 baseball cards
    4 cards on each page

    How many cards are on the last page?

13. 84 stickers
    5 stickers on each page

    How many pages will have some stickers on them?

Problem Solving

For **14–15**, use the table at the right.

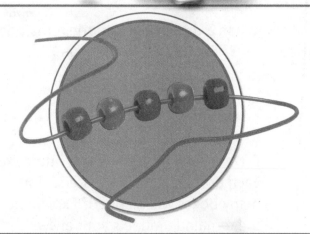

Ticket Exchange

Prize	Number of Tickets
Toy Car	8
Ring	9
Marble	7
Sticker	4

14. Samuel has 85 prize tickets. How many marbles can he get?

15. Inez chose 8 rings and 12 stickers. How many tickets did she use?

16. Keiko makes necklaces like the one in the picture at the right. She has 19 blue beads and 13 red beads. How many necklaces can Keiko make? How many of each color bead will be left over?

17. **Critique Reasoning** Amanda calculated $34 \div 8 = 3$ R10. Is Amanda's answer correct? If not, what is the correct answer? Explain.

18. **Higher Order Thinking** Write a problem that requires adding 1 to the quotient when interpreting the remainder.

✅ **Assessment Practice**

19. There are 39 children at a park. They want to make teams with 9 children on each team. Two of the children go home. How many complete teams can they make? Explain.

You can draw an array to help solve the problem.

184   **Topic 5** | Lesson 5-4

Name _____

Lesson 5-5
Use Partial Quotients to Divide

Solve & Share

Sally's bird feeder holds 6 cups of bird feed. How many times can Sally's bird feeder be filled using a 72-cup bag of bird feed? Use counters or draw pictures to solve this problem. Explain how you found your answer.

I can ...
divide by thinking about multiplication, estimation, properties, and place value.

Content Standard 4.NBT.B.6
Mathematical Practices MP.2, MP.4, MP.7

You can think about how many times you can take away groups of six from your original number.

Bird Feed
72 cups

Look Back! **Reasoning** How can you use multiplication to check your answer?

How Can You Use Partial Quotients to Solve Division Problems?

A

There are 3 seats in each row of an airplane for passengers. If there are 63 people boarding the airplane, how many rows of seats are needed for the passengers?

This bar diagram shows the problem, where *r* equals the number of rows.

You can divide by finding partial quotients until only a remainder, if any, is left.

How many groups of 3 counters can be taken away from 63?

63 counters

63 people

| 3 | *r* |

people in each row

B **One Way**

$$
\begin{array}{r}
1 \\
10 \\
10 \\
\hline
3)\overline{63} \\
-30 \\
\hline
33 \\
-30 \\
\hline
3 \\
-3 \\
\hline
0
\end{array}
$$

21   10, 10 and 1 are partial quotients.

Estimate: How many 3s are in 63? Try 10.
10 groups of 3 is 30. 63 − 30 = 33
Estimate: How many 3s are in 33? Try 10.
10 groups of 3 is 30. 33 − 30 = 3
How many 3s are in 3? 1
1 group of 3 is 3. 3 − 3 = 0

There are 21 groups of 3 in 63.

21 rows of seats are needed.

C **Another Way**

Sometimes you can use a different first estimate.

$$
\begin{array}{r}
1 \\
20 \\
\hline
3)\overline{63} \\
-60 \\
\hline
3 \\
-3 \\
\hline
0
\end{array}
$$

21   20 and 1 are partial quotients.

Estimate: How many 3s are in 63? Try 20.
20 groups of 3 is 60. 63 − 60 = 3
Estimate: How many 3s are in 3? 1
1 group of 3 is 3. 3 − 3 = 0

There are 21 groups of 3 in 63.

21 rows of seats are needed.

Convince Me! **Use Structure** How can you use the relationships between multiplication and division to check your answer?

Name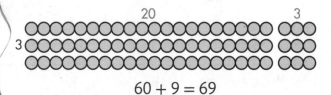

Another Example!

Break apart 69 using place value. Use the Distributive Property to show 69 ÷ 3.

20   3

3

60 + 9 = 69

$$69 ÷ 3 = (60 + 9) ÷ 3$$
$$= (60 ÷ 3) + (9 ÷ 3)$$
$$= 20 + 3$$
$$= 23$$

☆ Guided Practice

Do You Understand?

1. Harry used the model below to find 84 ÷ 4. Use the Distributive Property to show why Harry's strategy works.

20   1

4

Do You Know How?

For **2-3**, use partial quotients to divide. Use counters or draw pictures as needed.

2. How many groups of 4 are in 48?

4)48

3. How many groups of 6 are in 78?

6)78

☆ Independent Practice ☆

For **4-9**, use partial quotients to divide. You may use counters or draw pictures to help.

4. How many groups of 6 are in 90?

90 ÷ 6 =

5. How many groups of 5 are in 85?

85 ÷ 5 =

6. 2)78   7. 3)88

8. 2)84   9. 3)57

Problem Solving

10. Model with Math A collection of 64 stickers is placed into 4 equal piles. How many stickers are placed in each pile? Use the bar diagram to write and solve an equation.

64 stickers

| s | s | s | s |

↑
stickers in each pile

---

11. A chef is baking cookies for 3 parties. For each party, the chef uses the same number of eggs. She has 2 dozen eggs. What is the greatest number of eggs the chef can use for each party?

12. Show how to use the Distributive Property to divide 54 by 2 by breaking 54 into 40 + 14.

---

13. Higher Order Thinking Amanda wants to put some of her books on 4 shelves with 6 books on each shelf and the rest on 6 shelves with 3 books on each shelf. Can Amanda arrange her books this way? Explain.

42 books

---

14. Select all correct combinations of partial quotients that can be used to find 96 ÷ 3.

- ☐ 30, 2
- ☐ 30, 10, 2
- ☐ 10, 10, 10, 2
- ☐ 10, 10, 10, 6
- ☐ 20, 10, 2

15. Use the Distributive Property to find 84 ÷ 7. Which is the missing number?

$$84 \div 7 = (70 + \boxed{}) \div 7$$
$$= (70 \div 7) + (\boxed{} \div 7)$$
$$= 10 + 2$$
$$= 12$$

- Ⓐ 4
- Ⓑ 14
- Ⓒ 24
- Ⓓ 34

Name_____

Solve & Share

The new reading room in the library is 9 feet long. It is divided into a reading area and a help desk area. It has a total area of 153 square feet. What is the total width of the new reading room? Use the model to help solve this problem. **Solve this problem using any strategy you choose.**

	10 feet	f feet
9 feet	Reading area	Help desk area

You can use what you know about place value and the relationship between multiplication and division to help solve the problem.

Lesson 5-6
Use Partial Quotients to Divide: Greater Dividends

I can ...
divide by thinking about multiplication, estimation, and place value.

© **Content Standard** 4.NBT.B.6
Mathematical Practices MP.2, MP.7

Look Back! **Reasoning** If the area of the reading room was 216 square feet and the length was still 9 feet, would the width be more or less than 20? Explain.

Essential Question **How Can You Use Partial Quotients to Divide Greater Dividends?**

A

A total of 277 people signed up to audition for a talent show. Five people at a time were brought in for a group interview. How many group interviews were needed to audition all 277 people?

TALENT SHOW TRYOUTS

Interview Room

You can estimate and use partial quotients to divide.

There are 5 people in each group interview.

B Find 277 ÷ 5.

How many 5s are in 277?

Estimate:
$40 \times 5 = 200$
$50 \times 5 = 250$
$60 \times 5 = 300$
60 is too many.
There are at least fifty 5s in 277.

$$5)\overline{277}$$
$$-250$$
$$27$$

with quotient 50.

50	n
250	27

5

C How many 5s are in 27?

Estimate:
$5 \times 5 = 25$
$6 \times 5 = 30$
6 is too many.
There are at least five 5s in 27.

$$\begin{matrix}5\\50\end{matrix}\} 55$$
$$5)\overline{277}$$
$$-250$$
$$27$$
$$-25$$
$$2$$

50	5
250	25

5

D There are no more 5s in 277.

277 ÷ 5 = 55 R2

There were 55 group interviews with 5 people in each group. Two people remain. A total of 56 group interviews were needed to audition all 277 people.

Divide until the remainder is less than the divisor!

Convince Me! Use Structure How can you use multiplication and addition to check the answer above?

55
×5
275
+2
277

mulyply the qutent and the divisor Then add the

Another Example!

Find 1,968 ÷ 6.

	300	20	8
6	1,800	120	48

1,968 ÷ 6 = 328

$$\begin{array}{r} 8 \\ 20 \\ 300 \end{array} \Big\} 328$$

$6\overline{)1,968}$
$-\underline{1,800}$
$\quad\ 168$
$-\underline{\ 120}$
$\qquad 48$
$-\underline{\ \ 48}$
$\qquad\ \ 0$

There are at least three hundred 6s in 1,968.

There are at least twenty 6s in 168.

There are eight 6s in 48.

You can use multiplication, estimation, and place value to help solve division problems!

☆ Guided Practice

Do You Understand?

1. Hilary has 254 tokens to use for games at Pizza Mania. She would like to use an equal number of tokens for each of 3 visits she has planned. Will Hilary be able to use the same amount of tokens for each visit?

No she will use 84 tokens in 3 visits but have 2 tokens left over

84 R2
$3\overline{)254}$
$\underline{240}$
$\ \ 014$
$\quad \boxed{12}$

Do You Know How?

For **2-3**, use partial quotients to divide.

2. How many 4s are in 6,787?
6,787 ÷ 4

3. How many 5s are in 6,209?
6,209 ÷ 5

☆ Independent Practice

For **4-11**, use partial quotients to divide.

4. $9\overline{)153}$ 17

5. $8\overline{)450}$ 56 R 2

6. $3\overline{)2,826}$ 7

7. $7\overline{)9,428}$

8. $7\overline{)4,318}$

9. $4\overline{)8,457}$

10. $8\overline{)5,699}$

11. $3\overline{)4,567}$ 712 R 3

Remainder

Problem Solving

12. After a state fair, three 4th-grade classes volunteered to clean up the trash from the fairgrounds. In total, they collected 1,281 pounds of trash. If each class collected the same amount, how many pounds of trash did each class collect?

13. **enVision®** STEM An electric car can travel 4 miles on one kilowatt hour of electricity. How many kilowatt hours of electricity would it take for Shawn to drive his electric car to his grandmother's house and back? Shawn lives 156 miles from his grandmother.

For **14–15**, use the table at the right.

14. **Number Sense** Use estimation to find which material allows the students to make the least number of headbands.

15. **Higher Order Thinking** How many headbands can the students make? Explain.

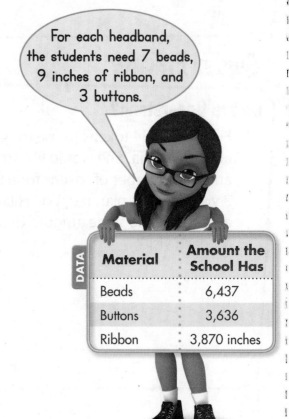

For each headband, the students need 7 beads, 9 inches of ribbon, and 3 buttons.

DATA	Material	Amount the School Has
	Beads	6,437
	Buttons	3,636
	Ribbon	3,870 inches

✅ Assessment Practice

16. Select all correct combinations of partial quotients and a remainder that can be used to find 4,567 ÷ 7.

- ☐ 600; 50; 2
- ☐ 500; 10; 50; R3
- ☐ 500; 100; 50; 2; R3
- ☐ 600; 50; R17
- ☐ 600; 50; 2; R3

17. Which is the quotient?
3,858 ÷ 8

- Ⓐ 4,082 R2
- Ⓑ 472 R2
- Ⓒ 482 R2
- Ⓓ 481 R8

Name _____

Activity

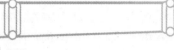

Lesson 5-7
Use Sharing to Divide

☆ ★ ☆
Solve & Share

A class collected $238 to be distributed equally to two charities. How much money will each charity receive? Use objects or draw pictures to help solve this problem. Explain how you found your answer.

I can ...
sort objects into equal-sized groups to divide.

© **Content Standards** 4.NBT.B.6 Also 4.OA.A.3
Mathematical Practices MP.4, MP.5

Using appropriate tools like place-value blocks, drawings, or money, can help you divide. What tool is easiest for you to use?

Look Back! When might you need to divide something into equal groups in everyday life?

How Can Place Value Help You Divide?

A

The craft club made 375 key chains. They sold 137 of the key chains at the school fair. The rest need to be packed into 2 boxes with the same number of key chains in each box. How many key chains will go in each box?

375 key chains

First, subtract to find how many key chains need to be packed.

$$375 - 137 = 238$$

You can use place-value blocks or draw hundreds, tens, and ones to show 238. Then divide.

B Find $238 \div 2$.

Divide the hundreds into two equal groups.

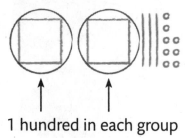

1 hundred in each group

C Divide the tens into two equal groups.

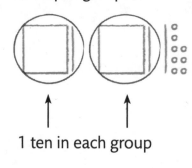

1 ten in each group

D Unbundle 1 ten for 10 ones. Divide the 18 ones into two equal groups.

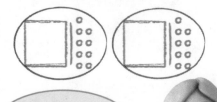

119 keychains go in each box.

Convince Me! **Use Appropriate Tools** Tell how you would evenly divide the money shown among 4 people using only $10 bills and $1 bills.

$64 \div 4 = 16$

Name _____

Another Example!

Find 55 ÷ 4.

Divide the tens equally into 4 groups.
Regroup 1 ten as 10 ones and then divide
the ones equally into 4 groups.
There are 3 ones left over.

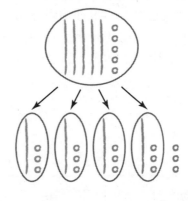

$55 ÷ 4 = 13\ R3$

☆ Guided Practice

Do You Understand?

1. Draw a picture to explain why
   $423 ÷ 3 = 141$.

2. The art teacher displayed 48 paintings
   on 3 walls. If each wall had the same
   number of paintings, how many
   paintings were on each wall?

Do You Know How?

For **3–4**, tell how many are in each group
and how many are left over. Use place-
value blocks or draw pictures as needed.

3. 176 magazines divided equally into
   5 boxes

4. 56 marbles divided equally into
   3 bags

☆ Independent Practice ☆

For **5–8**, use place-value blocks or a drawing to divide. Record remainders.

5. $71 ÷ \underline{3} = \underline{2}\ R2$

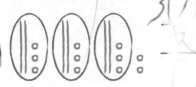

6. $\underline{44} = 176 ÷ \underline{4}$

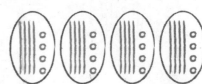

7. $46 ÷ 3 = 15\ R1$

8. $65 ÷ 4 = 16\ R1$

9. **Model with Math** A company with 65 employees is moving to a new location. All of the employees are divided into groups of 5 for the move. Write an equation and find g, the number of groups used for the move.

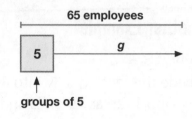

10. Maya used a drawing to divide 86. She made groups of 17 with 1 left over. Draw a picture to determine how many groups Maya made.

11. **Number Sense** A science museum has 2,400 gemstones displayed equally in 3 cases. How many gemstones are in each case? What basic fact did you use to determine the quotient?

12. Mr. Harold has 268 books on 4 shelves in the classroom library. He has the same number of books on each shelf. To find the number of books on each shelf, he divided 268 by 4. How many books are on each shelf?

13. **Higher Order Thinking** Five fourth-grade classes from an elementary school took a trip to the United States Capitol. There were 25 students in each class. At the Capitol, a maximum of 40 students were allowed on a tour at one time. What is the least number of tours needed so all the students were able to take a tour?

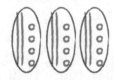 **Assessment Practice**

14. Which division equation is represented by the drawing below?

Ⓐ $72 \div 6 = 12$

Ⓑ $62 \div 3 = 24$

Ⓒ $64 \div 3 = 24$

Ⓓ $72 \div 3 = 24$

15. What is the missing divisor?

$2,244 \div n = 374$

Ⓐ 3

Ⓑ 4

Ⓒ 6

Ⓓ 7

Name_____

Solve & Share

Sara volunteers at a clothing recycling center. She packs T-shirts into bins for display. She packs the same number of T-shirts into 3 bins. How many T-shirts does Sara pack in each bin? She packs shorts into 2 bins with the same number in each bin. How many pairs of shorts does Sara pack in each bin?

I can ...
use place value and sharing to divide.

© **Content Standards** 4.NBT.B.6 Also 4.OA.A.3
Mathematical Practices MP.2, MP.4, MP.6

Be precise. You can use math symbols, numbers, or drawings to help. *Show your work in the space below!*

DATA		Plain T-shirts	Striped T-shirts	Shorts
	Number to Pack	34	48	45

Look Back! Explain how you can estimate answers to the problems above.

Essential Question

How Can You Record Division With a 1-Digit Divisor?

A

Helen has 55 postcards. As an art project, she plans to glue the same number of postcards onto 4 poster boards. How many postcards can Helen put on each poster board?

You can use place-value blocks to solve the problem.

B Divide the tens.

Estimate: 55 ÷ 4 is close to 60 ÷ 4 = 15.

Think: 5 tens divided into 4 equal groups.

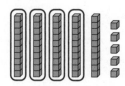

There is 1 ten in each group and 1 ten and 5 ones left over.

$$\begin{array}{r} 1 \\ 4\overline{)55} \\ -40 \\ \hline 15 \end{array}$$

C Divide the ones.

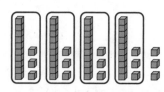

Trade the extra ten for 10 ones. The 1 ten and 5 ones make 15 ones. Think: 15 ones divided into 4 equal groups.

$$\begin{array}{r} 13 \ \text{R3} \\ 4\overline{)55} \\ -40 \\ \hline 15 \\ -12 \\ \hline 3 \end{array}$$

There are 3 ones in each group and 3 ones left over.

Helen can put 13 postcards on each of the poster boards. This quotient is reasonable since it is close to the estimate of 15.

Convince Me! **Reasoning** What does the remainder mean in the problem above?

Another Example!

Find 135 ÷ 2.

Estimate:
135 ÷ 2 is about
140 ÷ 2 = 70.

What You Show

- Regroup 1 hundred as 10 tens.

- Divide 12 of the 13 tens into 2 equal groups.

- Regroup 1 remaining or left over ten into 10 ones. Then, divide 14 of the 15 ones into 2 equal groups.

  There is a remainder of 1.

How You Record

$$
\begin{array}{r}
67 \text{ R1} \\
2\overline{)135} \\
-120 \\
\hline
15 \\
-14 \\
\hline
1
\end{array}
$$

13 tens divided into
2 equal groups
6 tens in each group
15 ones divided into
2 equal groups with
7 in each group.
Remainder of 1.

The quotient 67 R1 is reasonable since it is close to the estimate of 70.

☆ Guided Practice ☆

Do You Understand?

1. Explain how place-value blocks can help you with division.

Do You Know How?

For **2–3**, estimate, and then find the quotient. Use place-value blocks or draw pictures as needed.

2. 5)82   **3.** 7)659

☆ Independent Practice ☆

For **4–11**, find each quotient. Use place-value blocks or draw pictures as needed.

4. 3)78   **5.** 3)86   **6.** 8)417   **7.** 4)93

8. 8)526   **9.** 7)88   **10.** 3)761   **11.** 6)96

Problem Solving

12. Some of the tallest selenite crystals in a cave in Chihuahua, Mexico are 40 feet tall. Nathan is 4 feet tall. About how many times as tall as Nathan are the tallest crystals?

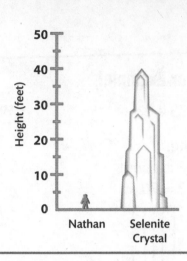

13. Model with Math The Galveston-Port Bolivar Ferry takes cars across Galveston Bay. One day, the ferry transported a total of 350 cars over a 5-hour period. The ferry took the same number of cars each hour. How many cars did it take each hour? Complete the bar diagram to help.

_____ cars

14. Zelda has a piece of fabric that is 74 inches long. She wants to divide it into 2 equal pieces. What is the length of each piece?

15. Higher Order Thinking Maggie is making trail mix. She makes 4 batches of the recipe shown. She divides it into 3 equal-sized bags. How many ounces are in each bag?

Tasty Trail Mix	
Granola	8 oz
Nuts	5 oz
Raisins	2 oz
Cranberries	3 oz

DATA

✓ **Assessment Practice**

16. Find the quotient.

7)784

Ⓐ 112
Ⓑ 114
Ⓒ 121
Ⓓ 122

17. Find the quotient.

60 ÷ 5

Ⓐ 10
Ⓑ 12
Ⓒ 25
Ⓓ 55

Name _____

Solve & Share

Choose a strategy to solve each problem. Explain your solutions.

Problem 1

There are 135 fourth-grade students. Each lunch table seats 6 students. How many tables are needed to seat all of the fourth graders?

Problem 2

A high school football stadium has 5 sections. Each section seats the same number of people. A total of 1,950 people can be seated in the stadium. How many people can sit in each section?

I can ...
follow a series of steps that breaks the division into simpler calculations.

© Content Standard 4.NBT.B.6
Mathematical Practices MP.2, MP.7

You can use reasoning and estimating to see if the answers are reasonable. *Show your work in the space below!*

Look Back! **Look for Relationships** Are either of the problems above easily solved using mental math? Explain.

Essential Question

How Do You Choose a Strategy to Divide?

A

What strategy should I use to solve the problems below?

Think about which strategy you can use to solve the problem.

Game Days Last Week	Number of Hot Dogs Sold
Saturday	834
Sunday	216
Monday	75

B How many packages of hot dogs were used on Saturday?

Think: I can use partial quotients.

```
      4  )
    100  } 104
  8)834
  − 800     There are at least one hundred 8s
   ────      in 834.
    34
  − 32      There are four 8s in 34.
   ────
     2
```

There were 105 packages of hot dogs used on Saturday.

C On Sunday, the 3 food stands each sold the same number of hot dogs. How many hot dogs were sold at each stand?

Think: I can break 216 apart and divide with mental math.

$$216 ÷ 3 = (210 + 6) ÷ 3$$
$$= (210 ÷ 3) + (6 ÷ 3)$$
$$= 70 + 2$$
$$= 72$$

72 hot dogs were sold at each stand.

You can use the Distributive Property.

Convince Me! **Reasoning** How do you decide which is the best method to use?

Name _____

Another Example!

Only 75 cookies were sold on Monday, Tuesday, and Thursday. The same number of cookies were sold each day. How many cookies were sold each day?

$75 \div 3 = c$

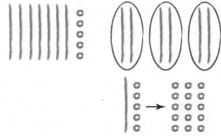

$$\begin{array}{r} 25 \\ 3\overline{)75} \\ -60 \\ \hline 15 \\ -15 \\ \hline 0 \end{array}$$

7 tens divided into 3 equal groups. 2 tens in each group.
Regroup 1 ten as 10 ones. Now there are 15 ones.
15 ones divided into 3 equal groups. 5 in each group.

25 cookies were sold each day.

☆ Guided Practice

Do You Understand?

1. Vickie's estimated quotient was 80. The actual quotient she calculated was 48. Is her actual quotient reasonable? Explain.

Do You Know How?

For **2** and **3**, divide.

2. $9\overline{)2,871}$ **3.** $4\overline{)468}$

☆ Independent Practice ☆

For **4–11**, divide.

You can use different strategies to divide.

4. $8\overline{)3,288}$ **5.** $5\overline{)247}$ **6.** $6\overline{)1,380}$ **7.** $5\overline{)3,980}$

8. $6\overline{)367}$ **9.** $3\overline{)3,582}$ **10.** $4\overline{)756}$ **11.** $6\overline{)999}$

Problem Solving

12. A family of four drove from San Francisco to New York. They drove the same number of miles each day for 6 days. How many miles did they drive each day? How can you interpret the remainder?

San Francisco | 2,906 miles | New York

---

13. Without dividing, how can you tell if the quotient for 5,873 ÷ 8 is greater than 700? Explain whether the quotient is less than 800.

14. Reasoning A square dance set is made up of 4 couples (8 dancers). There are 150 people at a square dance. What is the greatest number of sets possible at the dance? Describe the steps you would take to solve this problem.

---

15. Higher Order Thinking Is rounding or using compatible numbers a more useful method when finding quotients in division problems? Explain.

16. Ron's Tires has 1,767 tires for heavy-duty trucks. Each heavy-duty truck needs 6 tires. How many heavy-duty trucks can get all new tires at Ron's?

✓ Assessment Practice

17. Select all correct equations.

- ☐ 565 ÷ 8 = 70 R5
- ☐ 3,613 ÷ 6 = 600 R13
- ☐ 3,288 ÷ 4 = 822
- ☐ 218 ÷ 3 = 72 R2
- ☐ 6,379 ÷ 7 = 911

18. Find 6,357 ÷ 8.

- Ⓐ 814 R1
- Ⓑ 794 R5
- Ⓒ 794 R1
- Ⓓ 784

Name_____

☆ ⭐ ☆
Solve & Share

Allen set a goal to do at least 120 minutes of outdoor activities a day, Monday through Friday. He made a list of each activity and the amount of time he spends doing it every week. The same amount of time is spent every day doing the activities. Is Allen spending enough time each day on outdoor activities to meet his goal? What math can you use to solve this problem?

I can ...
use a drawing, diagram, or table to model a problem.

© **Mathematical Practices** MP.4 Also MP.1, MP.2
Content Standards 4.OA.A.3 Also 4.NBT.B.6

DATA	Activity	Weekly Time in Minutes
	Soccer	200
	Bicycling	150
	Walking	300
	Running	75

Thinking Habits

Be a good thinker!
These questions can help you.

• How can I use math I know to help solve this problem?

• Can I use pictures, objects, or an equation to represent this problem?

• How can I use numbers, words, and symbols to solve the problem?

Look Back! **Model with Math** What hidden question do you have to answer before you can determine if Allen met his goal? What math can you use to find the answer to this hidden question and the original question?

Essential Question

How Can You Apply Math You Know to Solve Problems?

A

A class is making decorations using same-size straws. They use the straws to make triangles, squares, pentagons, and hexagons. One package of straws is used for each group of polygons with the same number of sides. How many decorations can the class make?

1,500 Paper Straws

What math can you use to solve the problem?

I need to divide to find how many decorations can be made from one box of straws.

B **How can I model with math?**

I can

- use previously learned concepts and skills.

- find and answer any hidden questions.

- decide if my results make sense.

C Here's my thinking.

Each polygon has a different number of sides.

I will divide 1,500 straws by the number of sides for each polygon:

$1,500 \div 3 = 500$ triangles $1,500 \div 4 = 375$ squares

$1,500 \div 5 = 300$ pentagons $1,500 \div 6 = 250$ hexagons

I will add all the decorations together:

$500 + 375 + 300 + 250 = 1,425$

The class can make 1,425 decorations.

Convince Me! **Reasoning** Another class made 200 octagon-shaped decorations. How many straws did they use?

☆ Guided Practice

Model with Math

Miguel is going camping with 3 friends. He packed sandwiches for everyone to share equally. How many sandwiches did Miguel pack for each camper?

12 ham sandwiches

8 cheese sandwiches

20 peanut butter and jelly sandwiches

1. What hidden question do you need to solve first? Write and solve an equation to find the answer. Tell what your variable represents.

_____ sandwiches

2. Complete the bar diagram. Write and solve an equation to find the number of sandwiches, *s*, for each camper.

> You can use a bar diagram and write an equation to model with math.

Independent Practice ☆

Model with Math

Jodi delivers 54 newspapers on Saturday and 78 newspapers on Sunday. She makes bundles of 6 newspapers. How many bundles does Jodi make on Saturday and Sunday combined?

3. Explain how you could use a picture to represent the problem and show the relationships. Define variables.

4. Write and solve equations to represent the problem. Explain how you can check that your solution is reasonable.

Dog Grooming

Patricia and Antonio own a dog grooming business. To attract new customers, they offered free dog baths with the purchase of a grooming service. During the first 6 days of the promotion, they bathed 26 beagles, 12 boxers, 17 pugs, and 5 golden retrievers. Patricia and Antonio each bathed the same number of dogs each day.

Grooming Services

Nail Trim	$4
Teeth Brushing	$7
Ears Cleaned	$5
Flea Treatment	$5

5. **Reasoning** What are the quantities given in the problem?

6. **Make Sense and Persevere** What do you need to know to determine how many dogs Patricia bathed each day?

7. **Model with Math** Draw a bar diagram. Write and solve an equation to find d, how many dogs were bathed in all.

You model with math when you use a picture or equation to represent the problem.

8. **Make Sense and Persevere** Find how many dogs Patricia bathed each day. Explain how you were able to find the solution.

Name _____

Shade a path from **START** to **FINISH**. Follow the sums and differences that are between 1,000 and 1,200. You can only move up, down, right, or left.

I can ...

add and subtract whole numbers with regrouping.

 Content Standard 4.NBT.B.4
Mathematical Practices MP.2, MP.6, MP.7

Start				
314 + 707	7,020 − 5,001	686 + 304	1,064 − 145	1,201 + 289
4,300 − 3,200	1,220 + 99	4,054 − 3,913	909 + 402	1,509 − 519
999 + 200	3,099 − 899	484 + 750	1,580 − 670	1,010 + 1,101
3,455 − 2,305	807 + 499	3,704 − 2,544	725 + 460	1,388 − 209
623 + 500	2,010 − 1,009	800 + 350	1,577 − 368	1,050 + 99
				Finish

Vocabulary Review

A-Z
Glossary

Word List

- dividend
- division
- divisor
- equation
- partial quotients
- quotient
- remainder

Understand Vocabulary

Choose the best term from the box. Write it on the blank.

1. The answer to a division problem is called the
   quotent.

2. The number to be divided in a division problem is called the
   divi边den.

3. A way to divide that finds quotients in parts until only a remainder, if any, is left is
   using _partial qotents_.

4. The number by which another number is divided is called the _Divisor_.

5. The operation that tells how many equal groups there are or how many are in each group
   is called _division_.

For each of these terms, give an example and a non-example.

	Example	**Non-example**
6. equation	$27 \div 9 = 3$	$4 \cdot 20$
7. remainder	$\$53 \div 3 = 19 R_3$	$27 \cdot 1 = 23$

Use Vocabulary in Writing

8. Megan made 21 loom bracelets to share equally among her
   7 friends. How many bracelets will each friend receive?
   Write and solve an equation. Use at least 3 terms from the
   Word List to describe your equation.

megen need to do divition

megan needs to to divide $21 \div 7 = to$
find the Qutent.

The equation is $21 \div 7 = 3$

Name   F

1. Select all the equations that are reasonable estimates for the quotient 184 ÷ 8.

 ☑ $160 \div 8 = 20$

☐ $200 \div 5 = 40$

☑ $180 \div 9 = 20$

☐ $150 \div 5 = 30$

☑ $180 \div 6 = 30$

2. Draw a bar diagram for the equation, and then solve.

$2,400 \div 6 = m$

3. Mrs. Bollis has two pieces of fabric to make costumes. One piece is 11 yards long and the other is 15 yards long. Each costume requires 3 yards of fabric. How many costumes can Mrs. Bollis make? How do the remainders affect the number of costumes she can make?

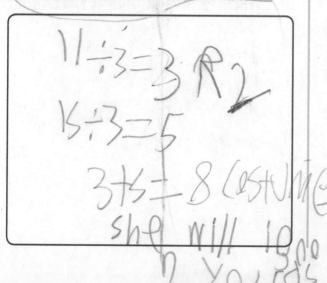
$11 \div 3 = 3\ R\ 2$
$15 \div 3 = 5$
$3 + 5 = 8$ costumes
she will ignore
2 yards

4. A. Write an equation to show how to divide 453 into 3 equal groups.

$453 \div 3 = R$

B. Complete the model to solve the equation in **A**.

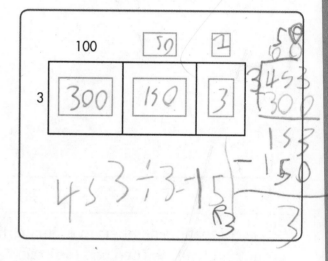
100   50   1

3 | 300 | 150 | 3

$453 \div 3 = 15$ R3

5. What is the best estimate for $3,350 \div 8$?

Ⓐ 600

Ⓑ 200

Ⓒ 400

Ⓓ 800

$3200 \div 8 = 400$

6. Draw an array and solve the equation.

$48 \div 9 = ?$

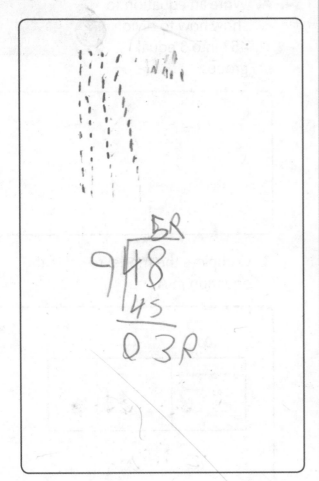

5R
9)48
$\underline{45}$
0 3R

7. Use compatible numbers to estimate the quotient $530 \div 9$. Then find the exact answer.

$549 \div 9 = 60$

$530 \div 9 = 58 R8$

8. Find $4,800 \div 6$ using a place-value strategy. What basic fact did you use?

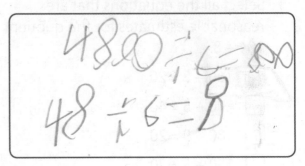

$4800 \div 6 = 800$

$48 \div 6 = 8$

9. Select all the equations in which the remainder is 5.

- ☑ $59 \div 9 = 6 R?$
- ☐ $352 \div 6 = 58 R?$
- ☑ $788 \div 9 = 87 R?$
- ☐ $1,486 \div 7 = 212 R?$
- ☑ $2,957 \div 8 = 369 R?$

10. Which of the following expressions does **NOT** have a remainder of 3?

- Ⓐ $52 \div 7$
- Ⓑ $123 \div 7$
- Ⓒ $451 \div 7$
- Ⓓ $794 \div 7$

11. Which of the following is **NOT** equivalent to $63 \div 3$?

- Ⓐ $(60 + 3) \div 3$
- Ⓑ $(33 + 30) \div 3$
- Ⓒ $(60 \div 3) + 3$
- Ⓓ $(60 \div 3) + (3 \div 3)$

12. Select all the quotients that are reasonable estimates for 472 ÷ 6.

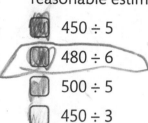
☑ 450 ÷ 5
☑ 480 ÷ 6
☑ 500 ÷ 5
☑ 450 ÷ 3
☐ 1,200 ÷ 6 = 200

13. Use partial quotients to find the quotient. Choose numbers from the box to complete the calculations. Use each number once.

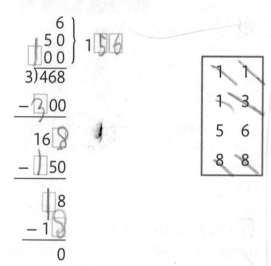

```
        6
      5 0  ⎫ 1 5 6
      0 0  ⎭
   3)468
   - 2 00
     16 8
   - 1 50
       1 8
   -  1 8
        0
```

1	1
1	3
5	6
8	8

14. Find 1,600 ÷ 8. What basic fact did you use?

```
1600 ÷ 8 = 200
16 ÷ 8 = 2
```

15. The fourth graders are going to the science museum.

Group	Number of People
Mr. Vorel's Class	30
Ms. Cahill's Class	32
Mrs. Winter's Class	29
Miss Meyer's Class	28
Teachers and Chaperones	18

Groups of 8 students can see a special exhibit on space travel. How many groups will be needed so everyone can see the exhibit?

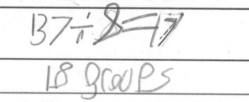

```
137 ÷ 8 = 17
18 groups
```

16. A. Divide.

432 ÷ 8 = 54

B. How can you use the answer from Part A to find 4,320 ÷ 8?

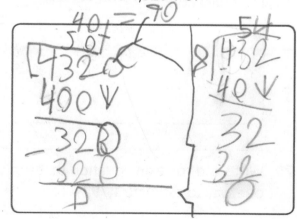

17. The Pizza Stand gives patrons a free pizza when they collect 8 coupons. How many free pizzas can Mrs. Fowler get if she has 78 coupons? How does the remainder affect the number of free pizza's she gets? How many more coupons does she need for the next free pizza? Explain.

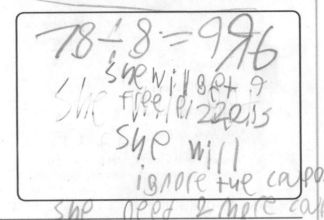

$78 \div 8 = 9$ r6
she will get 9
She free pizzas
She will
ignore the capons
she need 2 more capens

18. Estimate $257 \div 5$. Explain how you can use multiplication to estimate the quotient.

$250 \div 5 = 50$
$50 \times 5 = 250$

19. Use an equation to show how to separate 128 into 4 equal groups. Explain how to check the answer using multiplication.

20. Write and solve an equation that shows one way to estimate $1,792 \div 6$.

$1800 \div 6 = 300$

21. Draw a picture to explain why $657 \div 5 = 131$ R2.

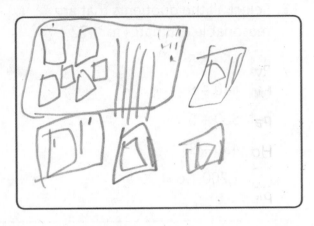

22. For each equation, mark a check to show the correct missing number.

	6	3	8	5
$4,\_00 \div 6 = 800$	☐	☐	☑	☐
$675 \div \_ = 135$	☐	☐	☐	☑
$360 \div 6 = \_0$	☑	☐	☐	☐
$98 \div 5 = 19R\_$	☐	☑	☐	☐

23. Holly uses 7 sheets of tissue paper to make one flower. If she bought a package with 500 sheets of tissue paper, about how many flowers will Holly be able to make? Use compatible numbers to estimate the number of flowers.

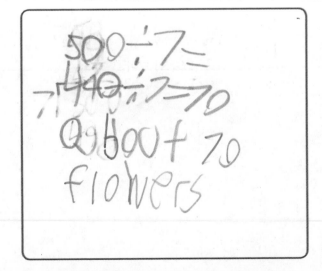

$500 \div 7 =$
$490 \div 7 = 70$
about 70
flowers

TOPIC
5

Performance
Task

Saving What You Earn

Trista's older brother Ryan got a job. Ryan would like to buy the items shown with his earnings. Ryan earns $8 for each hour he works.

1. Ryan is curious and wants to know the amount of time it will take him to earn enough money to buy the items shown.

Part A

How many hours does Ryan need to work to earn enough money to buy the computer? Explain how to use place value and mental math to solve.

$480

$341

$44

Part B

How many hours does Ryan need to work to buy the video game? Use a model to show how to find the quotient. Explain how to interpret the remainder.

Part C

How many hours will Ryan need to work to earn enough money to buy the smart phone? Use partial quotients to divide.

2. Ryan gets a raise. He now earns $9 an hour. Ryan decides to start saving for a car. He works 9 hours a week.

Part A

How many hours does Ryan need to work to earn enough money to buy the car, as well as pay for the taxes, title, and plates as shown? Draw bar diagrams to help write and solve equations.

Used car: $2,793
Taxes, title, and plates: $235

Part B

About how many weeks will Ryan need to work to buy the car and pay for the taxes, title, and plates? Explain.

Part C

How many actual weeks does Ryan need to work to buy the car and pay for the taxes, title, and plates? Show your work. Explain why your solution is reasonable.

Use Operations with Whole Numbers to Solve Problems

Essential Questions: How is comparing with multiplication different from comparing with addition? How can you use equations to solve multi-step problems?

Digital Resources

Interactive Student Edition   Activity   Visual Learning   Video   Practice

Assessment   Games   Tools   Glossary

It takes a lot of energy to power a neighborhood. Renewable energy can lower the pollution produced by powering these homes!

Some homes use solar power for energy. This type of renewable energy uses sunlight and is good for the environment!

Some of the energy is stored for nighttime or when it is cloudy. Here is a project on energy and multiplication.

enVision STEM Project: Energy and Multiplication

Do Research Use the Internet or other sources to find and describe 3 examples of renewable energy.

Journal: Write a Report Include what you found. Also in your report:

- Solar panels are made up of smaller modules or sections called cells. Find a picture of a solar panel. How many cells are in 6 solar panels? How many cells are in 9 solar panels? How many more cells are in the 9 solar panels than the 6 solar panels?

- Find examples of other items that use solar power.

Name_____

Review What You Know

Dividing by 1-Digit Numbers

Estimate each quotient.

4. $16 \div 3 =$ 5R1   5. $25 \div 4 =$ 6R1   6. $155 \div 4 =$ 39R1

7. $304 \div 3 =$ 10R1   8. $1,283 \div 6 =$ 213R5   9. $1,999 \div 4 =$ 491R3

Multiplying by 1-Digit Numbers

Find each product.

i dont know

10. $53 \times 9 =$ 477   11. $1,127 \times 7$ 12. $2,769 \times 5$

13. $3 \times 215 =$ 615   14. $914 \times 5 =$ 4670   15. $1,238 \times 5$

Problem Solving

16. **Construct Arguments** Explain why the array represents 3×21.

17. James multiplies 38 by 55. He finds three of the four partial products: 40, 150, and 400. Which partial product is James missing? What is the solution?

Name_____

PROJECT 6A

How tall is tall?

Project: Model the Height of a Redwood Tree

PROJECT 6B

What are some interesting number facts about a manatee?

Project: Make a Presentation with Manatee Number Facts

PROJECT 6C

How does temperature affect an alligator egg?

Project: Create a Bar Diagram

PROJECT 6D

How many eggs does the loggerhead turtle lay?

Project: Model a Turtle's Egg

Name _____

☆ Solve & Share ☆

Sarah is making a square pillow with edges that each measure 18 inches long. She needs a strip of fabric 4 times as long as one edge of the pillow to make a border around the pillow. How long does the strip of fabric need to be? **Solve this problem any way you choose.**

I can ...
use multiplication or addition to compare one quantity to another.

© **Content Standards** 4.OA.A.2 Also 4.OA.A.1, 4.NBT.B.5
Mathematical Practices MP.2, MP.3, MP.4

Use reasoning to make sense of the quantities in the problem. You can use a bar diagram to understand the relationship between the quantities.

Look Back! **Model with Math** How could a bar diagram help you write and solve an equation for the problem?

Essential Question How Is Comparing with Multiplication Different from Comparing with Addition?

A

Max said the Rangers scored 3 times as many runs as the Stars. Jody said the Rangers scored 8 more runs than the Stars. Could both Max and Jody be correct?

You can use multiplication or addition to compare the number of runs made by each team.

Let m = the runs scored by the Rangers according to Max. Let j = the runs scored by the Rangers according to Jody.

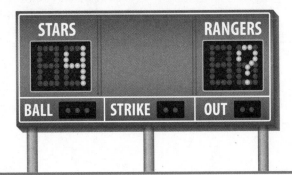

B **Compare with Multiplication**

Find 3 times as many as 4 runs.

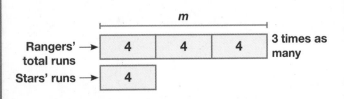

$m = 3 \times 4$
$m = 12$ runs

According to Max, the Rangers scored 12 runs.

C **Compare with Addition**

Find 8 more than 4 runs.

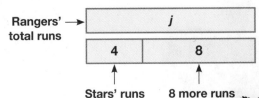

$j = 4 + 8$
$j = 12$ runs

According to Jody, the Rangers scored 12 runs.

Max and Jody are both correct.

Convince Me! **Construct Arguments** Describe when you would use multiplication and when you would use addition to make a comparison.

☆ Guided Practice

Do You Understand?

1. Use the information from the previous page. If the Rangers scored 5 times as many runs as the Stars, how many runs would the Rangers have scored?

a. Compare using multiplication. Write and solve an equation.

b. How could you use addition to compare the runs for the two teams?

Do You Know How?

For **2–3**, complete the comparison sentence. Find the value of the variable that makes the sentence true.

2. Sam's baseball team has 4 times as many helmets as Ed's team. Ed's team has 21 helmets. Let h = the number of helmets Sam's team has.

h is _____ times as many as _____.
h = _____

3. There are 128 more trees in the park than at Ty's house. There are 3 trees at Ty's house. Let t = the number of trees in the park.

_____ more than _____ is t. t = _____

Independent Practice ☆

For **4–9**, write a comparison sentence. For **4–7**, find the value of the variable that makes the sentence true.

Use *times as many as* or *more than* to compare the amounts.

4. Katy has 6 times as many nickels as Shaun. Shaun has 18 nickels. Let n = the number of nickels Katy has.

n is _____
n = _____

5. Kyle has watched 238 movies. Jason has watched 49 more movies than Kyle. Let m = the number of movies Jason has watched.

m is _____
m = _____

6. Amber tied 89 knots to make a macrame wall hanging. Hunter tied 3 times as many knots as Amber. Let k = the number of knots Hunter tied.

k is _____
k = _____

7. Tia sells 292 newspapers. Tess sells 117 more newspapers than Tia. Let n = the number of newspapers Tess sells.

n is _____
n = _____

8. Trent has 48 markers. Sharon has 8 markers.

_____
_____

9. Lucy has 317 bottles. Craig has 82 bottles.

_____
_____

Problem Solving

10. Model with Math Roger swam 19 laps in the pool. Anna Maria swam 4 times as many laps as Roger. How many laps did Anna Maria swim? Draw a bar diagram and write an equation to solve the problem.

11. Critique Reasoning Nina says the equation $600 = 12 \times 50$ means 600 is 12 times as many as 50. Julio says the equation means 600 is 50 times as many as 12. Who is correct? Explain.

12. (A-Z) Vocabulary The amount that is left after dividing a number into equal parts is called the _____.

$13 \div 4 =$ _____

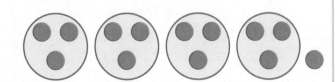

13. Higher Order Thinking A shirt is on sale for *d* dollars. The regular price is 4 times as much. Todd has enough money to buy 2 shirts at the regular price. How many shirts can Todd buy at the sale price? Explain.

✅ Assessment Practice

14. Select all the sentences that involve a comparison using multiplication.

- ☐ *k* is 26 times as many as 7.
- ☐ *u* is 18 more than 314.
- ☐ Tom ran 4 miles. Cindy ran 2 more miles than Tom. How many miles did Cindy run?
- ☐ Yuhan has 2 dogs and Jon has 3 times as many dogs. How many dogs does Jon have?
- ☐ Kris has 4 times as many pairs of shoes as her brother. Her brother has 8 pairs of shoes.

15. Select all the statements that can be represented by the equation $5 \times 9 = w$.

- ☐ *w* is 9 more than 5.
- ☐ *w* is 5 times as much as 9.
- ☐ Henry sang 9 songs during practice. He sang 5 times as many as Joe, who sang *w* songs.
- ☐ Greg carried 9 buckets of water to his sister's baby pool. His mother carried *w* buckets, which was 5 times as many.
- ☐ Tom has 9 pens. Joan has *w* pens, which is 5 fewer.

Name_____

Solve & Share

The students in Ms. Chang's fourth-grade class plant a tree every year. One tree they planted is now 288 inches tall. This height is 6 times as great as when the tree was first planted. How tall was the tree when it was first planted? **Solve this problem any way you choose.** Show your work.

Lesson 6-2
Continue to Solve Comparison Problems

I can ...
use multiplication or division to compare one quantity to another.

© **Content Standards** 4.OA.A.1 Also 4.OA.A.2, 4.NBT.B.5, 4.NBT.B.6
Mathematical Practices MP.1, MP.3, MP.4

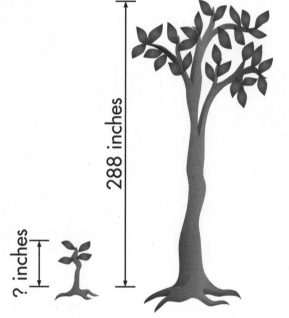

288 inches

? inches

You can model with math and use equations to compare the heights of the two trees.

Look Back! Compare the heights of the 2 trees using addition.

Essential Question **How Can You Solve a Problem Involving Multiplication as Comparison?**

A

Carla and Calvin are twins that attend different colleges. Carla's college is four times as far from home as Calvin's college. How far does Calvin travel to college?

Carla travels 192 miles to college.

Let m = the miles Calvin travels to college.

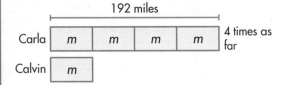

192 miles

| Carla | m | m | m | m | 4 times as far |

| Calvin | m |

Multiplication and division have an inverse relationship.

B The number of miles Carla travels, or 192 miles, is 4 times as far as Calvin travels.

Write a multiplication equation to find the number of miles Calvin travels to college.

$$192 = 4 \times m$$

What number times 4 equals 192?

C If $192 = 4 \times m$, then $m = 192 \div 4$.

$$\begin{array}{r} 8 \\ 40 \end{array} \Big\} 48$$

$$\begin{array}{r} 4\overline{)192} \\ -160 \\ \hline 32 \\ -32 \\ \hline 0 \end{array}$$

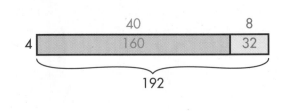

| 40 | 8 |
| 160 | 32 |

192

$m = 48$ miles

Calvin travels 48 miles to college.

Convince Me! **Use Structure** When do you use division to make a comparison?

☆ Guided Practice

Do You Understand?

1. Carla travels 3 times as far to college as her friend Mandy travels to college. Write and solve a related multiplication and division equation to find how far Mandy travels to college.

Do You Know How?

2. Complete the comparison sentence. Find the value of the variable that makes the sentence true.

If $3 \times m = 48$, then $m = 48 \div 3$.

_____ times as many as

_____ is _____.

$m =$ _____

Independent Practice ☆

For **3-8**, write a comparison sentence and an equation. Find the value of the variable that makes the sentence true.

3. Connor has 77 magazines. That is 7 times as many magazines Kristen has. How many magazines, n, does Kristen have?

4. Eric completed 75 math problems. That is 5 times as many math problems as Katie completed. How many math problems, m, did Katie complete?

5. Clare counted 117 different colors at the paint store. That is 9 times as many as the number James counted. How many different colors, c, did James count?

6. Alisa has 153 dominoes. That is 3 times as many dominoes as Stan has. How many dominoes, d, does Stan have?

7. Justin practiced piano for h hours. His sister practiced for 12 hours, which was 3 times as many hours as Justin practiced. Write and solve an equation to find how many hours Justin practiced piano.

8. Mary practiced violin for 2 hours and her brother practiced trombone t times as long or 8 hours. Write and solve an equation to find how many times as long Mary's brother practiced trombone.

Problem Solving

9. **Model with Math** Dave is making soup that includes 12 cups of water and 3 cups of broth. How many times as much water as broth will be in the soup? Draw a bar diagram and write and solve an equation.

10. Trevor wants to buy three light fixtures that cost $168 each. He has $500. Does he have enough money to buy the three light fixtures? Use a comparison sentence to explain your reasoning.

11. Miranda has 4 times as many leaves in her collection as Joy. Joy has 13 more leaves than Armani. Armani has 10 leaves in his collection. How many leaves does Miranda have in her collection? Explain.

12. **Higher Order Thinking** Jordan needs $9,240 for her first year of college tuition. Each of her two grandfathers said they would match what she saves. She has 8 years before she goes to college. How much does Jordan need to save on her own each year to have enough for her first year with the help from her two grandfathers?

Some problems require more than one operation.

13. Tina walked 20 miles for a fundraiser. Lia walked m miles. Tina walked 4 times as far as Lia. Which equation can be used to find m, the number of miles Lia walked?

   (A) $m = 4 \times 20$

   (B) $20 = 4 \times m$

   (C) $20 = m \div 4$

   (D) $m = 20 + 4$

14. Jason and Raul kept a reading log for the year. Jason read 7 books and Raul read 105. How many times as many books as Jason did Raul read?

   (A) 13 times

   (B) 14 times

   (C) 15 times

   (D) 16 times

Name_____

Solve & Share

Last year, 18 people went on a family camping trip. This year, three times as many people went. How many more people went this year than last year? Complete the bar diagram and show how you solve.

I can ...
find hidden questions and use bar diagrams and equations to model and solve multi-step problems.

Content Standards 4.OA.A.3 Also 4. OA.A.2, 4.NBT.B.4, 4.NBT.B.5, 4.NBT.B.6
Mathematical Practices MP.1, MP.3, MP.4

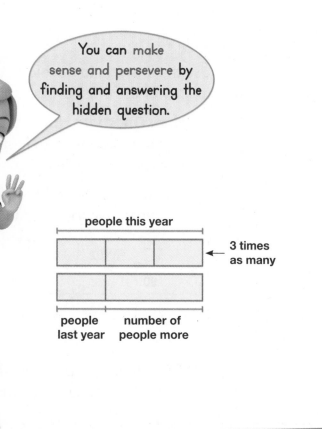

You can make sense and persevere by finding and answering the hidden question.

people this year

3 times as many

people last year   number of people more

Look Back! How can you use estimation to decide if your answer is reasonable?

How Can You Use Diagrams and Equations to Solve Multi-Step Problems?

A

A school uses 8 buses to transport the fourth-grade students and 6 vans to transport the third-grade students on a field trip. How many fewer third-grade students than fourth-grade students are on the field trip?

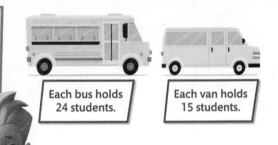

Each bus holds 24 students.

Each van holds 15 students.

You can use variables or letters to represent unknown numbers in equations.

B Step 1

Find and answer the hidden questions.

Hidden Question: How many fourth-grade students are on the field trip?

F = Number of fourth graders

| 24 | 24 | 24 | 24 | 24 | 24 | 24 | 24 |

$F = 8 \times 24$
$= 192$ fourth-grade students

Hidden Question: How many third-grade students are on the field trip?

T = Number of third graders

| 15 | 15 | 15 | 15 | 15 | 15 |

$T = 6 \times 15$
$= 90$ third-grade students

C Step 2

Use the answers to the hidden questions to answer the original question.

Original Question: How many fewer third-grade students than fourth-grade students are on the field trip?

$S =$ the number fewer third-grade students than fourth-grade students

192	
90	S

$S = 192 - 90$
$= 102$

102 fewer third-grade students than fourth-grade students are on the field trip.

Convince Me! **Construct Arguments** Amanda says she can solve the problem using the equation below. Do you agree? Explain.

$S = (8 \times 24) - (6 \times 15)$

Name _____

Another Example!

The Lopez family gets 2 pizzas and 4 hot dogs at Eat-It-Up. What is the total cost?

EAT-IT-UP

Hamburger $8	Pizza $18	Turkey Wrap $9
Hot Dog $6	Salad $16	Drinks $2

Step 1

Write expressions to represent the hidden questions.

What is the cost of 2 pizzas?

| 18 | 18 | 2×18
|---|---|

What is the cost of 4 hot dogs?

| 6 | 6 | 6 | 6 | 4×6
|---|---|---|---|

Step 2

Combine the expressions into an equation to find T, the total cost.

T = Total cost

18	18	6	6	6	6

Cost of Pizzas   Cost of Hot Dogs

$T = (2 \times 18) + (4 \times 6)$

Step 3

Solve.

$T = (2 \times 18) + (4 \times 6)$
$T = 36 + 24$
$T = 60$

The total cost is $60.

> 2×18 and 4×6 are expressions.
> $T = (2 \times 18) + (4 \times 6)$ is an equation.

☆ Guided Practice

Do You Understand?

1. Doug says he can use the equation $T = 18 + 18 + 6 + 6 + 6 + 6$ to solve the problem above. Is Doug correct? Explain.

2. Write one or more equations you could use to find the total cost C, of 2 turkey wraps, 2 hamburgers, and 4 drinks.

Do You Know How?

3. In the problem on the previous page, suppose the school fills 11 buses and lets the remaining students ride in vans. How many students ride in vans? Use one or more bar diagram and equation to show how you solve.

Independent Practice ☆

Draw a bar diagram, and write an equation to solve the problem. Use a variable to represent an unknown quantity and tell what the variable represents.

4. Four boys and five girls went to the movies together. Between them they had $120 to spend. Tickets cost $8 each. How much money did they have to buy refreshments?

Problem Solving

5. **Model with Math** A power plant has 4 tons of coal. A ton of coal produces 2,460 kilowatt hours of electricity. The plant reserves enough electricity to power 9 light bulbs for a year. How many additional kilowatt hours of electricity are produced? Draw bar diagrams and write one or more equations to show how you solve. Tell what your variables represent.

It takes 876 kilowatt hours of electricity to power a 100-watt light bulb for a year.

6. **Higher Order Thinking** You have $350 to buy 26 tickets for a baseball game. You need to buy some of each kind of seat. You want to spend most of the money. How many of each type of ticket can you buy? Find two different solutions to the problem. Use an equation to show each solution.

TICKET PRICES FOR HOMETOWN FIELD

Box Seats $18 Each
Upper Deck $12 Each

✓ **Assessment Practice**

7. The gym teacher has $250 to spend on volleyball equipment. She buys 4 volleyball nets for $28 each. Volleyballs cost $7 each. How many volleyballs can she buy? Explain how you solve. Use one or more equations and bar diagrams in your explanation. Tell what your variables represent.

Name_____

Solve & Share

Three eight-year-old children, one adult, and one senior had $125 saved to go to the Happy Days amusement park. After buying tickets, how much money did they have left to buy refreshments? Complete the bar diagram, and use it to write one or more equations to solve the problem. Tell what your variables represent.

I can ...
Solve multi-step problems by drawing bar diagrams and writing expressions and equations.

Content Standards 4.OA.A.3 Also 4.OA.A.2, 4.NBT.B.4, 4.NBT.B.5, 4.NBT.B.6
Mathematical Practices MP.1, MP.4

You can model with math by using equations and bar diagrams to find how much money the group had left.

HAPPY DAYS
TICKETS

Children under 5 **Free**
Children 6-12 **$12**
Teens **$20**
Adults 20 to 65 **$25**
Seniors **$18**

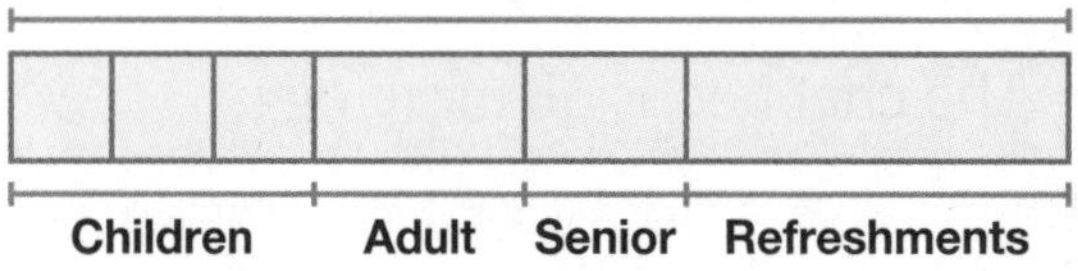

Children			Adult	Senior	Refreshments

Look Back! What expressions and equations did you use to solve this problem? What hidden questions did you need to answer?

Essential Question

How Can You Model and Solve Multi-Step Problems?

A

Chef Angela needs 8 cartons of eggs to make the cakes that are ordered. She has 2 cartons of eggs and 4 single eggs in the refrigerator. How many more eggs does she need to make all of the cakes?

A carton has 12 eggs.

Multi-step problems can often be solved in more than one way.

The chef estimates she needs about 6 cartons or about 6 × 12 = 72 more eggs.

B ## One Way

How many eggs does the chef have?

$(2 \times 12) + 4 = 24 + 4$
$= 28$ eggs

How many more eggs does the chef need?

$N =$ number of additional eggs needed

$N = (8 \times 12) - 28$
$= 96 - 28$
$= 68$

The expression 8 × 12 is how many eggs the chef needs in all.

The chef needs 68 more eggs.

Since 68 is close to 72, the answer is reasonable.

C ## Another Way

How many full cartons should the chef buy?

$8 - 2 = 6$ full cartons

How many more eggs does the chef need?

$N =$ number of additional eggs needed

$N = (6 \times 12) - 4$
$= 72 - 4$
$= 68$

The expression 6 × 12 is the number of eggs in 6 cartons.

The chef needs 68 more eggs.

Since 68 is a close to 72, the answer is reasonable.

Convince Me! **Model with Math** Draw bar diagrams to represent a solution to the problem above.

☆Guided Practice

Do You Understand?

1. Explain the meaning of the expression $(2 \times 12) + 4$ in the problem on the previous page.

2. In the problem on the previous page, how many eggs will the chef have left over? Explain.

Do You Know How?

3. Carrie's stamp book has 20 pages and each page can hold 15 stamps. She has 45 international stamps. She has 4 times as many U.S. stamps. Can all her stamps fit in her book? Use the bar diagram below to help solve this problem. Draw other bar diagrams as needed. Show the equations used to solve this problem.

?

| 45 | 45 | 45 | 45 | ← 4 times as many |

| 45 |

Independent Practice ☆

For **4–5**, draw bar diagrams, and write equations to solve each problem. Use variables to represent unknown quantities and tell what each variable represents.

4. Five toymakers each carved 28 blocks and 17 airplanes. Three other toymakers each carved the same number of airplanes and twice as many blocks. How many toys did the eight carve in all?

5. Kendra is using 27 blue patches and some white patches to make a quilt. The quilt has a total area of 540 square inches. Each patch has an area of 9 square inches. How much of the area of the quilt is white?

Problem Solving

6. Make Sense and Persevere A ticket to a movie for a student is $7. The cost for an adult is $2 more than for a student. How much would it cost 5 adults and 29 students for tickets to the movie?

7. (A-Z) **Vocabulary** Give an example of an expression. Then give an example of an equation.

---

8. Higher Order Thinking Cody and Max both solve the problem below correctly. Explain how each solve.

Emma has $79 to spend at the toy store. She wants to buy a building set, a board game, and 2 action figures from her favorite movie. What else can she buy?

Cody

$79 - 32 = 47$
$47 - 19 = 28$
$2 \times 8 = 16$
$28 - 16 = 12$

Emma can buy a doll or another action figure.

Max

L = the money Emma has left.
$L = 79 - (32 + 19 + 16)$
$L = 79 - 67$
$L = 12$

She can buy a doll or action figure.

Toy Shop	
Toy	**Cost**
Building Set	$32
Board Game	$19
Stuffed Toy	$15
Doll	$12
Action Figure	$8

DATA

✓ Assessment Practice

9. A company has 2 geothermal plants which can power a total of 2,034 homes. After they build 3 additional, more powerful, geothermal plants, they can power a total of 5,799 homes. How many homes does each of the new plants power? Explain how you solve. Use one or more equations and bar diagrams in your explanation. Tell what your variables represent.

Name_____

Solve & Share

A farmer needs $3,500 to buy a previously-owned truck. If she sells 45 maple trees and 27 pine trees, will she earn enough to buy the truck? If not, how much more money does she need? *Solve this problem any way you choose.*

Activity

I can ...
solve multi-step problems by finding and solving hidden questions and by writing expressions and equations.

ⓒ **Content Standards** 4.OA.A.3 Also 4.OA.A.2, 4.NBT.B.4, 4.NBT.B.5, 4.NBT.B.6
Mathematical Practices MP.2, MP.3, MP.4

You can use reasoning and think about the relationships between the quantities in the problem.

Rothacker
TREE FARM

SALE!
Maple trees $56
Pine trees $33

Look Back! In the question above, how many more of each tree could the farmer sell to get enough money to buy the truck? Explain.

Essential Question

How Can You Use Equations to Solve Multi-Step Problems?

Visual Learning Bridge

A

The students in the fourth and fifth grades are going to a concert. There are 178 students. How many rows are needed for the fourth graders?

Each row has 8 seats.
The fifth-grade students fill 12 rows.

To find the number of rows, you need to find the number of fourth graders. To find the number of fourth graders, you need to find the number of fifth graders.

Let s = the number of fifth graders, f = the number of fourth graders, and r = the number of rows of fourth graders.

B
Step 1

Find and solve the first hidden question.

Hidden Question:
How many fifth graders are there?

$12 \times 8 = s$
$s = 96$

There are 96 fifth graders.

C
Step 2

Find and solve the second hidden question.

Hidden Question:
How many fourth graders are there?

$178 - 96 = f$
$f = 82$

There are 82 fourth graders.

D
Step 3

Answer the original question.

Original Question:
How many rows are needed for the fourth graders?

$82 \div 8 = r$
$r = 10 \text{ R2}$

Ten rows will be filled with 2 fourth graders left over. So, 11 rows will be needed.

Convince Me! **Construct Arguments** Does the answer of 11 rows make sense for the problem above? Explain.

☆ Guided Practice

Do You Understand?

1. On the previous page, suppose there were only 11 rows of fifth graders, but the same total number of students. Do you need to solve the whole problem again to find how many rows are needed for the fourth graders? Explain.

Do You Know How?

2. Show another way to solve the problem on the previous page.

☆ Independent Practice ☆

For **3–4**, solve each multi-step problem. Write equations to show how you solve. Draw bar diagrams to help if needed. Use estimation to decide if your answer is reasonable.

3. Vanya bought 5 medium packages of buttons and 3 small packages of buttons. What was the total number of buttons Vanya bought?

Number of Items in Package

Item	Small	Medium	Large
Beads	32	64	96
Buttons	18	38	56

4. Vance bought 2 packages of large beads, 1 package of medium beads, 2 packages of large buttons, and 2 packages of medium buttons. How many more beads than buttons did Vance buy?

Problem Solving

5. **enVision® STEM** How much more does it cost to generate 9 megawatt hours of electricity with conventional coal than with wind energy? Write one or more equations to show how you solve. Tell what your variables represent.

It can cost up to $87 to generate 1 megawatt hour of electricity with wind energy.

It can cost $105 to generate 1 megawatt hour of electricity with conventional coal.

6. **Model with Math** Anna earns $8 an hour baby-sitting and $6 an hour working in the garden. Last month, she worked 15 hours baby-sitting and 8 hours in the garden. How much more money does she need to buy a robot which costs $199? Explain how you solve. Use one or more equations in your explanation. Tell what your variables represent.

7. **Higher Order Thinking** Show two different ways to find the answer to the problem below.

Dog and cat food are sold in 20-pound bags. There are 14 bags of dog food and 12 bags of cat food on the store shelves. How many pounds of dog and cat food are on the shelves?

✓ **Assessment Practice**

8. Chris needs $858 to buy a computer. She has already saved $575. She gets $15 an hour for babysitting and will babysit 12 hours in the next month. She can save $8 a week from her allowance. How many weeks of allowance will it take Chris to save enough to buy the computer? Explain how you solve. Use one or more equations in your explanation. Tell what your variables represent.

Name _____

Activity

Solve & Share

Ms. Valenzuela had her students design a snake house for the zoo. In the design shown, the anaconda has 538 more square feet than the python. The python has twice as many square feet as the rattlesnake. How much of the house's area does each snake have? **Solve this problem any way you choose.**

I can ...
make sense of problems and keep working if I get stuck.

© **Mathematical Practices** MP.1 Also MP.5, MP.6
Content Standards 4.OA.A.2 Also 4.OA.A.3, 4.NBT.B.5, 4.NBT.B.6

PYTHON
p square feet

RATTLESNAKE
r square feet

Viewing Area

ANACONDA
1,928 square feet

Thinking Habits

Be a good thinker!
These questions can help you.

• What do I need to find?

• What do I know?

• What's my plan for solving the problem?

• What else can I try if I get stuck?

• How can I check that my solution makes sense?

Look Back! **Make Sense and Persevere** How can you check that your solution makes sense?

Essential Question **How Do You Make Sense of a Multi-Step Problem and Persevere in Solving It?**

A

Bryan and Alex have to buy their own instruments for the band. Alex made $1,025 from a fundraiser. He has a part-time job that pays $8 an hour. How many hours does Alex need to work to have enough money to buy his instrument?

Bryan's trumpet costs $159.

Alex's tuba costs 9 times as much as Bryan's trumpet.

What do you need to do to solve this problem?

I need to determine how much Alex's tuba costs and how much Alex needs to earn to buy the tuba.

Here's my thinking.

B **How can I make sense of and solve this problem?**

I can

- identify the quantities given.
- understand how the quantities are related.
- choose and implement an appropriate strategy.
- check to be sure my work and answer make sense.

C Use the cost of the trumpet to find the cost of the tuba.

$$\$159 \times 9 = \$1,431 \quad \text{Alex's tuba costs } \$1,431.$$

Find how much more money Alex needs to earn.

$$\$1,431 - \$1,025 = \$406 \quad \text{Alex needs to earn } \$406.$$

Find how many hours Alex needs to work.

$$\$406 \div 8 = 50 \text{ R6}$$

Alex will not have enough money by working 50 hours, so he needs to work 51 hours.

Convince Me! **Make Sense and Persevere** How can you check to make sure the work and answer given above make sense?

Name_____

☆ Guided Practice

Make Sense and Persevere

In the problem on the previous page, suppose Alex wanted to know how many weeks it would take him to work 51 hours. Alex works 3 hours a day and 4 days a week.

1. What are you asked to find and what is the hidden question?

> Think about this question to help you persevere in solving the problem. What's a good plan for solving the problem?

2. Write and solve equations to solve the problem. Be sure to tell what each variable represents.

3. Does your answer make sense? Explain.

☆ Independent Practice ☆

Make Sense and Persevere

The high school tennis team is selling tennis balls to raise $500 for new equipment. They sell the balls for $2 each. Will they make enough money if they sell 4 cases?

4. What are the hidden questions? Write equations to solve each.

> A case has 24 packages.
> Each package has 3 tennis balls.

5. Will the team make enough money? Explain.

Designing a Flag

Rainey's group designed the flag shown for a class project. They used 234 square inches of green fabric. After making one flag, Rainey's group has 35 square inches of yellow fabric left. How can Rainey's group determine the total area of the flag?

Twice as much green as orange

3 times as much green as yellow

6. **Make Sense and Persevere** What hidden question(s) do you need to answer first?

7. **Appropriate Tools** Draw diagrams and write equations to represent the hidden question(s). Be sure to tell what each variable represents.

When you make sense of a problem, you check that your solution makes sense.

8. **Be Precise** Use your drawings and equations to find the total area of the flag. Explain carefully, using the correct units.

9. **Make Sense and Persevere** What information was not needed to solve the problem?

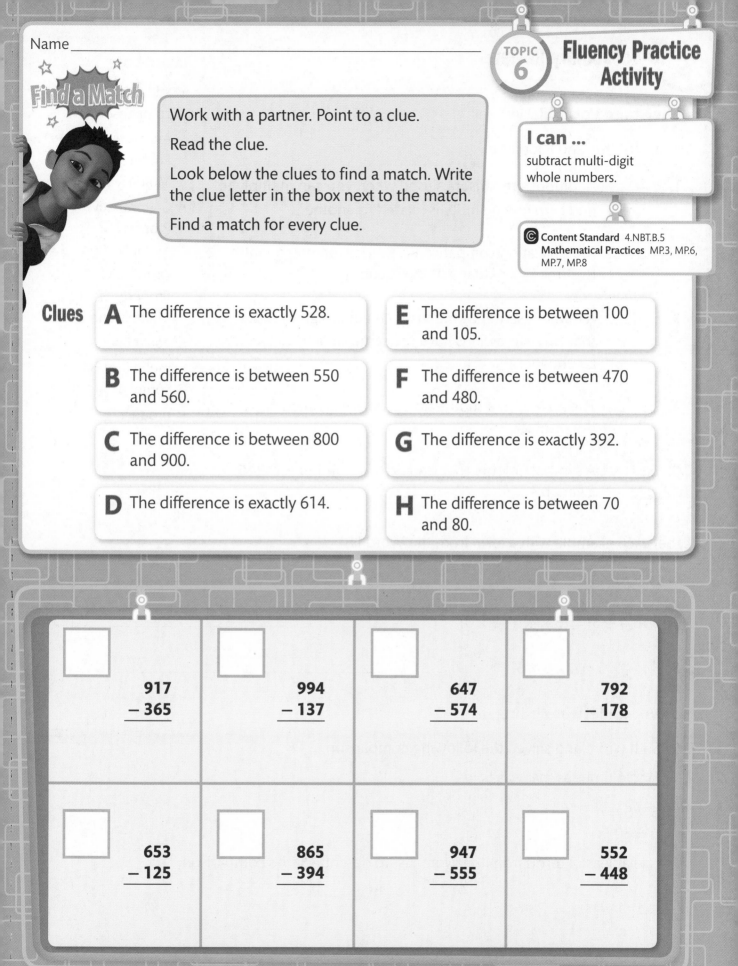

Find a Match

Work with a partner. Point to a clue.

Read the clue.

Look below the clues to find a match. Write the clue letter in the box next to the match.

Find a match for every clue.

I can ...
subtract multi-digit whole numbers.

© **Content Standard** 4.NBT.B.5
Mathematical Practices MP.3, MP.6, MP.7, MP.8

Clues

A The difference is exactly 528.

B The difference is between 550 and 560.

C The difference is between 800 and 900.

D The difference is exactly 614.

E The difference is between 100 and 105.

F The difference is between 470 and 480.

G The difference is exactly 392.

H The difference is between 70 and 80.

☐ 917 − 365	☐ 994 − 137	☐ 647 − 574	☐ 792 − 178
☐ 653 − 125	☐ 865 − 394	☐ 947 − 555	☐ 552 − 448

Vocabulary Review

Glossary

Word List

- addition comparison
- Associative Property of Multiplication
- Commutative Property of Multiplication
- Distributive Property of Multiplication
- equation
- multiplication comparison
- product
- variable

Understand Vocabulary

Write T for *true* and F for *false*.

1. _____ Addition comparison is used when you can multiply to find how one quantity is related to another.

2. _____ Multiplication comparison is used when one quantity is *x* times more than another quantity.

3. _____ A number sentence that uses an equal sign to show that two expressions have the same value is called an equation.

4. _____ The answer to a subtraction problem is called the product.

5. _____ A symbol or letter that stands for a number is called a variable.

Label each example with a term from the Word List.

6. $(3 \times 4) \times 5 = 3 \times (4 \times 5)$ _____

7. $3 \times (4 + 5) = (3 \times 4) + (3 \times 5)$ _____

8. $3 \times 4 \times 5 = 4 \times 3 \times 5$ _____

Use Vocabulary in Writing

9. Seth wrote and solved the following comparison:

Find 6 times as many as 5.

$6 \times 5 = n$
$n = 30$

Use at least 3 terms from the Word List to describe Seth's comparison.

Set A | pages 225–232

Write an equation for each comparison. Find the value of the variable that makes the equation true.

k is 9 times as many as 3.

$k = 9 \times 3$ $k = 27$

m is 6 more than 21.

$m = 6 + 21$ $m = 27$

There are 30 apples and 6 bananas in a basket. How many times as many apples as bananas are in the basket?

Let t = the number of times as many apples as bananas.

t times as many as 6 is 30.

$t \times 6 = 30$

Since $5 \times 6 = 30$, there are 5 times as many apples as bananas in the basket.

Remember to use addition or subtraction when you know how much more, and multiplication or division when you know how many times as many.

Reteaching

Write and solve an equation to match each comparison.

1. x is 21 more than 21.

2. Macon has 32 rocks in his collection. He has 4 times as many rocks as his brother. How many rocks, r, does Macon's brother have?

3. Pam has 24 pencils and 6 erasers. How many times, t, as many pencils as erasers does Pam have?

Set B | pages 233–240

At a restaurant, a children's meal costs $5, and an adult meal costs $9. Four children and 2 adults order meals. The family has a $25 gift certificate to use. How much will their total be before tax?

T = total cost of meals   *How much did the meals cost?*

$4 \times \$5 = \$20$ $2 \times \$9 = \$18$
$T = \$20 + \$18$
$T = \$38$

Using the gift certificate, how much is the total?

T

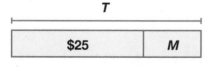

$\$38 - \$25 = M$
$M = \$13$

Remember to first find and answer any hidden questions.

1. There are 64 singers in the choir. The tenors and sopranos are in separate rows. There are 8 singers in each row. There are 4 rows of tenors. How many rows of sopranos are there?

2. Samantha has $600 saved for a trip. She buys an airline ticket for $120 and reserves a hotel room for $55 each night for 4 nights. If Samantha's trip lasts for 5 days and she spends the same amount each day, how much can Samantha spend each day?

There are 13 girls and 14 boys signed up to join volleyball. Each team needs 6 players. How many teams can be formed, and how many more players are needed to form one more team?

Find the total number of players signed up.

$13 + 14 = p$

$\qquad 27 = p$

Divide to find the number of teams that can be formed.

$27 \div 6 = t$

$\qquad 4\ R3 = t$

There are 3 students left not on a team. Subtract to find the number of players still needed to make a team.

$6 - 3 = p$

$\qquad 3 = p$

4 teams can be formed. 3 more players are needed to make one more team.

Remember to draw bar diagrams to help if needed.

Solve each multi-step problem. Write equations to show how you solve.

1. Keiva made $96 in necklace sales and half that amount in bracelet sales. How much money did Keiva make in necklace and bracelet sales?

2. A dog and cat rescue uses 40 pounds of dog food and 15 pounds of cat food to feed its animals each day. How many pounds of dog and cat food do they use in seven days?

Think about these questions to help you **make sense** of the problem.

Thinking Habits

- What do I need to find?

- What do I know?

- What's my plan for solving the problem?

- What else can I try if I get stuck?

- How can I check that my solution makes sense?

Remember to make sense of the problem before starting to solve it.

At a local shelter, each large dog can be adopted for $10 and each small dog for $5. There are 17 large dogs up for adoption. If all the dogs are adopted, the shelter will make $215. How many small dogs were at the shelter?

1. Find the hidden questions. Write equations to solve each.

2. How many small dogs are at the shelter?

1. Jason and his 3 brothers want to buy a gift for their mother. They have $314 saved. Each of them will save $17 a week until they have at least $515 for her gift. How much money will they save after 3 weeks? Will they have enough money to buy the gift?

A. What are the hidden questions?

B. Write an equation that can be used to answer each hidden question. Then solve.

C. Write and solve an equation to find how much money they will save after 3 weeks. Will they have enough to buy the gift? Explain.

2. Marco ordered 2 reclining chairs for $230 each and a coffee table for $350. The shipping cost is $100. Marco is going to pay off his bill in 5 equal payments. How much is each of Marco's payments?

---

3. Mitchell wants to beat the record for the most points scored in a season. This season, he has scored 51 points. If he scores 27 points at each of the next 7 games, he will break the record by 1 point. How many total points will break the record by 1 point?

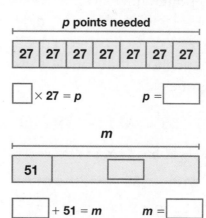

p points needed

| 27 | 27 | 27 | 27 | 27 | 27 | 27 |

$\boxed{} \times 27 = p$ $p = \boxed{}$

m

| 51 | | $\boxed{}$ |

$\boxed{} + 51 = m$ $m = \boxed{}$

Mitchell will break the record by 1 point if he scores a total of $\boxed{}$ points.

4. Select all the sentences that describe a comparison using multiplication.

☐ 9 is 3 times as many as *p*.

☐ 27 more than *r* is 41.

☐ A bus can travel 3 times as fast as a boat.

☐ It costs *d* dollars for 9 packages.

☐ There are 4 times as many girls as boys.

---

5. Choose the correct word from the box to complete each statement.

more than	times as many as

45 is 9 [＿＿＿＿＿＿] 5.

120 is 68 [＿＿＿＿＿＿] 52.

86 is 12 [＿＿＿＿＿＿] 74.

33 is 3 [＿＿＿＿＿＿] 11.

---

6. Dee has $120 to spend. She went to the grocery store and spent $55. She then bought 3 potted flowers for $18 each at the nursery. How much money did Dee have left? Select each correct equation or set of equations that could be used to solve the question.

☐ $120 − $55 = M; M − (3 × $18)

☐ $120 − $55 − (3 × $18) = M

☐ (3 × $18) − $55 − $120 = M

☐ ($120 − $55) − (3 × $18) = M

☐ $120 + $55 − (3 × $18) = M

---

7. Darcy ordered 18 boxes of red balloons and 12 boxes of blue balloons for a party. She ordered a total of 240 balloons. How many balloons are in each box?

Ⓐ 6

Ⓑ 8

Ⓒ 7

Ⓓ 9

---

8. Select all of the sentences that are true for the number 9.

☐ 18 × __ = 162

☐ 20 more than __ = 180

☐ __ times as many as 16 is 145.

☐ 315 is __ times as many as 35.

☐ 16 × __ = 128

---

9. Select all the expressions that are equal to the product of 14 and 9.

☐ (2 × 7) + 9

☐ 9 times as many as 14

☐ 14 × 9

☐ 14 more than 9

☐ 9 less than 14

---

10. Maggie collected 63 pounds of paper for recycling. Carl collected 9 pounds. How many times as many pounds did Maggie collect as Carl?

Ⓐ 3 times

Ⓑ 5 times

Ⓒ 7 times

Ⓓ 8 times

Name_____

Ski Jumping

Jackie and her older brother Robert went skiing. The **Ski Jumping** table shows their best jumps, including the distance they jumped and the total length of their run.

Ski Jumping		
Distance		
Feature	**Robert**	**Jackie**
Jump distance	297 feet	189 feet
Total length	3 times the jump distance	3 times the jump distance

1. Jackie wants to find how much farther Robert's run was than her run.

Part A

What is the total length of Robert's run? Draw a bar diagram and write and solve an equation to represent the problem. Does this situation use addition or multiplication to compare?

Part B

How much farther was Robert's run than Jackie's run? Write equations to represent each step of the problem. Tell what your variables represent.

2. Jackie's run was the same on two different jumps. In the first, she jumped 145 feet and went an additional 167 feet after the jump. In the second, she jumped 135 feet. How many feet, f, did she go after the jump?

3. Use the **Beginner Jump** information to find how much longer the total length of the ski jump hill for an advanced jump is than a beginner jump. The advanced jump distance is 408 feet.

> **Beginner Jump**
>
> The advanced jump distance is 8 times the beginner jump distance.
>
> The total length of a beginner jump hill is 3 times the beginner jump distance.

Part A

What are the hidden questions you need to answer to solve the problem? Name a variable for each question.

Part B

How much longer is d, the total length of an advanced jump hill, than a beginner jump hill? Write equations and explain how to solve the hidden questions and the original question.

Factors and Multiples

Essential Questions: How can you use arrays or multiplication to find the factors of a number? How can you identify prime and composite numbers? How can you find multiples of a number?

Animals have traits that allow them to survive in their habitats.

A penguins' dark feathers absorb heat from the sun to keep them warm in cold climates.

Penguins live in some of the coldest places on Earth! Here is a project on the animal kingdom and multiples.

enVision STEM Project: Analyzing the Animal Kingdom

Do Research As a defense against the cold, emperor penguins huddle together in large groups. Use the Internet or other sources to research how this helps them protect each other and their chicks.

Journal: Write a Report Include what you found. Also in your report:

- Suppose 64 penguins form a huddle to keep warm. Use a grid to draw all the possible arrays for 64.

- If a huddle of 72 penguins breaks apart, how many different ways can the penguins form equal groups? Is 72 prime or composite? Write the factor pairs of 72 to show all the ways the penguins can form equal groups.

Name _____

Review What You Know

Vocabulary

Choose the best term from the box.
Write it on the blank.

• dividend	• product
• divisor	• quotient

1. The _quotient_ is the answer to a division problem.

2. The number being divided is the _divisor_.

3. The _dividend_ is the number that tells into how many groups something is being divided.

Multiplication

Find each product.

4. $8 \times 4 = 32$ 5. $17 \times 6 = 102$ 6. $304 \times 9 = 2736$

7. $555 \times 5 = 2775$ 8. $22 \times 26 = 527$ 9. $33 \times 11 = 363$

10. $56 \times 70 = 770$ 11. $36 \times 91 = 3276$ 12. $27 \times 48 = 1296$

13. $56 \times 13 = 728$ 14. $12 \times 19 = 228$ 15. $36 \times 16 = 576$

Division

Find each quotient.

16. $27 \div 3 = 9$ 17. $56 \div 8 = 7$ 18. $36 \div 4 = 9$

19. $72 \div 9 = 8$ 20. $39 \div 3 = 13$ 21. $64 \div 4 = 16$

22. $105 \div 5 = 21$ 23. $824 \div 4 = 206$ 24. $942 \div 3 = 314$

25. $9,156 \div 3 = 3052$ 26. $2,156 \div 4 = 539$ 27. $4,136 \div 8 = 517$

Problem Solving

28. **Model with Math** Cecilia bought 2 sandwiches last week and 4 sandwiches this week. She spent a total of $42. If each sandwich costs the same amount, how much did Cecilia spend on each sandwich? Write and solve equations.

$4 + 2 = 6$ $42 \div 6 = 7$ each sandwica

Name_____

PROJECT
7A

Where is Mammoth Cave National Park?

Project: Model a Campground

PROJECT
7B

How many people can fill a college basketball arena?

Project: Create a Basketball Arena

PROJECT
7C

How many arrays of potted plants do you see?

Project: Design a Plant Array for a Store Display

Before watching the video, think:

People who work in a grocery store do many different jobs. Some employees make stacks of things for people to buy. Some employees clean up messes when people drop jars of tomato sauce. If an employee made a stack of jars, probably another employee would come around soon to clean up the mess.

I can ...
model with math to solve a problem that involves estimating and using factors and multiples.

ⓒ **Mathematical Practices** MP.4 Also MP.3, MP.7
Content Standards 4.OA.B.4 Also 4.OA.A.2, 4.OA.A.3, 4.NBT.B.6

Name_____

☆ ☆
Solve & Share

Fourth graders at Ames School have 24 carpet squares. What are all the different ways they can organize the carpet squares into a rectangular array? **Solve this problem any way you choose.**

I can ...
find the factor pairs of a whole number.

You can use grid paper or tiles, to find all the possible arrays.

© **Content Standards** 4.OA.B.4 Also 4.NBT.B.5
Mathematical Practices MP.2, MP.3, MP.7

Look Back! **Look for Relationships** What patterns do you see in the arrays?

How Can You Use Arrays to Find the Factor Pairs of a Number?

A

The music director is trying to find the best way to arrange the chairs for a performance. The chairs must be arranged in a rectangular array. How many different ways can the chairs be arranged into a rectangular array? Use grids to show all the ways the chairs can be arranged.

Pairs of whole numbers multiplied together to find a product are called factor pairs. Think about multiplication to decompose a number into its factors.

12 chairs

B 1 row of 12 chairs
12 rows of 1 chair

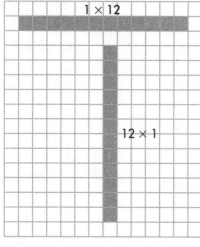

1 × 12

12 × 1

1 and 12 are a factor pair.

C 2 rows of 6 chairs
6 rows of 2 chairs

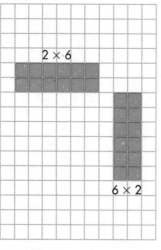

2 × 6

6 × 2

2 and 6 are a factor pair.

D 3 rows of 4 chairs
4 rows of 3 chairs

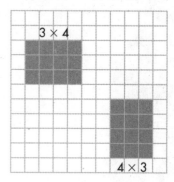

3 × 4

4 × 3

3 and 4 are a factor pair.

There are 6 possible ways the 12 chairs can be arranged.

Convince Me! Critique Reasoning Blake says, "Greater numbers will always have more factors." Do you agree? Explain.

Practice Tools Assessment

Guided Practice

Do You Understand?

1. How are the lengths of the sides of the arrays shown on the grids on the previous page related to the factors of 12?

2. What are the lengths of the sides of the arrays that show how 5 chairs can be arranged?

Do You Know How?

For **3–4**, find all of the factor pairs for each number. You can use grids to help.

3. 6   4. 16

For **5–6**, find the factors of each number.

5. 45   6. 30

Independent Practice

For **7–8**, use the grids to find all the possible arrays for each number. Use the arrays to help write the factors.

7. 9

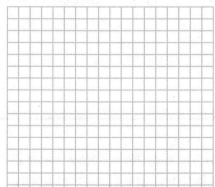

8. 14

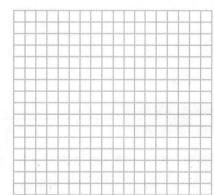

For **9–14**, use grids to find the factor pair or pairs for each number.

9. 5   10. 25

11. 8   12. 36

13. 23   14. 27

Problem Solving

15. Reasoning Use the grid to find two numbers that have 2 and 3 as factors.

Draw arrays with side lengths that have 2 and 3 as factors.

16. The dwarf planet Pluto takes about 90,403 days to orbit the sun. Write this number in expanded form and using number names.

17. David makes 17 dollars in an hour and works 25 hours each week. Linda makes 25 dollars in an hour and works 17 hours each week. How much do David and Linda make together each week? What property of multiplication does this represent?

18. What do you notice about the number of possible arrays and the number of factors of 22?

19. Higher Order Thinking Jane says 5 is a factor of every whole number that has a 5 in the ones place. Fred says 5 is a factor of every whole number that has a 0 in the ones place. Who is correct? Explain.

 Assessment Practice

20. Which of the following are factors of both 18 and 42? Select all that apply.

☐ 1
☐ 3
☐ 4
☐ 6
☐ 14

21. Which of the numbers below have 2, 3, and 4 as factors? Select all that apply.

☐ 86
☐ 72
☐ 36
☐ 32
☐ 24

Name _____

Activity

Solve & Share

Jared has 20 flowers. He wants to plant all of the flowers in equal rows in his garden. What are the different ways Jared can arrange the flowers in equal rows? **Solve this problem any way you choose.**

I can ...
use multiplication to find the factor pairs for a whole number.

© **Content Standards** 4.OA.B.4 Also 4.NBT.B.5
Mathematical Practices MP.1, MP.3, MP.4

You can use what you know about multiplying whole numbers to find equal rows.

Look Back! **Make Sense and Persevere** How can you check you have found all the different ways Jared can plant his flowers?

How Can You Use Multiplication to Find the Factors of a Number?

A

Jean wants to arrange her action figures in equal-size groups. What are all the ways Jean can arrange her action figures?

 Jean can think of all the factor pairs of 16. Factor pairs are two whole numbers that when multiplied give you a certain product.

16 action figures

B

1 group of 16

16 groups of 1

Jean can arrange 1 group of 16 figures or 16 groups of 1 figure.

$1 \times 16 = 16$
$16 \times 1 = 16$

So, 1 and 16 are factors of 16.

C

8 groups of 2

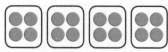

2 groups of 8

Jean can arrange 8 groups of 2 figures or 2 groups of 8 figures.

$2 \times 8 = 16$
$8 \times 2 = 16$

So, 2 and 8 are factors of 16.

D

4 groups of 4

Jean can arrange 4 groups of 4 figures. 4 is a factor of 16.

$4 \times 4 = 16$

The factor pairs for 16 are 1 and 16, 2 and 8, and 4 and 4.

Convince Me! **Construct Arguments** How do you know there are no other factors for 16 other than 1, 2, 4, 8, and 16? Explain.

Name _____

☆ Guided Practice

Do You Understand?

1. Jean bought 7 more action figures. What are the different equal-size groups she can make now?

2. What factor besides 1 does every even number have?

Do You Know How?

For **3–6**, write the factors of each number. Use counters to help.

3. 2   **4.** 20

5. 28   **6.** 54

Independent Practice ☆

> Remember, the factors of a number always include 1 and the number.

Leveled Practice For **7–12**, write the factor pairs for each number.

7. 34
_____ and 34
2 and _____

8. 39
1 and _____
_____ and 13

9. 61
1 and _____

10. 14
_____ and _____
_____ and _____

11. 22
_____ and _____
_____ and _____

12. 51
_____ and _____
_____ and _____

For **13–21**, write the factors of each number. Use counters to help as needed.

13. 6

14. 32

15. 83

16. 11

17. 49

18. 25

19. 30

20. 63

21. 19

Problem Solving

22. Irene wants to list the factors for 88. She writes 2, 4, 8, 11, 22, 44, and 88. Is Irene correct? Explain.

23. enVision® STEM The roots of a plant are often the largest part of the plant. Winter rye can grow combined root tissue well over 984,000 feet in length. Write this number in expanded form.

24. Model with Math A restaurant receives a shipment of 5,000 ketchup packets. In one week, they use 1,824 packets. The next week, they use 2,352 packets. Write and solve equations to find how many ketchup packets the restaurant has left.

25. Any number that has 9 as a factor also has 3 as a factor. Why is this?

26. Higher Order Thinking A mother manatee, pictured to the right, is three times as long as her baby manatee.

a. How long is her baby manatee? Write and solve an equation.

b. If a blue whale is 9 times as long as the manatee shown, how much longer is a blue whale than the manatee? Write and solve equations.

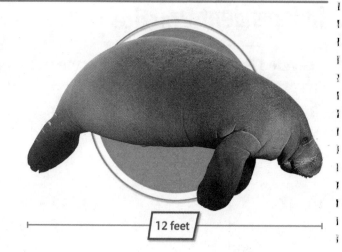

12 feet

✅ Assessment Practice

27. Which number has 3 and 29 as one of its factor pairs?

   Ⓐ 3

   Ⓑ 17

   Ⓒ 67

   Ⓓ 87

28. A store manager wants to display 45 cans of soup in an array. Which of the following shows 3 ways the cans could be displayed?

   Ⓐ $1 \times 9, 9 \times 5, 3 \times 15$

   Ⓑ $15 \times 3, 9 \times 1, 5 \times 9$

   Ⓒ $5 \times 9, 3 \times 15, 9 \times 5$

   Ⓓ $45 \times 1, 15 \times 1, 9 \times 1$

Name _____

Activity

★ Solve & Share ★

A closet company sells wooden storage cubicles. Jane bought 24 cubicles. She wants to arrange them in a rectangular array. What are all of the different ways Jane can arrange them, using all of her cubicles? Explain how you know you found them all.

I can ...
use repeated reasoning to generalize how to solve similar problems.

ⓒ **Mathematical Practices** MP.8 Also MP.1, MP.2, MP.3, MP.6
Content Standards 4.OA.B.4 Also 4.NBT.B.5

DATA

These cubicles are arranged in an array.	These cubicles are not arranged in an array.
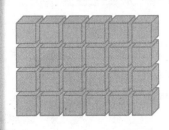	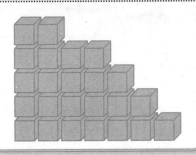

Thinking Habits

Be a good thinker! These questions can help you.

• Are any calculations repeated?

• Can I generalize from examples?

• What shortcuts do I notice?

Look Back! **Generalize** Do you need to try all numbers from 1 to 24 to be sure you have all the factor pairs for 24? Explain.

Essential Question

How Can You Use Repeated Reasoning to Find All the Factors for a Number?

A

A new city park is opening. The gardener needs to select 15 trees from a nursery and plant the trees in a rectangular array. What are all the different ways the gardener can plant the trees?

Select 15 trees to plant

Here's my thinking.

Can you look for a general method to solve this problem?

I can find all the possible factors of 15 that can be arranged in a rectangular array.

B

How can I make a generalization from repeated reasoning?

I can

- look for things that repeat in a problem.

- look for shortcuts.

- generalize from the example.

C

To find all of the factors of 15, I divide **15** by divisors starting with 1. Then I use the Commutative Property to write two multiplication equations.

$1 \times 15 = 15$ and $15 \times 1 = 15$
2 is not a factor
$3 \times 5 = 15$ and $5 \times 3 = 15$
4 is not a factor
$5 \times 3 = 15$ and $3 \times 5 = 15$

I already found the factor paired with **5**, 3×5 and 5×3.

When factor pairs start repeating, you can make a general statement, or generalize, that all the factors of a number are found.

The gardener has 4 different ways to plant the trees: 1×15, 15×1, 5×3, and 3×5 arrays.

Convince Me! **Construct Arguments** The diagram shows all the factor pairs of 24. Use the diagram to justify the conclusion that when factor pairs start repeating, you know you have found all the factors of a number.

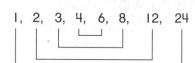

1, 2, 3, 4, 6, 8, 12, 24

Practice Tools Assessment

☆ Guided Practice

Generalize

Ms. Maribel wants to arrange the 20 desks in her classroom into rows with the same number of desks in each row. She wants at least 2, but not more than 8 rows.

When you generalize, you find general methods and shortcuts to help solve a problem.

1. What are the factor pairs for 20? Explain how you know you have found them all.

2. Find the ways Ms. Maribel can arrange the desks.

☆ Independent Practice ☆

Generalize

Kevin invited 15 friends to his birthday party. They played a game where everyone had to separate into groups. Each group had the same number of children. The game could not be played with all 16 children in one group and each group had to have more than 1 child.

3. List the factor pairs of 16 and then find the different ways Kevin and his friends could divide into groups.

4. Why does 16 have an odd number of factors?

5. Can you stop checking for factor pairs when you find a pair that repeats? Explain.

Problem Solving

Store Displays

A pet store needs 3 displays with the products shown. The boxes of kitty litter need to be stacked with the same number of boxes in each row. There needs to be at least 3 rows with at least 3 boxes in each row. What are all the ways the boxes of kitty litter could be stacked?

50 fish bowls

48 boxes of kitty litter

88 bags of dog food

6. **Make Sense and Persevere** What quantities are given in the problem and what do the numbers mean?

When you notice repetition in calculations, you can generalize to help solve problems.

7. **Reasoning** What are the factor pairs for 48?

8. **Be Precise** What are all the ways the boxes of kitty litter can be stacked with at least 3 rows with at least 3 boxes in each row?

☆ Solve & Share ☆

Max has 2 red tiles, 3 blue tiles, 4 yellow tiles, and 8 green tiles. How many different rectangular arrays of each color can Max make? Explain how you know you found all the arrays. **Solve this problem any way you choose.**

I can ...
use factors to determine if a whole number is prime or composite.

© **Content Standards** 4.OA.B.4 Also 4.NBT.B.5
Mathematical Practices MP.2, MP.3, MP.8

You can use reasoning. Find the factors of each number of tiles to help find the number of arrays.

Look Back! What do you notice about the factors of each number of color tiles and the number of arrays?

Essential Question

How Can You Identify Prime and Composite Numbers?

A

The data table lists the factors for 2, 3, 4, 5, and 6. What do you notice about the factors for 5? What do you notice about the factors for 6?

DATA

Number	Factors
2	1, 2
3	1, 3
4	1, 2, 4
5	1, 5
6	1, 2, 3, 6

A prime number is a whole number greater than 1 that has exactly two factors, 1 and itself.

A composite number is a whole number greater than 1 that has more than 2 factors.

B **Prime Numbers**

5 is a prime number.
It has only 2 factors, 1 and itself.

$1 \times 5 = 5$ $5 \times 1 = 5$

 The number 1 is a special number. It is neither prime nor composite.

C **Composite Numbers**

6 is a composite number.
The factors for 6 are 1, 2, 3, and 6.

$1 \times 6 = 6$ $6 \times 1 = 6$

$2 \times 3 = 6$ $3 \times 2 = 6$

Convince Me! **Generalize** Can a number be both prime and composite? Explain.

Name_____

☆ Guided Practice

Do You Understand?

1. What is the only even prime number?

2. Write an odd number that is not prime. What makes it a composite number?

3. Roger has 47 cars. Can he group the cars in more than 2 ways?

Do You Know How?

For **4–9**, tell whether each number is prime or composite.

4. 32   **5.** 51

6. 73   **7.** 21

8. 95   **9.** 29

A number is composite if it has more than 2 factors.

Independent Practice

Leveled Practice For **10–19**, tell whether each number is prime or composite.

10. 7

11. 10

12. 12   **13.** 97   **14.** 90   **15.** 31

16. 11   **17.** 44   **18.** 3   **19.** 59

Problem Solving

For **20-21**, use the graph at the right.

20. Which type of flower received a prime number of votes?

21. How many votes are represented by the picture graph?

Favorite Flowers

Daffodils	🌼 🌼 🌼
Daisies	🌸 🌸 🌸
Tulips	🌷 🌷 🌷 🌷 🌷

Key: Each flower icon equals 2 votes.

---

22. Critique Reasoning Maria says every number in the nineties is composite. Jackie says 1 number in the nineties is prime. Who is correct? Explain your answer.

23. Critique Reasoning Greta says the product of two prime numbers must also be prime. Joan disagreed. Who is correct?

---

24. Janelle has 342 pennies, 62 nickels, and 12 dimes. If Janelle exchanges her coins for dollars, how many dollars will she have? How many cents will remain?

25. Higher Order Thinking Why is 1 neither a prime number nor a composite number?

✅ Assessment Practice

26. Select all the groups of numbers that are prime.

- ☐ 17, 19, 53
- ☐ 37, 43, 79
- ☐ 52, 67, 99
- ☐ 63, 72, 83
- ☐ 59, 89, 97

27. Select all the expressions with sums that are composite.

- ☐ 17 + 25
- ☐ 33 + 51
- ☐ 16 + 83
- ☐ 29 + 32
- ☐ 47 + 29

Name _____

Activity

☆ ☆
Solve & Share

There are 9 players on the golf practice range. If each player practices with the same number of golf balls, how many balls might be in play at the same time? **Solve this problem any way you choose.**

I can ...
use multiplication to find multiples of a number.

© **Content Standards** 4.OA.B.4 Also 4.NBT.B.5
Mathematical Practices MP.2, MP.3

You can use reasoning. What do you notice about the number of balls in play?

Golf Balls in Play	
Balls per Player	**Balls in Play**
1	$1 \times 9 = 9$ balls in play
2	$2 \times 9 = 18$ balls in play
3	$3 \times 9 = 27$ balls in play
4	
5	

Look Back! Can you show all of the answers for the problem? Explain.

Essential Question

How Can You Find Multiples of a Number?

A

It takes 8 minutes for Car A to make one full turn on the Ferris wheel. If the Ferris wheel continues to turn at the same speed for the next hour, at what times during the hour will Car A return to the starting point?

Starting point

A multiple is the product of a given factor and a whole number.

B Step 1

One full turn takes 8 minutes.

$$1 \times 8 = 8$$

8 is a multiple of 1 and 8 because $1 \times 8 = 8$.

Car A is back at the starting point after 8 minutes.

C Step 2

Two full turns take 16 minutes.

$$2 \times 8 = 16$$

Car A is back at the starting point after another 8 minutes.

2 and 8 are factors of 16. 16 is a multiple of 2 and 8.

D Step 3

Car A is at the starting point every 8 minutes after that:

$$3 \times 8 = 24$$
$$4 \times 8 = 32$$
$$5 \times 8 = 40$$
$$6 \times 8 = 48$$
$$7 \times 8 = 56$$

During the hour, Car A returns to the starting point after 8, 16, 24, 32, 40, 48, and 56 minutes.

Convince Me! **Reasoning** What is the next multiple after 56? Explain why it is **NOT** used.

Another Example!

Factors are numbers that when multiplied together give a product.
A whole number is a multiple of each of its factors.

Factors of 24 are 1, 2, 3, 4, 6, 8, 12, and 24.
24 is a multiple of 1, 2, 3, 4, 6, 8, 12, and 24.

☆ Guided Practice

Do You Understand?

1. If the Ferris wheel in the example on the previous page turns at the same speed, will Car A return to the starting point at 75 minutes? Explain.

2. Suppose the Ferris wheel speeds up so it makes one full turn every 6 minutes. When will Car A return to the starting point if the Ferris wheel continues to turn for one half hour?

Do You Know How?

For **3–4**, write five multiples of each number.

3. 2   **4.** 9

For **5–6**, tell whether the first number is a multiple of the second number.

5. 14, 2   **6.** 3, 18

☆ Independent Practice ☆

For **7–14**, write five multiples of each number.

> You can skip count to find multiples of numbers. Be Precise.

7. 7   **8.** 4   **9.** 6   **10.** 5

11. 11   **12.** 1   **13.** 20   **14.** 15

For **15–18**, tell whether the first number is a multiple of the second number.

15. 44, 6   **16.** 25, 5   **17.** 30, 6   **18.** 54, 9

Problem Solving

19. Name all the numbers of which 45 is a multiple.

20. Critique Reasoning Lindsay says all numbers that are multiples of 4 have 2 as a factor. Is Lindsay correct? Explain.

21. Trisha bought bags of tennis balls. There are eight tennis balls in each bag. Could Trisha have 75 tennis balls? Explain.

22. Higher Order Thinking Gerri says that if a number is a multiple of 9 it is also a multiple of 3. Do you agree? Explain.

23. Describe how 20,000 and 2,000 are related.

24. Isabel wrote this mystery problem: The quotient is a multiple of 6. The dividend is a multiple of 9. The divisor is a factor of 12. Write one possible equation to Isabel's mystery problem.

Assessment Practice

25. Latifa and John played a game of multiples. Each player picks a number card and says a multiple of that number. Latifa picked a 9. Write all the multiples of 9 from the box.

9	17	29
36	45	51

Multiples of 9

26. A roller-coaster ride completes a full loop every 3 minutes. Seth listed multiples of 3 to determine when the ride would be back at its starting point. Write all the multiples of 3 from the box.

9	11	12
13	19	33

Multiples of 3

Shade a path from **START** to **FINISH**.
Follow the sums and differences that are
correct. You can only move up, down,
right, or left.

I can ...

add and subtract multi-digit
whole numbers.

Ⓒ **Content Standard** 4.NBT.B.4
Mathematical Practices MP.2, MP.6,
MP.7

Start				
573 + 417 **990**	685 − 559 **137**	808 + 123 **921**	609 − 541 **48**	501 + 469 **170**
491 − 188 **303**	347 + 607 **954**	948 − 558 **410**	505 + 125 **620**	987 − 696 **311**
764 + 346 **1,000**	994 − 405 **589**	874 + 721 **1,595**	894 − 455 **449**	369 + 290 **669**
668 − 485 **253**	762 + 901 **2,663**	941 − 725 **216**	640 + 89 **729**	537 − 271 **806**
119 + 679 **698**	977 − 239 **642**	987 + 111 **998**	812 − 99 **713**	335 + 25 **360**

Finish

Glossary

Word List

- array
- composite number
- factor
- factor pairs
- generalization
- multiple
- prime number
- whole number

Understand Vocabulary

1. Cross out the numbers that are **NOT** factors of 16.

   1   2   3   4   8

2. Cross out the numbers that are **NOT** multiples of 3.

   3   6   9   13   23

3. Cross out the numbers that are **NOT** whole numbers.

   $\frac{1}{4}$ $\frac{1}{2}$ 7 $17\frac{1}{5}$ 6,219

4. Cross out the numbers that are **NOT** factor pairs for 24.

  1 and 24   2 and 12   3 and 6   4 and 8   4 and 6

Label each example with a term from the Word List.

5. 13 _____

6. 12 _____

7. ●●● _____

8. When factor pairs begin repeating,
I have found all the pairs for a number. _____

Use Vocabulary in Writing

9. Marisol says 23 is both a prime and a composite number because 2 and 3
are both prime. Use at least 3 terms from the Word List to explain the error
in Marisol's reasoning.

Set A | pages 261–264

Draw arrays to find all the factor pairs for 8.

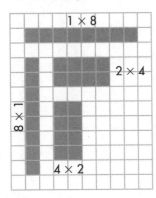

1 row of 8
8 rows of 1

2 rows of 4
4 rows of 2

The factor pairs for 8 are 1 and 8, 2 and 4.

Remember that 1 is a factor of every number.

Use grid paper to find the factor pairs for each number.

1. 26

2. 9

3. 37

4. 24

5. 19

Set B | pages 265–268

Find the factor pairs for 12.

1 and 12
2 and 6
3 and 4

The factors of 12 are 1, 2, 3, 4, 6, and 12.

Remember you can use counters or grids to make arrays and find the factors of a number.

Find the factors of each number.

1. 45

2. 40

3. 56

4. 63

Set C | pages 269–272

Think about these questions to help you use **repeated reasoning**.

Thinking Habits

• Are any calculations repeated?

• Can I generalize from examples?

• What shortcuts do I notice?

Remember to look for repeating factors when dividing to find the factor pairs of a number.

A valet has 34 cars to park in a rectangular array.

1. What are the different ways the valet could park the cars?

2. How do you know when you can stop looking for factors of a number?

Set D | pages 273–276

Is 49 prime or composite?

To determine if 49 is prime or composite, find whether 49 has factors other than 1 and 49.

49 is composite because it is divisible by 7.

$49 = 7 \times 7$

Remember you can use an array to determine if a number is prime or composite.

Tell whether each number is prime or composite.

1. 13
2. 25
3. 55
4. 2
5. 29
6. 23
7. 64
8. 99
9. 5
10. 21

Set E | pages 277–280

Find five multiples of 7.

Use multiplication.

$7 \times 1 = 7$

$7 \times 2 = 14$

$7 \times 3 = 21$

$7 \times 4 = 28$

$7 \times 5 = 35$

You can skip count to find multiples of a number.

Remember that to find multiples of a number, multiply the number by any whole number.

Find five multiples of each number.

1. 3
2. 6
3. 4
4. 9

Tell whether the first number is a multiple of the second number.

5. 22, 2
6. 29, 3
7. 25, 5
8. 40, 8

Name_____

1. Courtney has 36 photos to arrange on a gallery wall.

A. How many arrays can Courtney make with the 36 photos? List all the possible arrays.

B. How many factors are there for 36? Write them. What do you notice about the number of factors of 36 and the number of arrays Courtney can make with the photos?

C. Write all the factor pairs for 36. Is 36 prime or composite? Explain.

2. Determine whether the numbers in each list are **factors** or **multiples** of 16.

	Factors	Multiples
16, 48	❏	❏
1, 2, 4	❏	❏
8, 16	❏	❏
32, 64	❏	❏

3. Which statement is true?

Ⓐ The only factors of 3 are 3 and 1; therefore, 3 is prime.

Ⓑ The only factors of 4 are 4 and 1; therefore, 4 is prime.

Ⓒ The only factors of 5 are 5 and 1; therefore, 5 is composite.

Ⓓ The only factors of 8 are 8 and 1; therefore, 8 is composite.

4. Determine if each number is prime or composite. Then write all the factors for each number.

19, 33

5. Select all equations that have a dividend that is a multiple of 4 and a quotient that is a factor of 18.

☐ $8 \div 4 = 2$ ☐ $48 \div 8 = 6$

☐ $18 \div 6 = 3$ ☐ $16 \div 4 = 4$

☐ $36 \div 3 = 12$

6. Write 3 multiples and 3 factors for 24.

7. Write two multiples of 3 that have a factor of 7. Use equations to explain.

8. Select all the true statements.

☐ 33 has more than two factors.

☐ All of the factors of 34 are even numbers.

☐ 35 has exactly two factors.

☐ 3 is a factor of 36.

☐ 37 is a prime number.

☐ 38 is a composite number.

9. Martika says factors and multiples are related. Use the equation $6 \times 7 = 42$ to describe the relationship between factors and multiples.

10. Which lists all the factors of 25 that are also prime?

Ⓐ 1, 25

Ⓑ 5

Ⓒ 1, 10, 25

Ⓓ 5, 25

11. Carter lives on a street where all the house numbers are multiples of 6. Name two possible house numbers between 70 and 80. Explain.

12. Write the factors of 30 that are also prime numbers.

13. Javier says all odd numbers greater than 2 and less than 20 are prime. Find an odd number greater than 2 and less than 20 that is **NOT** prime. Explain why the number is not prime.

Name_____

Arranging Cars to Sell

Ms. Ortiz owns a car dealership. The dealership has the inventory of cars listed in the **Ortiz Car Dealership** table.

1. Ms. Ortiz wants to arrange all of the trucks in the front lot. She would like to have same number of trucks in each row.

Part A

How many different ways can the trucks be arranged in the front lot if the same number of trucks are parked in each row?

DATA	Ortiz Car Dealership	
	Type of Vehicle	Number Dealership Has
	Compact	40
	Sedan	36
	SUV	23
	Truck	15

Part B

What are all the ways the trucks can be arranged? Draw and label the different arrays.

Part C

Ms. Ortiz would like the arrangement to have more than 2 rows of trucks but less than 6 rows. What are the ways the trucks can be arranged? Explain.

2. As Ms. Ortiz sells sedans, those sedans remaining are parked in different arrangements.

Complete the **Arranging Sedans** table to find the number of ways Ms. Ortiz can arrange each number of sedans in the front lot so there are at least 2 rows with the same number of sedans in each row and more than one sedan in each row.

Arranging Sedans

Sedans Sold	Number Left	Number of Arrangements	Arrangements
1			
2			
3			
4			
5			
6			
7			

Glossary

A

acute angle An angle that is open less than a right angle.

acute triangle A triangle that has three acute angles.

addends The numbers that are added together to find a sum.
Example: $2 + 7 = 9$

Addends

algorithm A set of steps used to solve a math problem.

angle A figure formed by two rays that have the same endpoint.

angle measure The number of degrees in an angle.

area The number of square units needed to cover a region.

area model A rectangle used to model multiplication and division of whole numbers.

array A way of displaying objects in rows and columns.

Associative Property of Addition Addends can be regrouped and the sum remains the same.

Associative Property of Multiplication Factors can be regrouped and the product stays the same.

B

bar diagram A tool used to help understand and solve word problems.

bar graph A graph using bars to show data.

benchmark fraction A known fraction that is commonly used for estimating.
Examples: $\frac{1}{4}, \frac{1}{3}, \frac{1}{2}, \frac{2}{3},$ and $\frac{3}{4}$

billions A period of three places to the left of the millions period.

breaking apart Mental math method used to rewrite a number as the sum of numbers to form an easier problem.

C

capacity The amount a container can hold, measured in liquid units.

center A point within a circle that is the same distance from all points on a circle.

centimeter (cm) A metric unit used to measure length. 100 centimeters = 1 meter

century A unit of time equal to 100 years.

circle A closed plane figure in which all the points are the same distance from a point called the center.

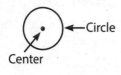
Circle

Center

common denominator A number that is the denominator of two or more fractions.

common factor A number that is a factor of two or more given numbers.

Commutative Property of Addition Numbers can be added in any order and the sum remains the same.

Commutative Property of Multiplication Factors can be multiplied in any order and the product stays the same.

compare Decide if one number is greater than, less than, or equal to another number.

compatible numbers Numbers that are easy to compute mentally.

compensation Choosing numbers close to the numbers in a problem to make the computation easier, and then adjusting the answer for the numbers chosen.

compose To combine parts.

composite number A whole number greater than 1 with more than two factors.

conjecture Statement that is believed to be true but has not been proven.

count down Counting down the lesser number from the greater number to find the difference of the two numbers.

count up Counting up from the lesser number to the greater number to find the difference of two numbers.

cube A solid figure with six identical squares as its faces.

cubic unit The volume of a cube that measures 1 unit on each edge.

cup (c) A customary unit of capacity. 1 cup = 8 fluid ounces

customary units of measure Units of measure that are used in the United States.

D

data Pieces of collected information.

day A unit of time equal to 24 hours.

decade A unit of time equal to 10 years.

decimal A number with one or more digits to the right of the decimal point.

decimal point A dot used to separate dollars from cents in money or to separate ones from tenths in a number.

decimeter (dm) A metric unit of length equal to 10 centimeters.

decompose To break into parts.

degree (°) A unit of measure for angles. $1° = \frac{1}{360}$ of a circle. Also a unit of measure for temperature.

denominator The number below the fraction bar in a fraction that represents the total number of equal parts in one whole.

difference The answer when subtracting two numbers.

digits The symbols used to write a number: 0, 1, 2, 3, 4, 5, 6, 7, 8, and 9.

Distributive Property Multiplying a sum (or difference) by a number is the same as multiplying each number in the sum (or difference) by that number and adding (or subtracting) the products. *Example:* $(3 \times 21) = (3 \times 20) + (3 \times 1)$

divide An operation to find the number in each group or the number of equal groups.

dividend The number to be divided.

divisibility rules The rules that state when a number is divisible by another number.

divisible Can be divided by another number without leaving a remainder. *Example:* 10 is divisible by 2

divisor The number by which another number is divided.
Example: $32 \div 4 = 8$
↑
Divisor

dot plot A type of line plot that uses dots to indicate the number of times a response occurred.

elapsed time The amount of time between the beginning of an event and the end of the event.

equation A number sentence that uses the equal sign (=) to show that two expressions have the same value. *Example:* $9 + 3 = 12$

equilateral triangle A triangle with three sides that are the same length.

equivalent Numbers that name the same amount.

equivalent fractions Fractions that name the same region, part of a set, or part of a segment.

estimate To give an approximate value rather than an exact answer.

expanded form A number written as the sum of the values of its digits.
Example: 2,476 = 2,000 + 400 + 70 + 6

expression A mathematical phrase.
Examples: $x - 3$ or $2 + 7$

fact family A group of related facts using the same set of numbers.

factor pairs Numbers that when multiplied together give a certain product.

factors The numbers that are multiplied together to give a product.
Example: $3 \times 6 = 18$
Factors

fluid ounce (fl oz) A customary unit of capacity. 1 fluid ounce = 2 tablespoons; 8 fluid ounces = 1 cup

foot (ft) A customary unit of length.
1 foot = 12 inches

formula An equation that uses symbols to relate two or more quantities.
Example: $A = \ell \times w$

fraction A symbol, such as $\frac{2}{3}$, $\frac{5}{1}$, or $\frac{8}{5}$, used to name a part of a whole, a part of a set, or a location on a number line.

frequency The number of times that a response occurs in a set of data.

frequency table A way to display data that shows how many times a response occurs in a set of data.

gallon (gal) A customary unit of capacity. 1 gallon = 4 quarts

generalize To make a general statement.

gram (g) A metric unit of mass.
1,000 grams = 1 kilogram

greater than symbol (>) A symbol that points away from a greater number or expression. *Example:* 450 > 449

hexagon A polygon with 6 sides.

hour A unit of time equal to 60 minutes.

hundredth One part of 100 equal parts of a whole.

Identity Property of Addition The sum of any number and zero is that number.

Identity Property of Multiplication The product of any number and one is that number.

inch (in.) A customary unit of length.
12 inches = 1 foot

inequality A number sentence that uses the greater than sign (>) or the less than sign (<) to show that two expressions do not have the same value. *Example:* 5 > 3

intersecting lines Lines that pass through the same point.

interval A number which is the difference between two consecutive numbers on the scale of a graph.

inverse operations Operations that undo each other.
Examples: Adding 6 and subtracting 6;
        Multiplying by 4 and dividing
        by 4.

isosceles triangle A triangle with at least two equal sides.

key Part of a graph that tells what each symbol stands for.

kilogram (kg) A metric unit of mass equal to 1,000 grams. 1 kilogram = 1,000 grams

kilometer (km) A metric unit of length equal to 1,000 meters.
1 kilometer = 1,000 meters

leap year A calendar occurrence that happens every four years when an extra day is added to February. Leap years have 366 days.

less than symbol (<) A symbol that points towards a lesser number or expression. *Example:* 305 < 320

line A straight path of points that goes on and on in opposite directions.

line of symmetry
A line on which a figure can be folded so both halves are the same.

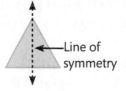
Line of symmetry

line plot A way to display data along a number line, where each dot or X represents one number in a set of data.

line segment A part of a line that has two endpoints.

line symmetric A figure that can be folded on a line to form two halves that fit exactly on top of each other.

liter (L) A metric unit of capacity.
1 liter = 1,000 milliliters

M

mass The amount of matter that something contains.

meter (m) A metric unit of length. 1 meter = 100 centimeters

metric units of measure Units of measure commonly used by scientists.

mile (mi) A customary unit of length. 1 mile = 5,280 feet

millennium (plural: millennia) A unit for measuring time equal to 1,000 years.

milligram (mg) A metric unit of mass. 1,000 milligrams = 1 gram

milliliter (mL) A metric unit of capacity. 1,000 milliliters = 1 liter

millimeter (mm) A metric unit of length. 1,000 millimeters = 1 meter

millions In a number, a period of three places to the left of the thousands period.

minute A unit of time equal to 60 seconds.

mixed number A number that has a whole number part and a fraction part.

month One of the 12 parts into which a year is divided.

multiple The product of a given whole number and any non-zero whole number.

N

number name A way to write a number in words. *Example:* Four thousand, six hundred thirty-two

numerator In a fraction, the number above the fraction bar that represents the part of the whole.

numerical expression An expression that contains numbers and at least one operation. *Example:* 35 + 12

O

obtuse angle An angle that is open more than a right angle but less than a straight angle.

obtuse triangle A triangle that has one obtuse angle.

octagon A polygon with 8 sides.

ounce (oz) A customary unit of weight. 16 ounces = 1 pound

overestimate An estimate that is greater than the exact answer.

P

parallel lines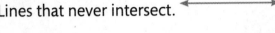
Lines that never intersect.

parallelogram
A quadrilateral that has
two pairs of parallel sides.

partial products Products found by
breaking one factor in a multiplication
problem into ones, tens, hundreds, and so
on and then multiplying each of these by
the other factor.

partial quotients A way to divide
that finds quotients in parts until only
a remainder, if any, is left.

pentagon A plane figure with 5 sides.

perimeter The distance around a figure.

period In a number, a group of three
digits, separated by commas, starting from
the right.

perpendicular lines Intersecting
lines that form right angles.

pint (pt) A customary unit of capacity.
1 pint = 2 cups

place value The value given to a place a
digit has in a number.
Example: In 3,946, the 9 is in the hundreds
place. So, the 9 has a value of 900.

point An exact location in space.

polygon A closed plane figure made up
of line segments.

pound (lb) A customary unit of weight.
1 pound = 16 ounces

prime number A whole number greater
than 1 that has exactly two factors, itself
and 1.

product The answer to a
multiplication problem.

protractor A tool used to measure and
draw angles.

Q

quadrilateral A polygon with 4 sides.

quart (qt) A customary unit of capacity.
1 quart = 2 pints

quotient The answer to a
division problem.

R

ray A part of a line that has one endpoint and continues on forever in one direction.

rectangle A quadrilateral that has four right angles.

rectangular prism A solid figure with 6 rectangular faces.

regroup To name a whole number in a different way. *Example:* 32 = 2 tens 12 ones

remainder The number that remains after the division is complete.

repeated addition A way to write a multiplication expression as an addition expression. *Example:* 3 × 5 = 5 + 5 + 5

repeating pattern Made up of shapes or numbers that form a part that repeats.

rhombus A quadrilateral that has opposite sides that are parallel and all of its sides are the same length.

right angle An angle that forms a square corner.

right triangle A triangle that has one right angle.

rounding A process that determines which multiple of 10, 100, 1,000, and so on a number is closest to.

rule A mathematical phrase that tells how numbers in a table are related.

S

scale Numbers that show the units used on a graph.

scalene triangle A triangle with no sides that are the same length.

second A unit of time. 60 seconds = 1 minute

sequence A set of numbers that follows a pattern.

side Each of the line segments of a polygon.

solid figure A figure with three dimensions that has length, width, and height.

solution The value of the variable that makes an equation true.

solve an equation Find a solution to an equation.

square A quadrilateral that has four right angles and all sides are the same length.

square unit A square with sides one unit long used to measure area.

standard form A way to write a number showing only its digits. Commas separate groups of three digits starting from the right. *Example:* 613,095

straight angle An angle that forms a straight line.

sum The result of adding numbers together.

survey Collecting information by asking a number of people the same question and recording their answers.

tablespoon (tbsp) A customary unit of capacity. 1 tablespoon = 3 teaspoons

teaspoon (tsp) A customary unit of capacity. 3 teaspoons = 1 tablespoon

tenth One part of 10 equal parts of a whole.

terms Numbers in a sequence or variables, such as *x* and *y*, in an expression.

ton (T) A customary unit of weight. 1 ton = 2,000 pounds

trapezoid A quadrilateral with only one pair of parallel sides.

triangle A polygon with 3 sides.

underestimate An estimate that is less than the exact answer.

unit angle An angle that cuts off $\frac{1}{360}$ of a circle and measures 1°.

unit fraction A fraction with a numerator of 1. *Example:* $\frac{1}{2}$

unknown A symbol or letter, such as *x*, that represents a number in an expression or equation.

variable A symbol or letter that stands for a number.

vertex (plural: vertices) The point where two rays meet to form an angle.

volume The number of cubic units needed to fill a solid figure.

W

week A unit of time equal to 7 days.

weight A measure of how heavy an object is.

whole numbers The numbers 0, 1, 2, 3, 4, and so on.

Y

yard (yd) A customary unit of length. 1 yard = 3 feet

year A unit of time equal to 365 days or 52 weeks or 12 months.

Z

Zero Property of Multiplication The product of any number and zero is zero. *Examples:* $3 \times 0 = 0$; $5 \times 0 = 0$

enVision® Mathematics
Common Core

Photographs

Every effort has been made to secure permission and provide appropriate credit for photographic material. The publisher deeply regrets any omission and pledges to correct errors called to its attention in subsequent editions.

Unless otherwise acknowledged, all photographs are the property of Savvas Learning Company LLC.

Photo locators denoted as follows: Top (T), Center (C), Bottom (B), Left (L), Right (R), Background (Bkgd)

1 MarclSchauer/Shutterstock; **3** (T) Cowardlion/ Shutterstock, (C) Dabarti CGI/Shutterstock, (B) Birgit Tyrrell/ Alamy Stock Photo; **4** (Bkgrd) Monkey Business Images/ Shutterstock; Ajt/Shutterstock, 24 Petr84/Fotolia. **33** forkART Photography/Fotolia; **35** (T) Sean Pavone/ Shutterstock, 35 (B) North Wind Picture Archives/Alamy Stock Photo; **36** (T) Naeblys/Alamy Stock Photo; **36** (B) Beata Bar/Shutterstock; **38** Richard Cavalleri/ Shutterstock; **50** Alexey Usachev/Fotolia; **54** Pavel L Photo and Video/Shutterstock; **60** Digital Vision/Thinkstock; **66** WaterFrame_mus/Alamy Stock Photo. **77** John Hoffman/ Shutterstock; **79** (T) Vm2002/Shutterstock, (C) DenGuy/E+/ Getty Images, (B) Viju Jose/Shutterstock; **80** (Bkgrd) Ivonne Wierink/Shutterstock; AlexLMX/Shutterstock, **98** Stevanzz/ Fotolia; **112** Andrew Breeden/Fotolia. **125** Majeczka/ Shutterstock; **127** (T) RosaIreneBetancourt 5/Alamy Stock Photo, (B) Rolf Nussbaumer Photography/Bill Draker/ Rolfnp/Alamy Stock Photo; **128** (T) John Green/Cal Sport Media/Alamy Stock Photo, (B) Christophe Petit Tesson/Epa/ REX/Shutterstock; **148** Steve Byland/Shutterstock; **152** 2011/Photos To Go. **165** Mark McClare/Shutterstock; **166** CristinaMuraca/Shutterstock; **167** (T) Stephen Vincent/ Alamy Stock Photo, (C) Colors and shapes of underwater world/Moment/Getty Images, (B) Tierfotoagentur/A. Mirsberger/Alamy Stock Photo; **168** (Bkgrd) Konstantin Gushcha/Shutterstock, Andrey Armyagov/Shutterstock. **221** ShutterStock; **223** (T) Itsik Marom/Alamy Stock Photo, (B) David Fleetham/Alamy Stock Photo; **224** (T) Brian Lasenby/Shutterstock, (B) Willyam Bradberry/Shutterstock; **236** (L) JackF/Fotolia; (R) Smileus/Shutterstock. **257** ShutterStock; **259** (T) Danita Delimont/Alamy Stock Photo, (C) Keith Birmingham/Pasadena Star-News/San Gabriel Valley Tribune/ZUMA Wire/Alamy Live News/Alamy Stock Photo, (B) Nikola Obradovic/Shutterstock; **260** (Bkgrd) Simon Belcher/Alamy Stock Photo; Ivonne Wierink/ Shutterstock, **268** Comstock Images/Jupiter Images; **270** Womue/Fotolia. **289** Kletr/Shutterstock;

291 (T) Robert Stainforth/Alamy Stock Photo, (B) T.W. van Urk/Shutterstock; **292** (T) Oksana Mizina/Shutterstock, (B) Elnur/Shutterstock; **296** Hamik/Fotolia. **329** Adrio Communications Ltd/Shutterstock; **331** (T) Goodluz/ Shutterstock, (C) Everett Collection Inc/Alamy Stock Photo, (B) Xuanhuongho/Shutterstock; **332** (Bkgrd) Rattiya Thongdumhyu/Shutterstock; AlenKadr/Shutterstock, **336** Oleksii Sagitov/Shutterstock; **364** Werner Dreblow/ Fotolia. **381** Pk7comcastnet/Fotolia; **383** (T) 123RF, (B) Monkey Business Images/Shutterstock; **384** (T) Hxdyl/ Shutterstock, (B) Realy Easy Star/Caterina Soprana/Alamy Stock Photo; **394** JLV Image Works/Fotolia. **413** NASA; **415** (T) Oliveromg/Shutterstock, (C) Radius Images/Alamy Stock Photo, (B) Tuasiwatn/Shutterstock; **416** (Bkgrd) Tom Wang/Shutterstock, (T) Yuliya Evstratenko/Shutterstock, (B) KK Tan/Shutterstock. **441** Bork/Shutterstock; **443** (T) Lynn Y/Shutterstock, (B) Evren Kalin Bacak/Shutterstock; **444** (T) Narin Nonthamand/Shutterstock, (B) Richard Brown/Alamy Stock Photo; **448** Hemera Technologies/ThinkStock; **461** StockPhotosArt/Fotolia; **475** (L) Proedding/Fotolia, (CL) Donfink/Fotolia (CR) Tim elliott/Fotolia, (R) Petergyure/ Fotolia; **476** Redwood/Fotolia. **477** Katrina Brown/Fotolia; **479** (T) Mark Winfrey/Shutterstock, (C) Borisov Studio/ Shutterstock, (B) Fototaras/Shutterstock; **480** (Bkgrd) John Dorado/Shutterstock, (T) Poznyakov/Shutterstock, (B) Billion Photos/Shutterstock; **489** (L) Glass and Nature/ Shutterstock, (C) Fesus Robert/Shutterstock, (R) Kseniya Abramova/123RF; **492** Duncan Noakes/Fotolia; 500 Sergio Martínez/Fotolia; **513** (T) Margouillat photo/Shutterstock, (B) LittleMiss/Shutterstock; **516** (T) Margouillat photo/ Shutterstock, (B) Little Miss/Shutterstock. **517** luchschen/ Shutterstock; **519** (T) David McGill71/Shutterstock, (B) Catarena/123RF; **520** (T) Homo Cosmicos/Shutterstock, (B) Matthew Wilkinson/Alamy Stock Photo; **524** Chinatown/ Alamy Stock Photo; **526** Photo24/Stockbyte/Getty Images. **545** James Kingman/Shutterstock; **547** (T) Oleksiy Avtomonov/Shutterstock, (C) Jules_Kitano/Shutterstock, (B) Petruk Viktor/Shutterstock; **548** (Bkgrd) Peter Etchells/ Shutterstock, Sarapon/Shutterstock; **579** WitR/Shutterstock. **581** Dja65/Shutterstock; **583** (T) Mukul Gupchup/ Ephotocorp/Alamy Stock Photo, (B) Sean Pavone/ Shutterstock; **584** (T) Mariia Tagirova/Shutterstock, (B) Edwin Godinho/Shutterstock; **586** Arina P Habich/ Shutterstock; **600** Gary Blakeley/Fotolia; **616** (T) Thampapon/Shutterstock, (B) Orhan Cam/Shutterstock